A Special Message from...
Dr. Arun Gandhi
- Grandson of Mahatma Gandhi -

I often wondered how our human society, so mired in materialism, greed, selfishness and all the attendant ills that are an integral part of these negative attitudes, can stop the madness of violence that is destroying the core of our being. My grandfather, Mohandas K. Gandhi, once enumerated what he called the Seven Social Sins that are destroying the world. They are:

1. **Wealth without Work**
2. **Pleasure without Conscience**
3. **Commerce without Morality**
4. **Science without Humanity**
5. **Knowledge without Character**
6. **Worship without Sacrifice**
7. **Politics without Principles**

My recent contribution to this list is: **Rights without Responsibilities**.

In *Awakening Perfection*, the authors, Audrone Wippich and Phil Brattain, have attempted to answer some of these issues. I am impressed by the way they have attempted to synthesize spirituality, technology and economics and opened yet another avenue for reflection and possible assimilation.

That societies around the globe need to change if we are to avert a disaster is obvious. This can, however, only come about with a better understanding and interpretation of our spiritual beliefs and the sincere internalization of those lessons so that we can create understanding and relationships between people based on mutual respect, love, compassion and acceptance. This book serves as a road map.

—Dr. Arun Gandhi, President,
Gandhi Worldwide Education Society, USA
www.gandhiforchildren.org and www.arungandhi.org

PRAISE FOR AWAKEN PERFECTION

"The authors speak from the fresh worldview of the planetary citizen, the young people growing up today with iPhones and instant global communications, about an authentic search for being and celebration. This book is sure to provoke discussion and creative response, hopefully at the level of being and play and celebration as humanity continues its surprising evolutionary journey."

—Matthew Fox, PhD, theologian and Episcopalian priest,
author of *Original Blessing*, *The Coming of the
Cosmic Christ* and *A New Reformation*

"Awaken Perfection offers a fresh perspective on the current cluster of crises we face and the paradigm shift that will resolve them. I like it, and if you have been thinking through the implications of what many call the "New Age," so will you. I highly recommend it."

—Amit Goswami, PhD, quantum physicist,
author of *The Self-Aware Universe*, *God is not Dead* and *Creative Evolution*

"As innovative and enthusiastic as it is authentic and challenging, Awaken Perfection *presents a real-time vision of what's possible right now for each of us, in this very moment, in our planetary spiritual journey."*

—Jordan Gruber, JD, MA, founder and CEO, Enlightenment.Com

"The authors have here presented us with a powerful new map of human existence to help us chart an enlightened course into the future. Theology, philosophy, art, technology, politics and economics are brought together into a shimmering portrait of both our past and our potential that is integral, mystical, scientifically sound and profoundly positive."

—Craig Hamilton, founder of Integral Enlightenment and Academy for Evolutionaries;former Senior Editor, *What Is Enlightenment?* (www.IntegralEnlightenment.com)

"A soulful call for awakening hearts and minds to the co-creative process in a planet-conscious age. The authors' acknowledgement of the celebration of life within the complexities of post-modern society point us to what Sufis have always regarded as the state of Tawhid, *the unity where truth is not learned but discovered in how we might be directed to see the manuscript of the God written in nature. Written in accessible style, this is a must read for all those interested in collective transformation."*

—Ana Chisti-Perez, PhD, professor, Institute of Transpersonal Studies; National Representative for the Sufi Movement International US

"In Awaken Perfection, *the authors pilot us as readers across dimensional realms of elevated consciousness, successfully illustrating our connection to a unified internal Source."*

—Robert Reneau, CEO, Aura iMedia

"The authors bring their journey of self-discovery, challenging our most basic notion of reality for a fuller and more spontaneous experience of life. One can appreciate their knowledge and synthesis of many spiritual traditions in a book accessible to everyone."

—Ale Gicqueau, president & CEO, The Business Bridge, Inc.,
Vice Consul of the Principality of Monaco,
InterFrench/SiliconFrench Founder & Chairman

"We have long considered ourselves human beings, but only measured ourselves in terms of human doings. Now, with climate change threatening to disrupt our very lives, we find that our doings have not only hurt the earth's delicate ecosystem, but also separated us from our original perfection, our essence, our being. Awaken Perfection *opens our eyes to our "paradise lost" and how we can recover our souls as fellow planetary citizens."*

—Sheridan Tatsuno, principal, Dreamscape Global,digital movie
producer and author, *Technopolis* and *Created in Japan*

"Who are we? Where did we come from? Where are we going? *These ultimate questions are courageously tackled and gracefully answered. We are all ONE, and the transformation of any one of us impacts the entire Being. We no longer live isolated in our villages, walled cities, islands; we live in a world that knows no boundaries. We built a global society that necessarily leads to planetary citizenship. Our true wealth lies in profound appreciation of one another."*

—Luis Velasquez, MBA and PhD, Louis Allen Worldwide

AWAKEN PERFECTION
The Journey of Conscious Revelation

By
Audrone Wippich
and
Phil Brattain

DEDICATION

To all of us who will never be satisfied
with anything less than the ultimate.

Our time has come!

ACKNOWLEDGEMENTS

Audrone Wippich is forever grateful to her extraordinary parents, Laimute and Raimundas Janusauskas, who gave her the wings to fly. Extreme thanks goes to her best friend and husband, Mark Wippich, who is the most beautiful and powerful soul she's ever crashed into. Also, she thanks Phil Brattain for his role in creating and sharing this vision with the world.

Phil Brattain would like to offer special thanks to Audrone for being the supreme inspiration behind this book, his partner every step of the way in pioneering a daring new consciousness for a transformed age. Phil would like to thank his late mother and father, Marian and Wesley Brattain, along with his uncles, aunts and cousins, especially Jim Brattain, who resurrected Phil's childhood faith, as well as his late uncle, Ray Heimburger, who encouraged him to be a visionary and think long term, and Ray's children, Pat, Carolyn and Hans. Phil wishes to thank all his friends and acquaintances along the way, including Wilbur Wong, Mary Stark, Janice Knetzger, David Bunnell, Paul Saffo, Toshi Ide, Farhad Nouri, Arjuna Noor, Christina Cheney, Sheridan Tatsuno, Majeed Shekarchi, Suresh Narayanan, Tenzin N. Tethong, Jordan Gruber, Lion Goodman, Keith Rayner, Ale Gicqueau and Dr. Manish Mehta.

Together we want to thank such early influences as Billy Graham, Arthur Katz, Francis Schaeffer, Baba Ram Dass, Dr. Lucille Green, Dr. Huston Smith, Dr. Mildred Henry, Dr. Wei-Ming Tu, Werner Erhard, Bucky Fuller, Alan Watts and Joseph Campbell.

We would also like to thank such contemporary thinkers and gurus as Dr. Deepak Chopra, Ken Wilbur, Gary Gach, Andrew Cohen, Craig Hamilton, Anodea Judith, Thich Nhat Hanh, The Dalai Lama, Dr. Matthew Fox, Michael Murphy, Tony Robbins and Mark Watts.

In addition, we would like to thank such leaders in authoring, publishing and information marketing as Guy Kawasaki, Mark Victor Hansen, Robert G. Allen, Tom Antion, Alex Mandossian, Janet Switzer, Dan Poynter, John Kremer, Ann McIndoo, Armand Morin, David Hancock, Brendon Burchard and Justin Sachs. Extra thanks goes to our editor Joanne Shwed as well as AuthorOneShop.com. Special thanks to our gifted illustrator, Lijana Saniukaite-Grebel.

Finally, we would like to thank all the independent, metaphysical and religious bookstores, including Kepler's, Passages, Bird & Beckett, East/West Books, Gateways and Open Secret.

Contents

Part I: The Megastory (History)

- From profoundly secular to profoundly sacred
- Finding our way through a twisted world where all the rules have changed
- Why our lives will never be the same

- Today's strange resemblance to the Traditional Age
- World master or world teacher?
- How the two hemispheres of our global brain shaped civilization

- How the Modern Age trumped everything before it
- When science and religion got a divorce
- Why the world is never enough

PART II: THE MEGADREAM (MYSTERY)

PREFACE:
Our Life as a Movie

We are right in the middle of a movie, a spectacularly divine love story. We hold it as real, and each of us takes our roles assigned from central casting seriously. We are quite attached to those roles. All the while, we are sitting in the seats in front of the silver screen smiling, crying, laughing ... quite beside ourselves with this amazing entertainment. We are very close to the climax of the cinema when all the fireworks go off, much like in the grand finale. Although we all are certain of the tragic consequences at this point, the script is about to turn into a glorious comedy.

*1: Life as a movie: We are both on the screen
and in the audience at the same time.*

What if all the world's great religious traditions, such as Christianity, Islam and Judaism, and Hinduism and Buddhism, were essentially true but incomplete? What if the entire humanistic tradition, originally inspired by the Greeks and coming out of the Nile River Valley, had a profoundly mystical edge, and the superstition of materialism is once and for all about to evaporate from our planetary society?

What if we have already entered a profoundly spiritual age — the Planetary Age — and the Modern Age in which many of us grew up is becoming increasingly irrelevant? What if the values, priorities, sensibilities and rules of the Modern Age have become obsolete and we are now scrambling to redefine those of the New Age? What if this New Age were as radically transformative to us as the Modern Age was to the traditional world? What if prospering and flourishing in this New Age requires a mystical awareness and deeper spirituality than most people imagine?

What if time was accelerating, and everything and everyone were coming together as orchestrated by a great story, a megaplot within the Megadream? What if, within this dream, everyone was dreaming everyone else, and everyone was playing everyone else? What if each of our dreams contains every other dream and there is ultimately only one dreamer?

What if we are all divine but deliberately chose to forget, to enter into the game and experience all the suspense? What if the Creator is experiencing it all right along with His creation? What if each of us was created to create? What if any of us at any point in the story could awaken to remember who he or she is and what this is all about, and then consciously re-enter the dream as creator?

What if there are just *three ultimate lessons* and they were never before fully graspable by the human race, even by the direct disciples of Krishna, Buddha and Christ? What if they were only graspable when the time had come, when we were about to collectively enter eternity? What if these lessons were: 1) All is One; 2) God IS Love; and 3) All is Perfect?

What if there were only four things to do in life, despite any and all appearances: 1) Awaken; 2) Create; 3) Play; and 4) Celebrate? And what if the whole thing were but one spectacular celebration?

What if God's hands have always been on the wheel, and He has never, ever made a mistake? That everything that ever happened has been a precious thread in a magnificent tapestry about to be unveiled?

The authors, Audrone Wippich and Phil Brattain, are two playful human beings of different ages and national origins with the privilege of mingling with people from almost every country in one of the furthest points West you can go in the continental United States, the Greater San Francisco Bay Area. Ever since the Gold Rush, this region has been inventing and re-inventing the future, including the recent Internet Boom, and shortly, a revolution in consciousness.

The authors point out that we are all "Sorcerer's Apprentices" who have messed up with our magic, and are awaiting the reappearance of our master to fix things up. While this illusion is the only thing that they rationally know, they intuit a truth far deeper.

The truth that lay underneath our daily soap opera to which we are all so addicted to. It is time we melt all of our masks and acting roles, and look beyond them. And in the process, we will realize that we are all at this very moment in a dream, in God's dream, and God is the producer, director, cast and audience.

FOREWORD

The book you now hold in your hands, view on your screens or hear on your speakers is a wonderful exploration of our individual and collective PERFECTION, a transformed vision of our past, present and future, a state akin to the classic enlightenment of the Buddhists. Its story goes well beyond our various faith traditions to unveil the underlying unity of all humanity, that divine aspect of ourselves that could take a lifetime to discover. It addresses our ultimate questions, skillfully pointing the direction to their intriguing answers.

The authors, Audrone Wippich and Phil Brattain, show us how the state of perfection is already within us, that it lies in our very *being*, in a whole new way of seeing, rather than in an endless cycle of *doing* or ever trying harder and harder. Surprisingly, it is ever available to us. They connect us both to the world's wisdom traditions and to the reality of our collective environment today, a globalized world and an increasingly endangered planet. They suggest that the latest advances in technology, far from diminishing our humanity, confirm the unique potential and mystery of being human.

Whether we hold it as the Supreme Being or primarily as the Supreme Force within the Universe, we are intimately connected to that Transcendent Mystery, even if we cannot bring ourselves to admit it. Others might see it as the ultimate nature of things, the force that mysteriously caused the Big Bang and the vast expanse of space and time, form and emptiness, as we know it, or even unknown universes we all have yet to explore.

Rather than being a simple rehash of ancient truths and philosophical ideas that have sustained us through the ages, it explores the relevance of our everyday experience as real human beings, how we emerged from the traditional world into the modern. From there, the authors prepare us for the next planetary phase of human consciousness, the burst of transformation opening up the planet and humanity to infinite possibility.

"What makes you so sure that we are actually entering a new global age?" you might ask. My direct knowledge and life experience as a Tibetan attests to that. My own people, on the verge of being utterly overwhelmed and engulfed within a much larger entity, actually survived against all odds and the stringent test of time. Collective cultural identity has invented new ways to overcome the traditional onslaught of subjugation and outwardly imposed change. The emergence of high technology with a consequent explosion in knowledge has made all that possible.

Our ultimate representative, His Holiness, the Dalai Lama, born in a tiny village in a remote corner of the Tibetan plateau, has become a truly global figure. Even more, he has been able to demonstrate in both word and action the relevance and richness of an ancient tradition. He shows how that very tradition can play in concert with our post-modern world and its advanced technology to address humanity's deeper needs. Science need not clash with spirituality, as there is much that the ancient world still has to offer to our emerging planetary civilization.

The Tibetan story of the last fifty years is, in itself, a journey of conscious revelation. *Awaken Perfection* reveals complementary developments that reinforce the theme. If you are at a point where you consciously want to transform your old disempowering perspective, this guide to the new Planetary Age before us will empower you to make your own journey into the ultimate fulfillment we call enlightenment.

—Tenzin N. Tethong
President, The Dalai Lama Foundation
Chair, Committee of 100 for Tibet
Distinguished Fellow, Tibetan Studies Initiative
Ho Center for Buddhist Studies, Stanford University

Introduction:
Our Discovery of
Ultimate Perfection

- We are witnessing the world rapidly coming to-gether at the very same time that it seems to be falling apart. Is this all by accident?
- We are recognizing that we are living in a whole new age where the old ways that we grew up with no longer work. Have we thought out WHY?
- We, humanity, and the planet itself, are facing unprecedented crises. What is the way to our collective transformation?

We have entered into a radically different age, demanding a whole new kind of consciousness. It is no longer an option but a necessity. This is all the more true when our religious beliefs and institutions are stuck in the past. Today, that new consciousness is proving to be our ultimate tool and bridge to transformation. It is highly inclusive, operating on a collective level.

We are speaking of a planetary consciousness for a plane-tary civilization in the Planetary Age. Why "Planetary" and not "Global"? By glancing at our current worldwide events, we see that we live in a period where the magnitude of our problems, as well as our opportunities, has gone planetary in scope, and where everything is taking an environmental twist. We now must view our home, Planet Earth, in a cosmic context.

It's All in How We Have It

Maybe our concept of reality is all messed up. Growing awareness of the quantum revolution, which unveils how our world acts at the subatomic level, and string theory, which bridges quantum theory, the infinitesimally small, with the cosmic theory of Einstein, the infinitely large, has taken the notion of reality and turned it upside down and inside out. Now, most of us are wrestling on the personal level with the issue of what constitutes reality, especially when we are actively trying to understand questions such as "Who am I?" and "What is the whole point of this collective story or dream in which I find myself?"

On a basic and nonquantum level, it is as if we choose to live in one of two universes: the "Universe of doing" or the "Universe of being." The grand prize is to be able to consistently enter life out of the Universe of being as opposed to the Universe of doing.

The Universe of doing is preoccupied with pure survival, what we mostly read in the newspapers or watch reporters declare on TV; all the facts that make up our collective story. It is a universe that keeps turning us into perpetual victims, utterly dependent on our surroundings and the thought that everyone and everything "out there" is out to get us. In other words, it is a universe of continuous shortage, with never enough to go around, and where you feel you must fight for every crumb on the table. It is void of any experience whatsoever of perfection or magic. But we all need magic in whatever shape and form might be available to us to truly relish life, much like having dessert after dinner.

On the other hand, the Universe of being belongs to little children and truly enlightened adults, people who can play all out and enjoy their everyday existence in any given circumstance. Audrone remembers when she was a little girl in Lithuania, running around with no worries, feeling that everything would take care of itself. For her, it was a truly magical time ... like Alice in Wonderland. But what if it is all ultimately an illusion and we are here to play by creating new fantasies? From a being level, there is literally nothing else to do but to create, play and celebrate our own masterpiece. Have you ever tried proving to a child that "playing" is not the way? He or she will look at you as if you were from another planet.

Just picture an actor playing multiple roles in a wide variety of movies and having fun with it. That's it folks ... that's life in its simplest form. We are not that aware of playing a role until we reach adulthood. The playing aspect shouldn't stop us here. The game only intensifies in terms of excitement, since it involves full participation and hands-on experience. When you play the game from the Universe of being, the passion for love and life multiplies by the nth power (to each his own) and it is simply perfect, even with all the bumps along the road. As human "beings," we belong in the being Universe and, if we don't live in our true element, we tend to suffer.

One Universe or Two: Your Choice

Once you fall into one of these two separate universes (the Universe of doing or the Universe of being), you get to live and relive its effects. In the survival Universe, perfection is not just a distant and impractical dream, it is utterly impossible. There is not one thing or person that can be seen as "perfect." In the being Universe, everyone and everything is inherently perfect. The notion that some are perfect and others are not is what keeps us stuck. Everyone is perfect in his or her own way. Perfection is the soul of the being Universe. It is like the Beatles' song, "Strawberry Fields Forever"—filled with joy, love, oneness and infinite possibility. In fact, it is the heart of every religion.

As the quantum revolution reveals, there is nothing fundamentally "out there." Thus, the world is an illusion and we are within that illusion, but who is the illusionist who created it all? Oh, could it be God? We are all "in the mind of God." The Creator is playing in His/Her creation and we are His/Her mirror reflections appearing in the flesh. Our differences and uniqueness make the illusion so much more fun and entertaining!

Suppose there is only God, that God IS Love, and that He/She can't be anything but PERFECT. When you enter the world of doing from the world of being, you can create your life out of the experience of perfection. Life then becomes a vibrant expression of your divine nature. To forget our divinity is to forget Whom we ultimately are, to forget our Supreme Identity. The divine pertains to our ability as human beings to live out of the being Universe, to come into life as sons and daughters of God, if you will.

You might have recognized the preeminent role of paradox and contradiction in every aspect of your life. Our entire creation and so-called "divine play" in this world are made of duality, or yin/yang, so that it is never dull and boring for us to stay engaged with it. However, in order to make any progress moving forward, we have to go beyond the duality to the reconciliation of opposites. It is all a journey, a continuous discovery of our core being and meaning.

Only through this journey of awakening are we able to arrive at a new consciousness, which is possible only through the realization of inherent perfection.

Everything that ever happened *had* to happen in a precise

order for us to get to this particular point in history. History has played a unique role in revealing this message to us. It disclosed some interesting patterns in the human psyche, and prompted us to investigate these patterns in the world that we commonly call "reality."

From Secular to Sacred

We are now in a collectivist era with strong elements of individualism that combine both capitalism and socialism. The new social media and networking embody this. As such, they are the foundation of a new global economy. Today, the importance of interrelationships and collective contribution is obvious. We need each other, on both individual and collective levels, to be able to grow, rebuild and move forward in all aspects of life. We are all reflections of one another within the same ultimate mirror.

Our current global economic crisis is a great example of how just one major country stumbling can bring down all the rest. The new technology has shrunk the world and brought us closer; it has also opened the door to an endless stream of information that has never before been so easily accessed. That is why this has so often been referred to as an "information age."

On the other hand, this age is profoundly spiritual, whether we like it or not. The East and West are rapidly converging, and each of them is bringing together a lot of powerful elements and insights that comprise our new unifying spiritual language. Until now, every faith was boxed within specific geographic walls and held secrets that would eventually inform every other. Humanity's puzzle was incomplete because the truth was hidden within different conceptual languages.

You can no longer afford to hold your own tradition in isolation. To be part of today's new consciousness requires holding it in a planetary context. You can cherish your tradition while you develop a keen appreciation of the other traditions. We made it really easy for everyone. The coming revelation has to do with the realization that every great tradition, including your own, was largely right but also incomplete. When the pieces of the puzzle all fall in place, we will find that the new whole is far greater than the sum of its parts.

How Story and Dream Interplay

Since history does play an important role in our overall lives, we decided to jump into a time capsule and take a sneak peek at how we arrived at this particular destination in time. We dove into the past and found answers to the perennial questions from truly spiritual and planetary perspectives: Who are we? Where did we come from? Where are we going?

Our book has two parts: 1) the Megastory (History); and 2) the Megadream (Mystery). You might be able to already see the correlation between the two separate universes of doing and being, which we just discussed.

Within the Megastory, we find ourselves within an intricate and eventful story where our Creator finds infinite value in each of our unique expressions. The Megastory is the Universe of appearances—what people take to be the "real world" or life itself. This part of the book will give you a better understanding of where we came from, laying a new foundation for viewing our future.

The Megadream is the alternative Universe of pure being, consciousness and bliss, where all form is seen to be but an intermittent dream. It fundamentally throws into question what we consider to be reality and shows us the power of creation within each of us. In other words, you will discover a fresh synthesis of the world's religions distilled to their mystical essence. We are sure that, if you quite simply open up your heart and mind, you will find it all to be magical.

We are going well beyond a new planetary framework to an ultimate transformational perspective or context that can turn your life upside down and inside out. This is beyond what was available in such powerful enlightenment programs as "est" (Erhard Seminars Training). We have collectively swung into the Planetary Age since the 1970s, and thus, today, we have a much deeper perspective as to how and why all the great traditions are converging and what that says about our destiny.

Recently, we received fresh revelation out of an open heart and open mind that puts things together in an unprecedented way. This new vision is unique in its completeness and can play a decisive role in individual and collective transformation. This work—our play—has emerged from intense conversation, scholarship, research and soul-searching over many years. We believe that we are not the only ones who now question the prevailing agreement around reality and existence. Never before has humanity been ready to accept the underlying truth that WE ARE ALL ONE.

Let the journey of awakening begin right here and right now!

Part I:

THE MEGASTORY (HISTORY)

When we look at the grand sweep of history, we must realize that we are narrating our collective story as humanity. As a story, it presupposes the questions "Who are we?," "Where did we come from?" and "Where are we going?" If history is a story, then the story, like the plot in a play, has a climax. It must leave the audience profoundly moved if the piece is to succeed as a work of art. There must be heroes and villains, wins and losses, sudden reversals, nuances and twists—all resulting in a supremely satisfying whole.

If the story is a play, we need a playwright, a director, actors and an audience (glance at Illustration No.1 in the Preface). The actors, even if they improvise, need to be informed of their roles and about how they fit into the course of action. The plot needs a theme that profoundly speaks to the audience. Even as the great director, Stephen Spielberg, confessed in the Academy Awards, "It all starts with the Word."

When we survey the grand tapestry of world history, we will indeed perceive both a play and a love story. Often—and in Shakespeare's immortal words, "Life is a tale told by an idiot full of sound and fury signifying nothing"— when you finally step back, you perceive an awesome panorama. You then come to appreciate the extraordinary opportunity our generation is facing at the culmination, having just entered the Planetary Age.

We are now actually in a position to rewrite our own stories because a story is a matter of how we interpret the past. As we learn to reinterpret our lives, we can actually reconstruct our past and even shape our future.

In Chapter One, we open up the panorama of the planet today and discuss how and why it is dramatically different from any time before it. In Chapter Two, we then dive into our ancient foundations to trace step by step exactly how we got here.

Chapter One:

WHERE WE ARE TODAY

We find ourselves in a profoundly different era than the one in which most of us grew up, with crisis after crisis … all global. When we really look at things, we'll find that nothing fits anymore the way it used to. The world is undergoing massive change at a frightening speed. All the crises that are coming up are planetary in scope—from the collapse of the monetary market to global warming to religious terrorism around the world. We are finding that the rules with which we grew up no longer apply, whether staying with one company for our entire career and retiring with social security or staying with one marriage for a lifetime with a happy family.

The old way no longer seems to work, and we are all left wondering what rules to make as we move along. It is almost as if we are strangers in a strange land, confronting a whole new landscape and then trying to figure it all out.

A New Story as the Old Transformed

Looking at the magnitude of the current environmental crisis, one prominent cosmologist, Dr. Brian Swimme, suggests that humanity needs a new story to discover a positive future. It is our view that this new story will not work unless it both includes and transcends the old one.

We can't just walk away from the past, no matter how much we would like to. We feel that if we look closely over the landscape of history, we will begin to see a larger story, a great story—

the Megastory—that is implicit in the old story, leading us into a whole new dimension of possibilities. We feel that we are at a unique point in what we call "history," where the time has come for everything to become clear, perhaps for the very first time.

If nothing else, we have to look at this moment and realize that everything that ever happened before has led us up to this very point.

Involution Replaces Evolution

While fundamentalists bitterly oppose evolution, modernists gladly champion it, rarely questioning what might be the nature of so-called "evolution." Our feelings are that both sides are right and both sides are wrong. The problem is that very few people have defined their terms. There is a mountain of assumptions behind each one. If we look at the mechanistic, scientific viewpoint, we find that it is an attempt to explain how things come to pass, and never answering the question "why" or where they are going.

As far as the religious right—the creationists—is concerned, it is readily apparent that the Earth was not created in six days, if for no other reason than the fact that you would have to decide whether or not it all happened in Greenwich Meridian time. It becomes very obvious that the primal language has to be considered symbolic. But how do we know that humanity has been here millions and millions of years? Can we absolutely trust carbon dating? It would seem as though we are willing to do anything to avoid confronting mystery.

Many issues have been glossed over, and both sides have assumed a very self-righteous stance. We propose a counter notion, brought up by the self-proclaimed avatar, Maher Baba. The idea is that, instead of things happening randomly and chaotically, our Source, the Creator of the Universe, God, or whatever we want to call this Higher Power, became the Universe, and is developing or exploring all the possibilities through us as the Universe.

Rather than being called evolution, this process is called "involution," where our innermost Source is working out the possibilities from within us and that, because the Source is the Universe, that Universe is both alive and conscious. If we look at evolutionary theory, what are the implications?

Evolutionary theory is fundamentally driven by a notion of random accidents where things just happen. Creationists offer the analogy of walking into an airplane parts factory, witnessing an explosion and seeing a fully assembled Boeing 747 right before our eyes. That whole scene is quite simply incredible, no matter how infinite the possibilities might be.

So, evolution, based on random mutation of genes, seems to be deficient as a theory, although it is very intelligently constructed. We come to a much deeper question: Is this all an accident or is it a fulfillment of our destiny? As we move through this book, we will suggest that things can appear accidental on one level and destined on a different level. Is there intelligent design at work? We feel that this is the case, but we also feel that the evolutionists have some points that the creationists need to hear.

Modern Age Bites the Dust

While the current landscape is unrecognizable from that of only several decades back, most people reflexively keep thinking that they are still part of the now defunct Modern Age. We can ask if we are still living in the Modern Age today. What was it about the Modern Age that made it "Modern"?

We feel that high technology has actually taken us well beyond the Modern Age, which we identify closely with the emergence of the Industrial Revolution. When we moved into an age driven by information—where intelligence was the value-add rather than further capital infrastructure-we were, from a material standpoint, in a whole new age. Coming out of the labs in Silicon Valley, we now find the emergence of nanotechnology. Crude materialism no longer works to explain the world or provide a rationale for life as it did in the mid-20th century CE.

The world has already started to come together whereas, in the Modern Age, the world was in a long, 500-year process of emerging through imperialism and colonialism, building out a global infrastructure. The world today is finally coming together because the infrastructure is now firmly in place, both in terms of transportation and communications.

If we look at President John F. Kennedy's "New Frontier," which he envisioned back in 1961, it is not so much that of outer space as that of inner space. We suggest that the entire value system of the Modern Age has been turned upside down and inside out.

Rational Empiricism/ Spiritual Materialism Out

The cultural war between the religious fundamentalists and the secular humanists seems tiresome only because the argument is now totally irrelevant: philosophic materialism is dead, having been defeated in the quantum laboratory.

If we look at the cultural war that has happened recently under the religious right, under both the Ronald Reagan and George W. Bush presidential administrations, we see that this entire cultural clash is based on a massive misunderstanding. The far left, being driven by secular agnostics and atheists out of the major universities, uncritically based their worldview around a physics that has been completely outmoded, which was pre-Einsteinian—let alone prequantum—and certainly not in accord with string theory.

On the other hand, on the religious right, the entire fundamentalist outlook emerged out of a reaction against an excessively materialistic society. If we look at the hard facts, the view of scientific materialism is now obsolete, like an old technology of computers that no longer fits the paradigms coming out of the quantum research labs. The religious materialist view is also obsolete; a whole new spiritual outlook has superseded it.

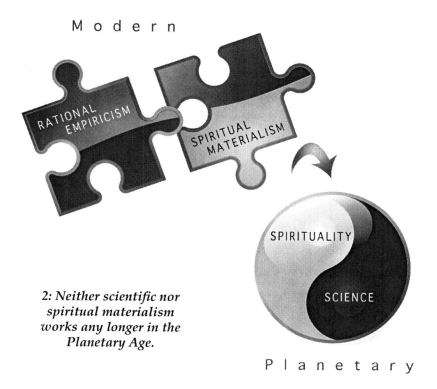

Modern

RATIONAL EMPIRICISM

SPIRITUAL MATERIALISM

SPIRITUALITY

SCIENCE

2: Neither scientific nor spiritual materialism works any longer in the Planetary Age.

Planetary

People keep seeing the world through their childhood conditioning. It is very hard for any of us to shake off how we grew up, whether baby boomer from the 1950s and 1960s or Generation X and Y from the 1970s and 1980s. We are now living in a profoundly different world. When both sides of this cultural war fully realize this, the cultural war will be over. The fundamentalists will be heard, and the intellectuals in the academic world will not be quite so reactionary.

Why Planetary?

You might wonder why we call this new age "Planetary" and why all the crises humanity is now confronting are global in scale. If we look at what the Planetary Age denotes, it is basically the assertion that the common denominator of the current environment is humanity united on a worldwide level. All the consequences of our botching up, if you will, are environmental in impact. It is now—not just being stuck on a globe but also owning *our* planet in *our* solar system in *our* galaxy in *our* Universe. We can no longer think of ourselves as simply innocent bystanders. We are actively involved in the whole process of creation.

We are now in a cosmic age. Humanity has finally grown up and functions at a planetary level. It is much too early to say that we are in a galactic or interstellar age. We certainly have sent probes out beyond the solar system, but the fundamental common denominator now needs to be our planet itself, and not our city, country or corporation.

The Modern Age was that period when the world started coming together; it was a very long haul entailing ever-increasing complexity and development. The whole thrust of the Modern Age was expansion arising from the three ships of Christopher Columbus in 1492 opening up a new world. It was a continuous growth of largely Western European, and later, American, civilization that assumed a dominant position around the world.

We have now built out an interdependent global society. We know it is a Planetary Age because of the infrastructure and its domino effect on the economy. We recently saw how the global monetary crisis jeopardized every single nation in the world. It wasn't just a question of the American economy collapsing but of the entire global monetary system collapsing.

We now have no choice but to approach all of these crises from a new planetary perspective and a new planetary consciousness.

Planetary Citizenship

Barack Obama is the first U.S. president to call himself a global citizen, although President John F. Kennedy hinted at this concept back in the early 1960s, calling himself "a Berliner." No single country is truly independent in "the new world order."

George H. W. Bush asked, "You don't want America to be another country A to Z, do you?" He was commenting on a quirk in computer technology where, upon being given an alphabetical list of 120 nations, you would always have to scroll to the bottom to find the U.S. This was actually poor functional design because it shows no respect for the size of the countries, just their place in the alphabet. The prejudice of America first got us into big trouble when we assumed we could be independent of other countries. Just look at the war in Iraq—a total boomerang.

We must now play together to prosper. We really have no choice at this point. We are now in a world system where both the individual and the collective matter equally. If you oppress individuals long enough, you will get religiously inspired terrorism that will rock the economic cart. Think of how few people it took to knock out the Twin Towers in New York. It is now appropriate to consider citizenship on a much higher level.

Barack Obama called himself a global citizen before he was elected president. Any of us can. If we truly are global citizens, why can't we start to do something about it, building meaning into it, starting today?

Three Megacrises

If we step back, we find three overwhelming issues superseding every other. At first glance, the global monetary crisis might seem to be the supreme issue, followed closely by the environmental crisis and then followed by religiously sanctioned terrorism and warfare.

The monetary crisis happened when it happened very quickly, although it was shaped over several years. Because our very ability to function within society and institutions requires money, the collapse of our entire economic system would bring about anarchy and chaos. A much more serious danger is the environmental crisis, which will certainly have the greatest long-term impact. The true capital of the planet is not paper money or even digital exchange. Our true capital lies in our environment of plants, animals, birds and the weather—our ecosystem—which we cannot easily repair. Then we look at religious warfare as a wildcard that could erupt at any moment. We look at many nations going nuclear, including Pakistan, Iran and most likely Israel. To get into any kind of religious warfare could very quickly bring about thermonuclear war.

If we look at other issues—and there are myriads of other issues worthy of discussion including abortion, child abuse and animal rights—they are superseded by these three megacrises. What is our way out? Each one is uniquely pressing; each is uniquely demanding. It would take a genius of a president to handle any one of these three issues, let alone all three simultaneously. This is what we are facing today.

Four Cultural Directions Converge

If we look at San Francisco, where the United Nations actually began before it was moved to New York City, we can imagine four cultural (and symbolic) directions figuratively converging upon it:

1. The northern direction of humanism (humanistic mysticism)
2. The southern direction of shamanism (shamanic consciousness)
3. The eastern direction of realization (enlightened realization)
4. The western direction of revelation (mystical revelation).

While there are shamanic people on virtually every continent of the planet, and humanistic mysticism on virtually every continent, by and large these four directions do correspond to actual regions of the world. Certainly, the Western tradition of mystical revelation belongs mainly to Europe and America. The northern direction of humanistic mysticism emerged in the Greek and Roman Empires but ultimately supersaturated the modern world. If we look at the Eastern tradition of enlightened realization, we

3: Today, four different mystical perspectives cross in San Francisco to form a revolution in consciousness.

see South and East Asia. As for shamanic consciousness, shared by indigenous people living close to our mother Earth, it is most readily found in the Southern Hemisphere.

What is humanistic mysticism? It is the awareness of quantum mechanics; that the observer and the observed, as well as the very process of observing itself, are all the same. If you don't look at an object, it is not really there in any truly objective sense of the word.

What is shamanic consciousness? It is the acute appreciation of the web of life, the feeling that the Earth is feminine in some way; that in a very real and meaningful sense, it is our Mother; that human beings share both consciousness and being with animals and plants—even rocks—and with each other; that all of nature, all of creation, is spectacularly alive.

What is enlightened realization? It is an awareness of pure consciousness, pure being and pure bliss. Underneath all appearances, there is an underlying reality that transcends everything, more relevant than anything else. That underlying order of being is our true self. Who and what we think we are—our nametag, our body and even our mind—are secondary.

What is mystical revelation? Here we look at the realization that our ultimate Source is actively communicating with us in various ways and through various media. In the Western tradition, it is widely viewed that God spoke and created the world and that God speaks to us primarily through sacred scriptures. To use the terms of Christian theology, "natural revelation" is seen as the splendid witness of creation to the Creator; "special revelation" is seen as the Creator's own words to humanity through the prophets.

Each of these four directions is now converging to form a whole new planetary consciousness: the focus of our discussion.

Four Revolutions in San Francisco

San Francisco is still the world's leading city and region for revolution:

- Its first revolution was economic in the Gold Rush of 1849.
- Its second was social and cultural with the Summer of Love in 1967.
- Its third was technological with the dot-com boom, starting in Silicon Valley in 1994.
- Its fourth is the growing green revolution around consciousness itself, as demonstrated by Eckhart Tolle's spectacular success with his recent book, *A New Earth: Awakening to Your Life's Purpose,* as well as his earlier work, *The Power of Now.*

Tolle told Oprah Winfrey, in his unprecedented 10-session video webinar with her, that he couldn't have written his first book without having been in San Francisco. He suggested that there is something about the energy and space of San Francisco that inspires conscious revolution.

So, if we look at the greater San Francisco Bay Area as a whole, we see—as in the case of Silicon Valley—that it really is in a very meaningful sense where the future is continually being invented. If we look at the 1849 Gold Rush in more detail, we realize that this discovery brought people from every country together in pursuit of economic freedom. In the process, almost as an afterthought, it built up early industry such as the textiles of Levi Strauss, which helped create the "Golden State" of California.

1. gold rush/economic - 1849

2. summer of love/culture - 1967

3. dotcom boom/technological - 1994

4. green/consciousness - 2001

4: San Francisco seems to be ground zero when it comes to innovation.

We look at Chinese Americans today who largely came in during the Gold Rush. If we look at the Love Generation, what did the hippies do? They introduced the concept of "pluralism," an appreciation and a value of traditions and cultures other than Western and, most certainly, other than American. This embodied an acute sense of the importance of spirituality and a willingness to start over and create an entirely new culture or civilization, along with an incipient world consciousness.

If we look at the Internet boom, we see people who have carved out a bold new world of cyberspace and have linked the world together in real-time. Today, we have broadband mobile communication, which in theory is available to anyone on any continent, uniting humanity for the first time in a very real and fundamental way.

Why now would we postulate a revolution of consciousness, again coming from the very same area of San Francisco? We are looking at the rise of biotechnology and pharmaceuticals in the Greater Bay Area. We are looking at a critical mass of people from India, South Asia as well as East Asia, who are beginning to let their sensibilities be known. As China and India emerge as superpowers, we are taking in a new appreciation of their cultures and civilizations, which place a higher value on awareness and consciousness than was the case in the modern West.

If we look at these four revolutions, each one of them changed the world. The last one, the green revolution around consciousness, is about to change the world in the most profound way imaginable.

Individual versus Collective Transformation

The Planetary Age invites a new type of enlightenment, dreamt of in ancient times, but never before fully realized: "collective enlightenment." As mentioned, the world is coming together through advanced communications. It is not only possible to call somebody on a dedicated phone line but to also walk down the street sending video clips around the world to anybody at will.

We now have a much higher order of problems today than ever before. We can no longer tackle these problems on a strictly individual level, even though each of us inadvertently contributes to them, as in the case of global warming. The time has come for a form of collective enlightenment, as no one can be ultimately enlightened in this era without also enlightening everyone else in the process.

Thus, the fantasy of going into a cave to awaken is now obsolete. It once served a useful function but, until that person actually comes out, informs and transforms the rest of society, it might be looked at as a failed effort.

Why Does This Matter?

Our world is changing very rapidly. Not just the economy but also the entire planet. This shift will permanently impact the way we think, assess, approach and do everything. Now, the question is this: Who wants to be left behind? If we want to live to the fullest extent, we need to surf the waves of change rather than struggle to come up for air while drowning.

Humanity's journey into the unknown has led us up to this very point. History is our witness. Mankind keeps progressing with every new age, but the Planetary Age holds special significance. We are back to a very spiritual age—much like the Traditional Age, only planetary in scope. East and West are converging as we speak, and so are all of the religious traditions that go with them.

Speaking of cause and effect, the external world is the direct reflection of our internal world. Every one of us is actively involved in the process of creating the world that we witness today, whether consciously or unconsciously.

Now, the focus shifts from external to internal, from evolution to involution and from materialism to spirituality. God is playing throughout history as each one of us. All forms that appear to be material are simply expressions of the Supreme Being. The time has come to reevaluate what we take to be real.

For the first time in history, collective enlightenment and transformation are truly possible. A mystical consciousness resonates with the age in which we now find ourselves, as opposed to the rational humanism of the past.

Chapter Two:

HOW WE GOT STARTED
The Traditional Age (pre-1500 CE)

In order to comprehend the nature of the newly emerging planetary consciousness, we must go all the way back to the ancient period when the great religious traditions began and take a fresh look at the Western Middle Ages. Everything before the Modern Age was prescientific and traditional in nature. The Modern Age truly changed everything in its wake. The consciousness of the Traditional Age was dramatically different.

We then might ask, "Why is the Traditional Age so important if we have just come out of the Modern Age?" It is because the Traditional Age is the age that inspired all the great religious traditions, which collectively house the spiritual wealth of humanity. The Traditional Age includes the Western Middle Ages, and we maintain that the Planetary Age we are in today shares certain uncanny resemblances to this period.

Spiral Dynamics Theory of History with Dialectic

Humanity has had two conventional conceptions of history: a circle, as in South and East Asia, and a straight line, as in Western Europe and the United States. We maintain that history is not simply a circle or a straight line, or even a straight upward line implying either an evolutionary development or a steady elaboration of human civilization. We need to combine the two into a spiral theory called the "Spiral Dynamics Theory."

A spiral goes upward, but it also goes around in circles, so

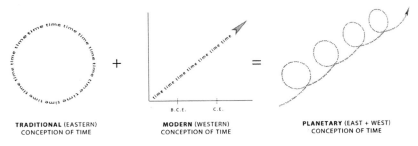

| TRADITIONAL (EASTERN) | MODERN (WESTERN) | PLANETARY (EAST + WEST) |
| CONCEPTION OF TIME | CONCEPTION OF TIME | CONCEPTION OF TIME |

5: Why time seems such a mystery to us today.

you are always going up and down. A spiral is interesting be-cause you emerge at a place where the low of one era is higher than the high of previous eras, which is the entire point. A gradual development happens, yet you have all these ups and downs that must be accounted for, such as finding ourselves right back in a major recession.

We also maintain that there is another dynamic going on in history, which is the "dialectic." Are we talking about the dialec-tic materialism of Karl Marx? Karl Marx was actually inspired by his professor, Georg William Friedrich Hegel, who devel-oped the dialectic. Ultimately, the dialectic came from Socrates way back in Ancient Greece, where he was asking questions as a means to establish the truth.

The dialectic theory implies that our awareness of truth ex-pands as a process, in which we emerge into ever-higher real-izations of that truth. You advance an idea, which we can call the "thesis" and that idea itself inspires a counter idea called the "antithesis." They then duke and clash it out, emerging with a higher view—a "synthesis."

The evolutionary theory can be thought of as a thesis. We have its antithesis in intelligent design. We might then anticipate a new synthesis combining elements of both. The idea is that the discov-

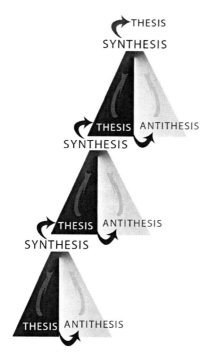

6: *What Karl Marx got right.*

ery of truth is not static but found in a dynamic process of ever-higher realizations. History, also, is not static but is a process where we keep moving to higher and higher truths but, in every major development, there is opposition that emerges, resulting in a counterthrust. For example, the French Revolution ended up with Napoleon taking over, in a way reinstating the monarchy, and then there emerged the democratic and republican values of contemporary France.

Things are not so simple; they do not just go straight up. That's most apparent. This is a critical insight when we examine the whole thrust of history, that we bear in mind both the spiral and dialectic theories.

The Divine Mother—Planet Earth as Goddess

Anthropology and archaeology suggest that primal humanity has had a profound appreciation of Planet Earth as its divine Mother—a green goddess, if you will. The first consciousness in the caves must have been of the awesome scope of creation. We look at people such as Native Americans. We look at folklore around the world, including that of the Aborigines in Australia.

All over the world, indigenous people had an awesome respect for nature, both plants and animals.

American mythologist, writer and lecturer, Joseph Campbell, pointed out that ancient people, when they sacrificed an animal to eat it, actually gave thanks—not to God the Creator, but to the animal itself that had forfeited its own life. There was a profound respect for life itself. Life was sacred, and the Earth was sacred. The Earth was literally seen as a goddess.

If you look at the Garden of Eden story in the Bible, the notion of paradise is also implied. You could extrapolate this to the notion that the early human environment was seen as paradise. The Earth was seen as a gorgeous goddess. So, we might speculate that our initial, primal consciousness was of the Earth as a divine Mother, a goddess.

Emergence of Traditional Consciousness

When we think of consciousness before modern times, such as in the Middle Ages, we have to go back to the ancient river valley civilizations when people shifted from being hunters and gatherers or tillers of the soil, in conjunction with simple hunting and gathering, to being agricultural workers in fertilized and irrigated fields along the great river valleys, which supported substantial populations.

As humanity grew, it emerged from region to region and continent to continent, and began to cluster around areas that allowed for water transportation, which sustained larger groups, which became villages, town and cities. People constructed housing rather than putting up the equivalent of tents. They wandered and began concentrating in certain regions where they were able to create a simple currency, which would allow for trade to go up and down the waterways, while their major economy was built on agriculture.

This was the foundation of material civilization as we think of it, including the development of astronomical observatories, such as the ziggurats in ancient Babylon, which were monumental terraced platforms much like pyramids, where people studied the movements of the sun and planets and developed a solar, rather than lunar, calendar.

Out of all this ferment, literacy emerged, either as sacred writing or, perhaps on a more pragmatic scale, as a means of keeping an accurate record of trades and financial transactions. Literacy emerged to record human thought, providing us with an early appreciation of history, endowing civilization with an historical sensibility.

Two River Valleys/Two Civilizations/One Destiny

The world has seen civilizations on virtually every continent, including the ancient Mayan, Aztec and Incan civilizations of the Western Hemisphere. We also see important civilizations in China and the Middle East, including the fertile crescent of Babylon and Persia.

While Planet Earth has hosted dozens of civilizations, the two most pivotal civilizations stand out: the one that formed around the Nile River Valley, giving birth to Western civilization, and the one around the Indus and Ganges River Valleys, giving birth to Eastern civilization, most particularly South Asian culture.

If we really look at the cultural divide, this is where it begins: East versus West. The Western civilization coming out of Egypt was linear and rational. We know that the ancient He-

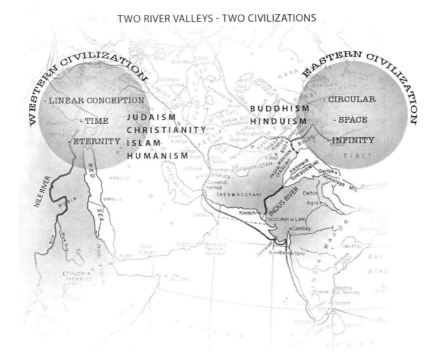

TWO RIVER VALLEYS - TWO CIVILIZATIONS

7: Where East and West actually began.

brew's migrated into Egypt in the face of starvation, eventually winding up as slaves and then winning their freedom back again. We look at the massive pyramids, the cult of Pharaoh, the whole court buried together, along with the ideal of everlasting life. We witness a linear, time-based perspective.

In the East, we see a proliferation of gods. Ultimately, India developed 330 million separate gods, along with a very intuitive and space-oriented approach. So, if we look at ancient Hindu thought, it already had a concept of trillions of years and infinite expanses in multiple worlds and multiple universes. It was truly vast and awesome in scope.

When we look at the primary focus of Western civilization,

it was time and eternity as opposed to space and infinity, East versus West, where one was linear and the other circular or spatial. The West began to understand God in terms of a story; hence, the importance of the *Torah* (foundation of Hebrew scripture, the books of Moses, including Genesis and Exodus), or the Pentateuch (Greek for "five books") in the Old Testament. The East understood God as pure being, a quality of being or consciousness, even energy. We began to see God, on one hand, in terms of a story with personality and, on the other hand, in terms of a type of consciousness and dimension of reality.

The West, therefore, grew into a much more materialistic approach as a civilization; the East retained and developed to a very high degree the spiritual qualities of civilization. We thus have two master civilizations—one materialistic, the other spiritual—that have remained so for millennia, not just for the last few centuries.

Five Great Religious Traditions

When we look at the great religious traditions that have survived and flourished right up to today, we find Hinduism, Buddhism, Christianity and Islam—not counting Judaism, which is the foundation of both Christianity and Islam. When we consider humanism as a possible sixth tradition, it was absorbed into Judaism, Christianity and Islam, and transmitted through the centuries, but broke loose to become an independent force in the Modern Age.

The East gave rise to the two major traditions of Hinduism and Buddhism, along with a number of minor traditions. The West gave rise to Judaism with the emergence of what we call "monotheism," or belief in one God, forming the conceptual foundation of Christianity and, later, that of Islam.

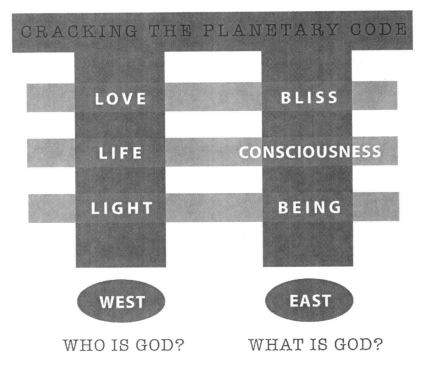

CRACKING THE PLANETARY CODE

LOVE	BLISS
LIFE	CONSCIOUSNESS
LIGHT	BEING

WEST | EAST

WHO IS GOD?   WHAT IS GOD?

8: Opposite approaches to the same Supreme Being.

Hinduism is an outlook not too dissimilar to the indigenous, shamanic outlook that the Universe is alive, the world is alive and there is a sacred web of life. Hinduism in its multidimensional thought is way beyond what you might find in shamanic culture with multiple gods and myriad expressions of the divine.

There is a stress on diversity, that there are multiple types of revelation, multiple types of consciousness. There is a very vast feeling about it all. Hinduism is orchestrated by major epics, the *Mahabharata* and the *Ramayana*, which unite the people with a common list of gods and goddesses.

Buddhism was an outgrowth of Hinduism. Some people see

it as Hinduism stripped to its bare essentials for export. The focus of Buddhism was to relieve suffering. Buddhism is actually more psychological, and Hinduism is more metaphysical. Buddhism had a very pragmatic approach from the very beginning to relieve the inherent pain, confusion and frustration of being human and find an elegant way out of it through a process of detachment to conditions of life and circumstances.

In Judaism, we look at the incredible gift of seeing one ultimate God as well as the emergence of destiny as being backed by God, Himself, if you will, which was exclusive to the Jewish people. The Jewish race has been preserved with odds that no other ethnic group might have imagined surviving. The concept of destiny implies that the Jewish people are special people. The Authorized King James Version of the Bible refers to them as "peculiar" people, but these people have a unique destiny in the world. That concept of destiny was picked up by other cultures, especially Christianity and Islam.

When we look at Christianity, there is a different accent: divine love. Here we see a remarkable departure from monotheism and the notion of incarnation, that Jesus is the Son of God and that we are all children of God. Neither Orthodox Judaism nor mainstream Islam would ever allow such a possibility. Christianity, however, recognizes divinity in human beings; human beings become, as it were, the gods of ancient Greece and Rome with the possibility of immortality, enjoying unlimited knowledge and power.

When we move to Islam, we see an accent on the unity of God as the overriding factor. The name *Allah* means "*The* God," referring to the supreme God, carrying the implication that God is beyond any definition. The Qur'an has 99 separate names for God.

Going back to ancient Judaism, it is very interesting that the name given for God in the flaming bush on Mount Sinai is "Yahweh," which means "I AM" or "I AM THAT I AM." We see Judaism introducing the notion of a supreme identity, that identity can only be defined in terms of Himself, Herself or Itself. The same would be true of Islam.

The amazing thing, as we look at the Abrahamic religions of Judaism, Christianity and Islam, is that we are looking at about two-thirds of the people living on the planet who identify with this tradition, nominally or otherwise. Many of them may not go to church, mosque or synagogue, but they still identify with monotheism.

We are thus looking at the majority of humanity sharing an underlying belief in one God, Who is seen as personal in a meaningful sense of the word.

Three World Masters Set the Stage

We find three world masters who forever altered the course of history:

- Siddhartha Gautama paired with Emperor Ashoka
- Aristotle paired with the conqueror Alexander the Great
- Jesus of Nazareth paired with the emperor Constantine

Why these three and not others? For example, Muhammad had a phenomenally vast impact on history. While he was actually born much later than the pivotal axial age of Siddhartha Gautama, coming in at the late 6th century CE, he helped shape the whole contour of the planet and civilization. Despite Muhammad's spec-

tacular accomplishments, we still have to look at these three con-
quers and spiritual masters as setting the foundational ideas that
would be essential for three different approaches to reality.

These three great masters gave birth to three separate
worldviews. You might say that Siddhartha Gautama, called
the Buddha (a title meaning "the man who woke up" or "the
awakened one") invented enlightenment, *per se*, as something
that anyone could achieve rather than being limited to a handful of elite people. The amazing thing is that, in the wake of
his mission of wandering throughout North India for decades
teaching every class of people, Siddhartha's message was later
institutionalized into a religion through Emperor Ashoka, who
came several hundred years later.

Ashoka was a truly remarkable conqueror who unified
most of northern and southern India. When Ashoka invaded
the nearby province of Kalanga in 265 BCE, he was disheart-
ened at the number of people killed because they fought back
so hard for their freedom. Ashoka became utterly disillusioned
with warfare and adopted Buddhism, institutionalizing it. The

Three World Masters and Three World Conquerors

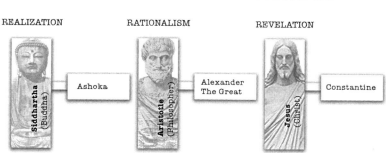

*9: It takes both a spiritual and political
master to conquer our imagination.*

circle we see today on the flag of India is that of the Buddhist wheel of dharma, the Noble Eightfold Path, Siddhartha Gautama's prescription for enlightenment.

Aristotle introduced a system of philosophy that was ultimately institutionalized throughout the world, being inspired by his direct and indirect masters, Plato and Socrates. We remember that Socrates invented the dialectic, which was picked up thousands of years later by Georg Wilhelm Friedrich Hegel, but Aristotle institutionalized the instruction of the philosophy of Socrates and Plato, making it into an institution. First, it was simply an academy in Athens; eventually, it would catalyze the institution of the university and establish philosophy, along with scientific thinking, as a discipline.

The interesting thing was that Alexander the Great was a conqueror who was groomed by his father Philip of Macedonia. Philip unified Greece and then prepared his son to conquer the known world. So, Alexander, in his early 20s, embarked on a crusade to take out the world, and did so to most of the known world at that time, taking a total of 13 years. He tragically died in Babylon just before the age of 33.

What happened in the wake of Alexander's exploits was that the Greek language and culture were standardized as "Hellenism" throughout all of the conquered territory, which included Ancient Egypt, unifying most of the known world. There was actually a Greek overlay into the Ancient Egyptian tradition. Alexander may have impacted India to some degree, but he found the Ancient Indian culture so robust that he could barely make a dent in it. It is noteworthy that Greek mercenary soldiers stayed on there for centuries.

Alexander the Great shaped the ancient world, inspiring

Julius Caesar and the Romans. The Greco-Roman civilization became the foundation, along with Judeo-Christian civilization, of the modern civilization in which most of us grew up.

We then turn to Jesus of Nazareth, born 4 or 5 BCE under Roman Emperor Augustus in Palestine—a remote part of that empire, which had been repeatedly conquered and had known violence and warfare throughout its history, being the gateway to Asia. Jesus most brilliantly enunciated the principle of non-violence in His famous "Sermon on the Mount" where He admonished His disciples to turn their cheeks, pray for their enemies and resist not evil, to actually love their enemies.

If we look at the cross from a very human standpoint, as in the recent film, *The Passion of the Christ*, we see its overwhelming statement as the ultimate display of divine love, a love that is beyond our reckoning. At first, this movement was almost entirely Jewish. It was quickly picked up by more and more Greek and Roman people through the influence of the Apostle Paul and other early missionaries. Over a 300-year period, it became dominant throughout the Roman Empire. Then, in 313 CE with the Edict of Milan, Constantine legalized Christianity, and a little later made it the official religion of the Roman Empire. At that point, one could say that Christianity truly "conquered" the Roman Empire.

It is interesting in each case that you find a spiritual master paired with a conqueror. In the case of Siddhartha, he was set up to be a king by his father, left as a prince, went out as a wondering monk, went into an extreme privation and ended up becoming a world teacher.

In the case of Jesus, if you believe the Gospels, He was born to be a king who also became a world teacher. Jesus was a king who never got to be a king, just as Siddhartha never actually became a king, leaving his kingdom as a crown prince. Both were picked up by later conquerors who took their teaching worldwide—Ashoka in the case of Buddha and Constantine in the case of Jesus. The same thing happened in terms of Aristotle and Alexander the Great.

We see a marriage, if you will, of a world master and a world conqueror that drove each of these three worldviews.

Western Mystical Traditions: Judaism/Christianity/Islam

The Western mystical traditions focus on divine redemption and rebirth, sharing a view of all creation as an infinite expression of the eternal love of God. In these traditions, the human story can only be understood in relation to a personal God. The Bible, if you look at it as a document, is replete with history. God is realized primarily in the context of human experience as well as in dreams, visions and revelations.

The focus is on our relationship with God and the need for spiritual rebirth. The underlying notion is that there is the Creator and the created. The Creator is trying to communicate with the created who, in some sense, are rebelling against their Creator. That is the underlying premise of Judaism, Christianity and Islam.

These traditions came out of the life experience of the ancient Hebrew patriarch, Abraham, who migrated out of Babylonia into the "Holy Land" of Palestine. Abraham, by all rights, can be considered the world's first monotheist, leaving behind the gods of Chaldea for The One True God. Interestingly enough, the most sacred name Yahweh was not revealed until the time of Moses. Early on, God is addressed as the Lord or El Shaddai. All these traditions are built on Abraham's vision, including Christianity and Islam.

What is the mystical element? The mystical element in Judaism might be the name of Yahweh, Himself, "I AM THAT I AM," which implies that the Supreme Being is an absolute mystery. It also has to do with the revelatory nature of experience, dreams and visions. It is mainly based on an inner realization that accompanies revelation in various forms, documented by scripture.

The Christian mystical experience focuses on the love of Christ, tuning within to become a reflection of that divine love on a transcendent level. The Islamic mystical experience, like the Christian, focuses on love but, in Sufism, it is seen as the rapturous love of the devotee for the Creator as friend, on an extremely high level as in the work of Rumi, the Persian poet and philosopher.

So, in the entire Western tradition, God is experienced primarily in terms of a voice or a vision rather than as an interior realization or feeling. God is understood to be a person, even if the ultimate reality is transpersonal, going beyond personality.

In summary, the Western tradition is built upon a relationship with the Supreme Being. There is a deep mystical tradition that has to do with The One God; that, ultimately, there are not multiple gods but one God, Who is infinite and absolute. The mystical side is that The One God is ultimately a single reality and that there is *only* God, God is all that exists and God is our ultimate true Self. This has been a subtle undercurrent in Western civilization. To openly profess and claim that you were one with God often meant heresy and, in many cases, death. God is seen as the ultimate true reality, which is more readily recognized in the East. In the West, it is found in what might be referred to as the "esoteric tradition," which implies that which is subtle, or hidden, with just a few people realizing it. This is in contrast with the "exoteric tradition," which is the public view that you might find in churches, mosques or synagogues in a typical suburb.

Northern Tradition of Mystical Humanism

The mystical tradition of the North, started by the Greeks as "humanism," was first expressed in the esoteric saying, "As within, so without; as above, so below," which was ultimately refined into the infinite possibility of quantum mechanics that unifies observer and observed.

The Greco-Roman tradition inspired the development of democracy, philosophy and science as well as most of the institutions that define the modern world. It was a brilliant tradition, ultimately stemming from Ancient Greece. Most often, 5th century BCE Athens is considered the pivotal time and place where we saw Socrates and Plato, along with the Greek tragedians and comedians, as well as the institution of direct democracy.

The mystical element underlying this Western tradition was found in a variety of directions. One was the philosophical notion of "the True, the Good and the Beautiful." The "True" ultimately became science, the "Good" ethics and the "Beautiful" what we consider aesthetics, entailing the fine arts of painting, sculpture, music, poetry, dance and theater.

In the ancient philosophical understanding, the ultimate reality was the True, the Good and the Beautiful. The surrounding day-to-day reality in which we lived was only a weak approximation of the truth, reflecting the ultimately True, Good and Beautiful. That was mystical. Implicit in the perception of the Beautiful was the notion of perfection, that fully realized art, ethics and philosophy, including mathematics, held the potential of being perfect. The ideal world was most certainly held to be perfect. The whole idea of perfection itself might be attributed to the ancient Greeks. The Modern Age picked up these values to a large degree. People applied the scientific method to such an extent that they eventually arrived at seeing how everything is integrally related in quantum theory. We finally got into a very profound mysticism that echoes both East and West, thanks to the post-Newtonian physicists such as Albert Einstein, Werner Heisenberg and the quantum and string theorists of the 20th century CE.

Southern Mystical Tradition of Shamanism

The mystical tradition of the South, championed by the shamans of Earth's indigenous traditions past and present, celebrates the sacred web of life, "the Great Spirit." Worldwide, even today, there are approximately 350 million people still living as hunters and gatherers, very often moving from place to place with the most basic agriculture, tilling the soil without the benefit of animals or machinery.

Their lifestyle, in many cases, such as the tribes of the Amazon basin, is not that different from the lifestyle of prehistoric people. They look at the natural world and all of life as being inherently sacred, with a shamanic consciousness. The Earth is seen largely in feminine terms as our divine Mother, with the implication that the sky is our divine Father. We can actually go to places like the Costa Rican rainforest and the Amazon, which is a kind of paradise. The world is reverenced as paradise. Humanity's purpose is not to bulldoze it but to live in harmony with a profound appreciation of its beauty.

These people remain the true custodians of the Earth, the only people who can truly save us from an environmental perspective. By giving us the intricate sensibility required to love the Earth, the indigenous people can help put us in harmony with the ecosystem and align ourselves with all the other species of plants and animals.

In a nutshell, the Southern mystical tradition views all of life, as well as the Universe, itself, as sacred and very much alive. Even rocks have a primitive form of consciousness, as is also seen in the Eastern tradition of Hinduism.

Why Does This Matter?

We can't fully appreciate the present without knowing the past. The Traditional Age infused the world with all of our great religious traditions. Compared to the Modern Age, it was a very spiritual era. The Planetary Age in which we are living today bears a strange resemblance to that period in its openness to mystery and magic. Spirituality has returned but, this time, it is much more focused on unity and much more powerful in its breadth and depth.

This shows us that history is not static. It keeps moving on and on to ever-higher truths. As per the Spiral Dynamics theory, we emerge at a point where the low of one era is higher than the high of the previous era, which applies not only to civilization but also to our own spiritual consciousness. We gradually develop, with ups and downs all along the way that prompt us to search and discover the deeper meaning of our existence.

Chapter Three:

HOW WE WENT MAD
The Modern Age *(1500-1945 CE)*

When we ask ourselves how humanity veered so far off course as to create a megacrisis of the magnitude of global warming, we need to go all the way back to the Crusades and the discovery of America by Christopher Columbus. This is a story of how Western Europe and America came, stage by stage, to dominate geopolitics while inadvertently bringing humanity together.

This is the first period in history to witness the sharp break between religion and science, where science actually came out ahead. In the process, Western "man"—humanity, in effect—lost his soul. We will recount the last 500 years that led us right up to our recent past and show you how this very complex material civilization came together, and how we fell into world wars and emerged with a brand new civilization and age.

The Crusades Inspire the Age of Discovery

As the Roman Empire declined and succumbed to Germanic invasions, Islam rose to create a magnificent civilization of its own, effectively upstaging Western Europe. As we look back at the Roman Empire, we wonder why it collapsed. Rome was held to be the empire that would last a thousand years. If you actually count the Eastern Empire under Constantine, it did continue for more than a thousand years; however, the city of Rome itself was sacked by Vandals and Goths, raiding Italy in the 5th century CE, and then rebuilt.

If you wonder why this happened to Rome, we have to look back at Emperor Constantine's decision to split the Roman Empire by having two separate capital cities. Constantine, after he became a Christian, made Christianity—not only the legal religion but also set the stage for it to become the official religion of the Roman Empire. He then moved to what is now Istanbul, Turkey, forming a city there—Constantinople, named after himself and closer to the Holy Land. This decision strategically weakened the Roman Empire on the West, enabling the Germanic hordes to later successfully advance on Rome.

As we move forward, we look at a vacuum as Islam emerged as an alternative to Christianity, a profoundly prophetic movement with a deeply radical concept of monotheism, where there is no god but "God." In other words, *Allah* offered a unified conception of God, as the very name means "*The* God." This movement proceeded to conquer much of the known world at a much faster rate than did Christianity, taking not much more than a century.

The Muslims, in the wake of Christianity, developed an initially superior civilization in terms of art, philosophy, science, medicine and engineering. In the West, that same period was looked upon as a falling into the "dark ages," awaiting revival in the Middle Ages. Thanks to the monasteries, Western civilization was nursed back to life. The Muslims, however, did not suffer any such relapse but grew and proliferated right up until the industrial age.

As time elapsed, Western Europe began to reunify and, at one point, the Muslims were preparing to take all of Europe, bringing it all under the aegis of Islam; however, the armies of Charles Martel, a Frankish military and political leader, stopped the Muslim troops in Tours, France, in 732 CE. This brought

Western Europe into the Middle Ages with the Holy Roman Empire, a Germanic federation modeled after the original Roman Empire. As the Holy Roman Empire was built, we saw the great cathedrals come out of nowhere, rivaling the great mosques of Islam as well as picking up the institution of the university, which the Muslims had pioneered, borrowing from the ancient Indian university of Nalanda, which was a Buddhist institution.

The West wanted to regain its position in the Holy Land as it reasserted its power. A series of crusades lasted some 150 years, declared by various popes, which largely backfired and proved ultimately futile. However, the result of Western Europe flexing its muscles was the emergence of a spirit of adventure. The underlying economic reason for the crusades was Western Europe's keen interest in direct access to India, not having to go through Muslim traders.

In those days, there were no ice chests. Europeans had nothing with which to preserve their meats except the spices from India. The nobility, of course, had also acquired a taste for the silks and textiles from the East. Out of this turbulence, a new concept of the world was emerging. Columbus successfully sold to royal patrons the proposition that the world was not flat but actually round and, therefore, Spain could reach India from the opposite direction. He then set sail with three ships to discover the alternate route to India. What he actually did discover, of course, became known as the "New World" or the Western Hemisphere, launching the "age of exploration." At first, Spain was content to simply mine gold and silver from the Native Americans, but it ultimately colonized much of the Americas.

As this age emerged, Europe began to unite through nationalism and the modern world along with it. This group of nations would produce the greatest material civilization ever seen, while unfortunately stripping Earth of her natural resources and devastating much of the environment in the process.

Renaissance Man as "The Measure of All Things"

As the classical Greek and Roman texts were recovered by the Crusaders and Islamic scholarship, a new conception of humanity emerged echoing ancient philosophy. We saw the little Italian states emerge out of the Middle Ages, which had begun to explore beyond the Mediterranean Sea. There was world travel. Most everyone is intrigued by the adventures of Marco Polo, who went from Venice to China and back, and there was increasing interest in other civilizations and lifeways.

There was a rediscovery of the classics through the Muslims, particularly the work of Aristotle and Plato, which began to have a measurable impact on European civilization. There was a rising merchant class as a result of the trade, along with a rapidly growing appreciation of, and taste for, the finer things in life; one thinks ultimately of Renaissance Italy. The rediscovery of Aristotle and Plato had a remarkable impact in building a whole new conception of the world. In this view, there was an emphasis on placing humanity, rather than God, at the very center of the world.

As the Renaissance ideal went, "Man is the measure of all things." In essence, the Renaissance philosophy developed the school of thought referred to as "humanism," which suggests that the sole concern of humanity should be humanity itself. The implications of this to the environment should by now be apparent.

Democracy was reinvented in Italy at the level of the city/state and the arts flourished as never before. There were small republics that thrived for a matter of centuries. They were overshadowed by the great monarchies of France and England. In London, during the Northern Renaissance, we saw Shakespeare reinvent theater and literature, enlarging the English language in a truly remarkable way, with a universal humanistic outlook that would shape future generations. In the American tradition, Shakespeare's plays ranked second only to the Bible in literary influence.

For the first time, the individual in Western civilization was given ultimate importance over society, and romantic love as an ideal was born. We see this earlier in the troubadours of ancient France where, in the Middle Ages, knights would court their aristocratic lovers and go into chivalrous jousts, which were contests. More particularly, one thinks of the play, "Romeo and Juliet"—the ideal of individual love with the conviction that marriage should be based on romantic love; that children should be allowed to choose their own mates rather than allowing their parents to do so. In India, even today, this is referred to as a "love marriage." This fits in with the whole notion of "Renaissance Man"—that humanity is the measure of all things and the individual can do anything.

Reformation—Freedom of Faith Established

The invention of movable type and the printing press enabled affordable copies of the Bible to be passed on to the Church and, increasingly, to the educated elite. We see the emergence of the printing press with movable type in the late 1400s CE. The implications were immense, because it allowed multiple books to be produced. With movable type, one did not have to take out a wood block and carve it; one could simply move the type around, which gave rise to newspapers and periodicals as well as books.

With rapid printing, there was the ability to create more and more copies of printed books, making them less and less of a rare item. The focus initially, because of its supreme religious importance, was to print the Bible. As the Bible began to be distributed, the literacy of the clergy, and gradually the literacy of the aristocracy, increased. Even the celebration of the mass, in the case of Protestantism, began to be delivered in the common languages of German, French and English. People were finally free to find the truth for themselves and develop their own beliefs.

The implications of Martin Luther's stand were to establish the devout believer's right to question Church doctrine. He rejected any notion of buying indulgences to win merit in the afterlife and began to carefully examine the New Testament, which became the final authority. As the Bible became variously interpreted, it led to sharp divisions within Christianity. These divisions became acute in countries like England, leading to violent religious wars, such as the Civil War under Oliver Cromwell in the 1600s CE. The various religious wars lasted for decades, shaking Europe to its very foundation.

The early Puritans who settled Boston and New England had left England for the Netherlands. From there, they sought greater religious freedom in the New World to worship in their own way, as opposed to submitting to the orthodoxy established by the Anglican Church. They put a premium on religious freedom. As the American colonies were built, America became known for institutionalizing various freedoms that would include the Declaration of Independence, the U.S. Constitution and the Bill of Rights.

As the religious civil wars throughout Europe subsided, there was a standoff between Protestants and Catholics. An ideal of tolerance emerged in what became known as the "Age of Enlightenment," that is, the European enlightenment of the 18th century CE.

Scientific Revolution — Creation as an Open Book

As Nicolaus Copernicus and Galileo Galilei stumbled upon a whole new paradigm in astronomy that contradicted early Ptolemaic thought, which asserted that the Earth revolved around the sun rather than the sun revolving around the Earth, the stage was set for a final showdown with the Roman Catholic Church.

The Copernican Revolution overthrew the medieval conception of humanity as the center of the Universe, where the Earth was now seen to revolve around the sun. The ancient idea was that the planets all revolved around the Earth in a convoluted fashion. This tradition, because it was Greek, was upheld by the Catholic Church, which had come to accept the natural philosophy of Aristotle, Ptolemy and the other Greeks as authoritative, treating it as if it were unquestionable dogma.

Beginning in the 1400s CE, scientists began to question the Latin Church's stand. Galileo had worked out a brilliant theory of gravity, but he was literally forced by the Roman Catholic Church to recant his heliotropic views. By 1600 CE, another great physicist, Giordano Bruno, was killed for maintaining his scientific views as well as his mystical views, being burned at the stake in Rome.

In Protestant countries, the scientific method was perfected, as the breakout with the Roman Catholic Church led to greater freedom of thought, stressing empirical observation and measurement. The scientific method is unique in world history in the sense of it being based on direct observation with very precise measurement, along with the notion that any experiment must be publicly verifiable and repeatable. It is interesting that the French word for experiment is *experience*; it is an experiential approach to discovering the truth.

With the printing industry expanding through movable type, scientists were now able to formally share their ideas all around Europe and a whole body of scientific knowledge built up rather quickly. When we come to Sir Isaac Newton, he not only invented the very calculus that allowed us to go to the moon but was also able to precisely trace the planets, stars and solar system, coming up with a vision of the solar system and the Universe as one vast clock. There was increasing fascination with seeing all aspects of the Universe in terms of an intricate mechanism.

In Louis XIV's Palace of Versailles, there was a gorgeous little model of the planets and the Earth as a clock. It was deeply built into the modern mindset that the Universe is a wound-up clock with the Creator, as watchman, having walked away. As science advanced, so too did physics and chemistry, leading right up to the Industrial Revolution, which would enable modern civilization to eclipse Islamic civilization.

The ability to harness equipment, beginning with steam power, would change everything. It put the European civilization on a par with Islamic civilization and would enable it to finally overtake Islamic civilization militarily, politically and economically.

Democratic Revolutions in the European Age of Enlightenment

Western Europe moved from religious wars into a period of enlightened rationalism that inspired the intelligentsia of the 18th century CE to determine their destiny through democratic revolution.

In the wake of the bloody religious wars, particularly the Civil War in England, rationalism, along with education and literacy, was seen as a form of social enlightenment. In other words, people should not kill in the name of religion or God because we all have a common humanity and we should work for that.

The American colonies began to question the legitimacy of their British masters on rational grounds, launching a successful political revolution. If we look at the Declaration of Independence, drafted by Thomas Jefferson, we will see a document of divorce issued unilaterally against the British Empire. The American colonialists' success with the American Revolution inspired the French Revolution, which ultimately collapsed on itself, but whose values haunted the 19th century CE in the person of Emperor Napoleon, who adopted many of its ideals, exporting them in his conquests throughout Europe.

It is amazing when you think about these little American colonies winning over the mighty British Empire, but you have to remember that Britain was in the process of conquering India while in severe competition with France. In an ironic quirk of history, Britain chose to give up America in turn for keeping India.

At the heart of all these revolutions was a free press that encouraged broad, public education. As early as the 19th century CE, we began to see serious education among women in upper classes and a growing literacy that would spark the popularity of American novels and operas. These revolutions established modern political and social values on a widespread basis, which became nearly universal by the 20th century CE.

Industrial Revolution—
The West Surges Ahead of the Islamic World

With the emergence of steam power, Western Europe and the United States began developing machinery that would weave textiles and transport people with railroads and ships, surpassing anything that the Islamic world had ever seen. For the first time in a thousand years, European civilization surpassed Islamic civilization on multiple levels. Because of economic superiority, it was able to unify the world and build an advanced military, which enabled it to prevail over the various Islamic countries.

The expansion was very rapid in the 19th century CE, particularly in Africa and all parts of Asia. Europeans could now successfully challenge and defeat the Islamic armies. Their steamships and huge guns could pound major cities from offshore. Steam power enabled engines to be built, which revolutionized transportation and warfare. Steamships emerged as well as, of course, the locomotives and trains that dotted Europe, America and, ultimately, India.

Factory production enabled widespread material affluence to an unprecedented degree. We saw mass production along with the industrial innovations of Henry Ford, who made his famous Model T. Parts were made universal and replicable, so factories were able to generate a massive amount of goods and materials.

When applied to agriculture, the Industrial Revolution made slavery obsolete because the machinery could more efficiently pick cotton, ultimately leading to the abolition of slavery. Were it not for the invention of the cotton gin, it might not have been economically feasible to work large fields without servants or slaves. The entire impact of the Industrial Revolution was phenomenal, shaping every aspect of the Modern Age and forming the basis for the great modern economic wave.

Western Imperialism and Social Darwinism

It is strangely ironic that the revolutionary fervor of Napoleon set the stage for an unparalleled period of colonial exploitation in Africa and Asia, justified by a very twisted form of Darwinism. Western Europe dominated the known world through their steamships, gunboats and superior cannon, and began to colonize everywhere around the world.

It was in the context of that colonial expansion that Charles Darwin boarded the *H.M.S. Beagle* and began to observe the weird life formations in the Galapagos Islands. In this model, the occupied colonies provided raw materials, which were shipped right back to Europe to be produced in factories, most obviously in terms of the textile industry. The amount of goods was prolific and the impact on the native environments was devastating. Many of the forests of Africa and India were systematically stripped and mined.

Charles Darwin's new "theory of evolution" emerged at the height of this age of Western imperialism at a time when imperialism was placed in question. Emerging when it did, it strangely served as a convenient rationale for further exploitation. The Darwinian concept of "survival of the fittest" was seen as the way of nature, that only the fittest species could survive over other species. There was an implicit justification and rationale for European aggression. Along with this, there was the notion of "might makes right," a doctrine espoused by Kaiser Wilhelm, who invaded Belgium on the eve of World War I, rationalizing his actions by commenting, "What is a treaty but a scrap of paper?"

Modern Western philosophy was heavily influenced by a whole stream of evolutionary thought with an undercurrent of hostility towards the great East and West religious traditions. The prevailing idea was that nature was strictly materialistic, the Universe was a vast clock and humanity was the measure of all things. What was the point of God? Hostility against all forms of religion developed in the academic institutions, which became increasingly secular, setting the stage for the fundamentalist revolt that we would see in the 20th century CE.

Capitalism, Socialism and the Multinationals

The 19th century CE witnessed the emergence of powerful corporations under laissez-faire capitalism and socialist fervor under a young Karl Marx in the aborted Revolution of 1848.

With the growth of capitalism, more and more factories emerged, employing an endless stream of people from the farms. There was mass migration into the cities. The great cities of Europe, and increasingly in America, grew larger and larger, eventually developing into urban areas. More and more people were displaced, taking poorly paying jobs with 12-hour days and six-day work weeks.

In these conditions, children were often compelled to work these long hours because education was not yet universal. Public education was very basic in the 19th century CE. In the 20th century CE, we would finally see kindergarten through 12th-grade education standardized in Europe and America.

In the midst of all this exploitation, Karl Marx created socialism as a theory, which maintained that workers have the inherent right to own the means of production. Marx created the *Communist Manifesto* as a new vision for the working class to participate in the capital infrastructure as a reward for their labor. Before this time, raw capital was less and less of an issue. By "capital," we are referring to the money involved as well as the physical plants required to create and operate the machinery itself, along with the raw materials.

As the industrial age increased, the average workplace became a factory rather than a field. In the information age, the factory would increasingly give place to the office. The irony is that Karl Marx died protesting, "I am not a Marxist!" A whole revolutionary ideology formed around his masterpiece, *Das Kapital*, a brilliant analysis of the capitalism of his age. Ironically, Karl Marx underestimated the success of the Industrial Revolution in freeing up more and more workers to create a healthy middle class.

Colonialism, in supplying raw materials to the world, set the stage for the multinational corporations of today. As this industrial economy moved further and further, we began to see the emergence of the multinationals that would become more powerful than many nations. Tragically, capitalism sided with the church, especially in Catholic countries, inadvertently exploiting workers, while socialism sided with the workers against the capitalists and the church. Therefore, on economic grounds, we began to see increasing hostility toward religion, particularly coming from countries that would eventually become socialist.

"The Belle Epoque"– Rule of Reason and the Fundamentalist Reaction

Western Europe had convinced itself that its polite society, with impressive refinement in the arts and sciences, was here to stay before the outbreak of World War I. Under colonialism, nationalism emerged among the European powers over who owned which territory. As we basically saw, Europe emerged to dominate most of the planet, ironically with a handful of countries: Great Britain, France, the Netherlands, Belgium, Portugal, Spain and, to a lesser degree, America.

In the 19th century CE, America was largely content with going across the continent and staking out the land. For example, California came in the wake of the shameless Mexican-American War, as did Arizona, Texas and New Mexico. We witnessed an era of unparalleled greed and disregard for other civilizations and cultures.

In this era, when we look at high societies, like Paris, we see a society naively assuring itself that it lived on rational grounds; that there was every reason to suppose that war as an institution would fade away. The government was still led by a privileged ruling class but, increasingly, there were democratic institutions such as Parliament. Alliances were formed in the early 20th century CE all over Europe where, if any one nation were attacked, all of its allies would be drawn into the war. Thus, each country felt protected.

It is ironic that, just before World War I, many of the leading European monarchs were German in blood, including the monarchs of Great Britain, the wife of the Czar and, of course, Kaiser Wilhelm, himself. We had the United Kingdom, Russia and Germany all fighting against each other, sharing the same ancestry, making it a very tragic war that nobody anticipated. Because of all of these entangling alliances, a multisided war was precipitated by the assassination in Serbia of Archduke Ferdinand of Austria. The number of deaths in World War I totaled over 20 million. In the wake, the League of Nations was formed through the efforts of U.S. President Woodrow Wilson to put an end to war. It was tragic that, despite President Wilson's impassioned efforts to enlist the support of his own country, America refused to join.

At the time of World War I, Russia was full of disillusioned troops and the early communists were propagandizing workers. Vladimir Lenin returned from Paris and began to precipitate the Communist Revolution. In the case of Russia, the Mensheviks formed a polite revolution where they threw out the czar but kept him and his family alive. A little later, the Communist Bolshevik Party came in and literally took over with machine guns, ordering the Mensheviks out.

It is ironic that most of the people in the countryside actually supported the czar over either revolutionary government. Because of mismanagement and brutal politics, millions of Russians died of starvation under Lenin and Stalin. As World War I raged on, the veneer of polite society grew thin and many people began to seek spiritual values. The whole idea that we could put an end to war itself, which is how World War I had been sold to America under Woodrow Wilson, grew thin and lost its credibility.

Modern Consciousness Culminates in the Atomic War

If we question the development and detonation of the atomic bomb, ultimately leading to the hydrogen bomb in the wake of World War II, we find a peculiar mindset that allowed both the conception and execution of such a monster. The Modern Age instigated the greatest changes humanity had ever seen, providing the foundation for a truly global civilization.

The early divorce between the scientists and the church set

the stage for a secular society with fervent development of all the sciences. In this standoff, the scientists ironically won through the spectacular technology they enabled, which upstaged the church and its religious values. The standards of living emerged beyond anything the world had ever seen. Western Europe, America and other countries began to share a strong humanistic framework, and democracy became the prevailing idea all around the world.

Education emerged as universal in many of the Western countries during the 20th century CE. We saw the emergence, thanks to Germany, of the great Western secular universities, which established new standards of scholarship and research. On the West Coast, we may think of such institutions as Cal Berkeley, which were explicitly nonreligious. In many cases, teaching religion was formally excluded, whereas the early universities in the Middle Ages were actually formed in cathedrals such as Notre Dame, Cambridge and Oxford.

As the potential for good exploded, so also did the potential for destruction. Under the pressure of World War II, the famous American Manhattan Project was formed and conducted in top secrecy, resulting in the detonation of two atomic bombs over Hiroshima and Nagasaki, instantaneously liquidating hundreds of thousands of people.

As Japan was decisively defeated, and American law was instated throughout Japan and much of the Far East, China fell vulnerable to the communist insurgents during their Long March. The insurgents took advantage of the vacuum of power since the Japanese invasion and withdrawal to assume control in Beijing, converting the former empire systematically exploited by European powers into a massive communist state with an ideology of radical egalitarianism and scientific materialism that left no room for either individuality or religious differences. It is important to realize that, prior to the revolution, China had suffered starvation in the millions and massive floods.

After Mao-Tse Tung assumed power, his first decisive move was to attempt to take over Tibet, even though the average height of this land mass, the size of the western United States, is over 12,000 feet. The pressure on the reigning monarch, the Dalai Lama, was intense. The growing presence of Chinese troops continued for years, making Tibet a vassal territory. Ultimately, in the late 1950s, the Dalai Lama, with a few members of his court, fled Tibet for his life, while the Chinese armies decisively closed in.

Thousands of monasteries were stripped and destroyed, while hundreds of thousands of people were harassed, humiliated and tortured. Literally millions of Tibetans ended up dying in the ensuing years in a country with a population of just five million people. India gave refuge to the Dalai Lama in Dharamsala, along with thousands of refugees who escaped down the Himalayas. While the Dalai Lama was able to create a government in exile, he was forbidden to speak out against China due to the danger of fatally exacerbating the severely strained relations between India and China.

It wasn't until 1989, as a Nobel Peace Prize recipient, that the Dalai Lama got the critical traction he would need to become the world's foremost spokesman, ceaselessly advocating nonviolence and demonstrating consummate compassion to the very Chinese who persecuted him and nearly destroyed his country and people.

After World War II, we also saw the emergence of Christian neo-orthodoxy and neo-evangelicalism. There was growing recognition of a spiritual vacuum and many people were appalled at the devastation of over 40 million lives. In response, the United Nations was first formed in San Francisco and then transferred to New York City. There was a conservative reaction against the excesses of World War II, with a belief in sin, judgment and biblical values.

Billy Graham emerged as the world's foremost evangelist. Thanks to radio and television, he spoke to more people worldwide than any Christian before him. He preached the Gospel on every continent except Antarctica, directly touching at least half a billion people. Graham gradually shifted the emphasis from hell and brimstone toward what was the audience's relationship with God through Christ and its eternal implications. The impact of Billy Graham can hardly be overestimated if we consider his cumulative impact on the Nixon, Reagan and Bush administrations. The Christian Right would have not been possible without the groundwork he laid.

We look at the culmination of the Modern Age in the formation of an atomic bomb that would devastate human beings. This endeavor would proliferate—thanks to the Cold War between the United States and the U.S.S.R.—to the point where we collectively had 50 times the firepower to destroy the entire human race. The upside was the realization that unlimited warfare could no longer work and thus was no longer a feasible policy. If there were any advantage in building a nuclear stockpile, it was the realization that nobody wins in a thermonuclear exchange.

Why Does This Matter?

The Modern Age was filled with adventurism and discovery. During that time, humanity "evolved" in so many ways while we lost what was so essential—our blissful soul. We brushed spirituality aside, becoming empty, and got exceedingly preoccupied with material abundance.

Every "yin" has a "yang," and there is a sweet counterpart to every sour note. Let us not overlook the positive side of this age and why it was a necessary phase. The Modern Age set the stage for a truly global civilization. Due to early misunderstandings, science and religion got a divorce that lasted for several hundred years, resulting in a schizophrenic spirituality, a dualistic worldview. Colonialism and imperialism laid the groundwork not only for the Industrial Revolution, which effectively ended slavery, but also for the global infrastructure that would finally enable humanity to come together.

Chapter Four:
WHAT WOKE US UP
Early Transition—Pluralism *(1945-1980)*

When we consider the post-World War II era, which led into the social and cultural revolutions of the 1960s and 1970s, we witness the apogee of white Western civilization that would set the very conditions for its decline, with the subsequent emergence of true pluralism.

The world balance of power gradually shifted away from Western white people in favor of other nations and ethnic groups in America, which was known to be a melting pot of countries. This concept was superseded in the 1960s with ever-increasing interest in multiculturalism such as Black Power, La Raza and Women's Rights.

The Cold War between the Soviet Union and the United States introduced the space race, taking humanity literally out of this world. As the Industrial Revolution peaked, we began to see some developments that would take us well beyond an industrial framework. The preoccupation with science and technology began to shift in this period toward social and cultural values, and material progress itself was questioned.

One need think only of the Beatles wearing granny glasses in their *Sergeant Pepper's Lonely Hearts Club Band* album, which highlighted 1967. The Beatles focused on the present rather than the future and, as Timothy Leary famously declared in Golden Gate Park, "Turn on, tune in, drop out."

Gandhi Topples the British Empire

Although Mohandas Karamchand "Mahatma" Gandhi's nonviolent revolution took a lifetime to prepare, it all culminated within a couple of years after World War II with the formation of the British Commonwealth. Gandhi was the first person in all of history to free an entire nation through nonviolent methods.

When we look at the remarkable case of Christianity, even when Romans were throwing Christians to the lions in the coliseum, we don't see an entire nation using nonviolent methods. We've never seen this, to our knowledge, in history, until Mahatma Gandhi successfully deployed these methods—first in South Africa among the Indian population and then throughout all of India in the 1920s through the 1940s.

A free India and Pakistan would result in the liberation of virtually all the British colonies within a decade or two, all becoming independent in the newly formed British Commonwealth. The newly formed United Nations gave these independent nations recognition and a voice. The U.S. prestige and influence growing out of the United Nations, along with the U.S. success in ending World War II, gave the United States unparalleled power in the 1950s and 1960s. This was increasingly countered by the ideological challenge of the Soviet Union that would emerge as the Cold War and the space race.

Gandhi's spirituality inspired a deep wave of interest in the West by first influencing Martin Luther King, Jr., with the Civil Rights Movement and then increasing interest in spirituality, including various forms of Hinduism in California and a growing interest in all kinds of Eastern traditions.

American Civil Rights Movement Brings Democracy to the Streets

Gandhi's revolutions inspired Martin Luther King, Jr., to launch the Civil Rights movement in 1954, leading to his famous march on Washington where he gave his "I have a dream" speech, echoing the Bible, just as Mahatma Gandhi had earlier echoed the Bhagavad Gita. It is noteworthy that there is a parallel between the lives of Mahatma Gandhi and Martin Luther King, Jr. Unfortunately, Dr. King's life was tragically ended much earlier than was the life of Gandhi. It actually took a little over a decade for Dr. King to liberate America, whereas it took decades for Gandhi to liberate India.

Dr. King deployed the very same techniques, including peaceful demonstrations, marches, chanting and sit-downs, that Gandhi successfully deployed in India. Because of the difference in the sensibility of America, King incorporated largely Christian values and symbols, attracting liberals from the North. This antagonized the deeply conservative and fundamentalist South.

The liberals in the North had organized the Civil Rights movement and, joining the Democratic Party, brought about a kind of revolution in civil rights, which would set the entire agenda for the 1960s. While Dr. King's demonstrations actually made their way into a constitutional amendment under President Johnson, he was tragically assassinated in 1968, as was Bobby Kennedy, who had won the Democratic primary.

The extremes of affirmative action inspired a white backlash under Republican President Richard Nixon. This actually began in the Boston schools, where people in that liberal bastion were upset about their own children having to be bussed into black neighborhoods and vice versa. In carrying forth the ideals of the Civil Rights movement, it was a very bumpy experience, creating much resentment and opposition.

For the first time in American history, we see the Civil Rights movement with the emergence of what we call the "subculture," a culture within a culture, which diverges from the main culture. The liberal concern over civil rights in terms of white/black relationships would ultimately inspire standards for human rights around the world, beginning with Mexican American rights, Asian American rights and women's rights, and eventually leading to gay rights, handicapped rights and animal rights.

The Space Program Inspires High Technology

As part of the Cold War, both the Soviet Union and the United States in the 1960s found an exciting way to test their rockets and missiles—not with nuclear payloads but through a high-profile space race. President Kennedy's "New Frontier" was outer space with a stated mission of "landing a man on the moon in this decade."

In this context, Russia had launched Sputnik as a satellite, well ahead of the United States, and had actually launched a man, Yuri Gagarin, into near space. America was caught trailing Russia in technology. The implications of this were thought to be strategic in that America appeared to be losing the Cold War. America rallied behind President Kennedy, putting a much greater emphasis on education, especially in math and science, and beginning a megaproject of building space rockets and capsules with payloads sufficient to send a small crew to the moon and back.

This was an eight-year effort requiring billions of dollars, which unified America in an unprecedented way. From the standpoint of the space race, it is of interest that America placed an emphasis on manned missions, rather than relying on animals, and leveraged smart technology. America also gave increasing priority to the development of electronic components, which actually gave birth to the high-technology industry.

In this context, we should note that AT&T Bell Labs invented the transistor in 1948, which is the underlying technology for the microprocessor. Americans thus enjoyed a hidden advantage over the Soviets in the space race. Innovations in aeronautics through the development of space technology reduced the cost and travel time for commercial transport, stimulating widespread international tourism. During the late 1960s, college students would begin touring Europe, which before was economically unthinkable for the average American.

From the Soviet Sputnik on, satellite communications emerged to allow real-time communication around the world in one-way television broadcasts. The implications of this were phenomenal. The world was united around analog technology, with mass printing of paperback books, real-time global satellite broadcasts of television, high-fidelity stereo cassettes, portable radios and a mass culture that was becoming increasingly sophisticated.

This late-modern culture sparked the dreamers and cultural creatives but, even more important, from this whole effort a new planetary symbol was unveiled: Planet Earth shot from outer space. While America did win the space race over the Soviet Union by successfully deploying a man on the moon, the unanticipated outcome was the visualization from not only outer space but from satellites, of the nature of the planet itself as a unified sphere. This had a deep spiritual impact upon many early astronauts, setting the stage for a new planetary consciousness.

Vietnam: America's Most Unpopular War— Questioning Authority

After the shocking assassination of President John F. Kennedy on November 22, 1963, the United States ill-advisedly plunged into a massive escalation of the war in Vietnam under President Lyndon B. Johnson, with the pretense of stopping the expansion of communism, dictated by the so-called "domino theory."

After World War II, Western allies—particularly Britain, France and Russia—broke up the German empire. In the wake of this, almost every country in the world was aligned economically with one of the two superpowers. The prevalent view was that, if any additional nation fell, even a modest nation like Vietnam, then other nations, such as Cambodia and Thailand, would also fall. There was an intense interest in maintaining a strategic balance between the superpowers, which literally meant sending American troops to the battlefield.

During the Cold War, paranoia on both sides emerged around nuclear weaponry because America developed the first hydrogen bomb. Disaffected Americans had earlier sold the atomic secrets to Russian spies, and Russia then developed its own atomic bomb in retaliation. If we actually look at the situation, there was no need for America to develop the hydrogen bomb. Japan had been conquered, the war was over, yet America continued to develop nuclear technology. You can draw your own conclusion as to who was the true aggressor.

The Soviet Union retaliated, developing an increasingly robust military capability, first by deploying missiles, which were gradually enhanced to be intercontinental ballistic missiles (ICBMs), which could reach any location on the planet.

In the case of the Vietnam War, America felt that Vietnam was strategic. President Kennedy sent a limited number of military "advisors" to bolster France. France withdrew and America filled the gap under President Johnson. It has to be recognized that, while many of the Vietnamese were indeed communists, they were also freedom fighters. Vietnam had been a French colony for a hundred years. They simply wanted to be free, and communist ideology provided a convenient rationale for revolution. America, however, mostly chose to forget that fact.

President Johnson committed 500,000 troops to Vietnam against the guerilla fighters, which lasted an entire decade. A 1965 newspaper article showed an American general predicting that the land war would last 10 years. The general was right on the money; however, he didn't foresee that America would actually lose the conflict. Back in 1965, nobody wanted to believe that could happen. So, America as a whole eventually suffered the consequences.

Half a million American youths were drafted and the war stretched on and on, weakening the perceived value of patriotism. Some 60,000 Americans died and some 160,000 were wounded. American youth, in the wake of the Vietnam War, used the same methods that they had in the Civil Rights movement. Millions took to the streets in massive protests throughout the country. There was a vigorous conflict in American colleges and universities. We saw the birth of sit-downs, street theater and other radical approaches to protesting, along with increasing disenchantment of the youth against the dominant culture, which they called "the System" and "the Establishment."

Some youth, particularly in California, actually began to identify with Chairman Mao and the concurrent Cultural Revolution in China. Many even felt that the North Vietnamese communists were being oppressed and openly sided with North Vietnam.

The Vietnam War tore America in half, resulting in a deep questioning of authority that has lasted to this very day. The Democratic Party went through a value crisis and lost traction for decades from this whole experience.

Birth of the Liberation Movements

When the Civil Rights movement merged with the peace movement, the alienation of American youth to what they considered "the Establishment" reached an all-time high. Concern with African American rights that emerged from the Civil Rights movement was then applied to Latinos, Asian Americans and Native Americans in a broad-based activism.

One of the more humorous incidents was that of Native Americans capturing the San Francisco Bay island of Alcatraz, the famous penal colony, claiming it belonged to Native Americans. No one in the liberation movements was ready for the Women's Liberation movement, which ended up, not only tearing America in half, but all of humanity for an entire generation. It was interesting how the early anti-war activists were not very sensitive or sympathetic with the feminists and the whole Women's Liberation agenda. From a male standpoint, the temporary popularity of the sexual revolution and the notion of "free love" were even more interesting.

This permanently altered the female role in society with the rapid emergence of women in the workforce. Today, the economic requirement for most Americans is to have a two-income family, the development of which actually stemmed from that period. Affirmative action drove black economic rights as well as those of women and other ethnic groups. These quotas focused on Fortune 1000 companies and government. The affirmative action quotas allowed corporations to select not only black people but also Latin Americans, Asians and women to fulfill their quotas. Whether or not black people were chosen, we began to see a demographic shift in large corporations and the government.

The role of the housewife was imperiled economically as American families required two incomes. The majority of youth at that time had access to a college education, yet the housewife was still subject to ridicule. These liberation movements grew to ever more far-reaching areas, such as gay and handicapped rights.

The Love Generation Blows Its Mind

As part of the disillusionment over the war in Vietnam and the growing interest in exploring alternative cultures and societies, San Francisco's "Flower Children" dropped out and began experimenting with psychedelic drugs. San Francisco's famous "Summer of Love," which actually lasted six months, marked the deep phase of social and cultural revolution.

Back in 1967, reporters would go to San Francisco posing as people trying to "find themselves," as a way to get into the hippies' heads. A lot of people from the East Coast would come to simply hang out. Welfare was universal. With food stamps and low rent, one could live on precious little. This was long before the price of housing soared in California after Proposition 13. At the time, it was relatively inexpensive to live.

The Beatles came out with provocative songs like "Baby You're a Rich Man" and "Revolution." There was a feeling that it's all about right now, and the past and future are irrelevant. The increasing availability of psychedelics encouraged people to experiment with their own consciousness and "trip out." Taking drugs soon became illegal; hence, there was increasing paranoia associated with them. At that period in time, people were either "straight" or "hip"; there was nothing in between. The very last thing you wanted to be seen as was a straight person. "Narc," short for narcotics agent, was the ultimate dirty word.

For a brief period of time, there was serious interest in exploring all realities. After the tragic deaths of Janis Joplin, Jimi Hendrix and Jim Morrison, there was a loss in credibility that psychedelics could lead people to any kind of ultimate realization. In the case of Timothy Leary, he did literally hundreds of LSD "trips," as did Richard Alpert, now called Baba Ram Dass. Ram Dass went to India to seriously explore what the psychedelic experience had revealed and to gain a cognitive map of the inner experience.

These experiments with altered consciousness allowed the hippies within a welfare environment to form experimental communes and try multiple partnerships, open relationships in marriage and alternative economic systems. This led to an increasing interest in producing American crafts, in doing anything so long as it was not corporate, multinational or institutional. For a short period of time, it looked like the whole institution of marriage itself, especially with the dawning sexual revolution, would be jeopardized because only straight people actually married.

People would refer to their mates as "my old man" or "my old lady." It was all a very casual, not-too-serious perspective on life. There was also increasing interest in altered states of consciousness that might be attained with a variety of drugs as well as an active exploration of Buddhism and other forms of Eastern religion and philosophy. Various forms of Hinduism and astrology became extremely popular, spilling out to all sectors of American society. People wore their hair long. There was growing interest in mythology and Native American traditions, which included males reenacting tribal myths and rituals.

We saw in the case of the Beatles' delightful animated movie, *Yellow Submarine*, incipient interest in the theory of relativity, Albert Einstein and cutting-edge physics. The irony about relativity was that, while Einstein developed it back in 1905, only a handful of people in the world understood the theory; by the late 1960s, it was still too early for a broad understanding. People found the theory thought-provoking, particularly in conjunction with recent space exploration where people could see for themselves that the planet literally was a sphere and that it all depends on how you look at things as to what you consider real.

Phrases like "do your own thing," "drop out" and "you create our own reality" embodied a profound shift in outlook that led to the growth of the transformational movement, which directly followed in its wake.

Re-enchanting the World:
Mythology and the Birth of the Commune

Along with 1967's "Summer of Love" in San Francisco came a wave of Eastern gurus, including the Beatles' Maharishi Mahesh Yogi and A. C. Bhaktivedanta Swami Prabhupada, who inspired the Krishna people. Everything *but* rational, scientific thought was suddenly "in" on the college campus.

Early interest in Joseph Campbell's mythology was sparked at that time, with hippies trying out various forms of tribalism and discovering a keen interest in shamanism. Dee Brown's book, *Bury My Heart at Wounded Knee,* came out, as well as Carlos Castaneda's famous *Teachings of Don Juan,* which offered a contemporary account of actual shamanism in Mexico. For the first time in American history, shamans became known and were eagerly sought after.

Astrology, reincarnation and psychic phenomena began to be studied with immense interest and would spill over in the 1980s to celebrities like Shirley MacLaine, who opened up broad interest in past lives and channeling. The whole Human Potential movement emerged just after this as an alternative to drugs, including Esalen encounter groups, Werner Erhard's est and Transcendental Meditation (TM). Encounter groups were meetings, inspired by the great nondirective psychotherapist Carl Rogers, where people would sit around in a circle and talk. They could not talk about their stories. They could not talk about their ideas. They could only talk about their feelings toward one another in the current moment.

Esalen became ground zero for all kinds of experimentation in alternative ways of life, and est developed as a more institutional approach, where hotel ballrooms were used to train people, using workshop methods, in what amounted to a fusion of Eastern metaphysics and human potential thinking. est was heavily influenced by Zen, Scientology, creative visualization and a variety of radical new psychotherapies. We had TM from the Maharishi, where people were practicing 20 minutes in the morning and 20 minutes in the evening. We look at many famous and well-known people going to India as the thing to do. It is noteworthy that Steven P. Jobs returned from a trip to India in the mid-1970s only six months before forming Apple Computer. He apparently had gone there to find himself.

Interest in enlightenment and transformation boomed in South and East Asia, where we saw the emergence of serious study in Hinduism, Sikhism, Zen and Taoism. All these religions found their home in the United States in ashrams, communes and communities of all sorts. Many people with yellow and white robes came to the United States in jet airplanes. We saw the first American ashrams formed across the board, including the Zen Center in San Francisco.

This was a time in which America opened up to world culture, and the San Francisco Bay Area in particular fast became a microcosm of the entire planet.

It Is All Relative — "Yellow Submarine" Celebrates Einstein

One of the Beatles' last movies was a delightful cartoon feature done in the Netherlands featuring a journey in a yellow submarine with "Nowhere Man" exploring different worlds, including the famous "theory of relativity." The general spirit of 1960s and 1970s was profoundly relativistic, celebrating Einstein's famous theory.

This actually fell into a kind of amoral relativism that your viewpoint is your viewpoint and my viewpoint is my viewpoint. As the famous *Gestalt Prayer* by Fritz Perls said:

> *I do my thing and you do your thing.*
> *I am not in this world to live up to your expectations,*
> *And you are not in this world to live up to mine.*
> *You are you, and I am I, and if by chance we find each other, it's*
>   *beautiful.*
> *If not, it can't be helped.*

There was a celebration of the individual at all costs, even at the price of relationships. This relativism went across the board to all kinds of intellectual studies. The academic institutions loosened in terms of opening up new programs. There was a lot of interest in interdisciplinary studies around such programs as "the humanities," which were launched in major universities.

There was also keen interest in addressing the spiritual aspects of contemporary science as people began to question the aging Newtonian worldview, beginning to critique the mechanical nature of modern society and facelessness of the huge corporations. Increasingly, people in the United States and the West felt like cogs in a giant machine, dying to get out. No doubt, this was a common feeling in the Soviet Union as well.

Fritjof Capra's *Tao of Physics* inspired a generation of scientists to build out quantum mechanics, setting the foundation for exotic string theory. Capra found a strange correlation between cutting-edge quantum theory and the discovery of Daoism, where it was all about intervals among relationships. Capra pointed to the fact that there was nothing there until you observed it. How could you know it really was there? Hence, the observer, the observed and the process of observing were all one. This type of thinking was emerging about the time that string theory was first being formulated.

The "New Age" came to be more than just the Age of Aquarius. It was also a total transformation in perception, sensibility, values, standards and rules. We saw it coming basically in the 1960s and 1970s with moral relativism and situational ethics. There would be pluralism, an increasing questioning of the Western tradition, religion and values, along with increasing interest in world civilization and culture. A little later on, this very generation that experimented heavily with drugs questioned authority and marched, demonstrated and sat in colleges would invent the world's first personal computer (PC) as a revolutionary force that might truly give power back to the people.

If you saw a photograph of Bill Gates taken back in 1975, you would see that he looked like a young, blonde-haired boy with his hair down to his waist, much like a stereotypical Jesus. The early pioneers back then looked more like hippies than serious computer scientists. They actually dreamed of putting a computer on every desk. The early Apple II computer made its way to small businesses in San Francisco and around the country. Apple computers blazed the way for the home office, education and personal use. When IBM moved into the PC market, Apple actually took out a full page ad in *The Wall Street Journal* welcoming the behemoth as a kind of validation.

The Ecology Movement
Ignites the Green Revolution

The hippies picked up on Rachel Carson's *Silent Spring*, which portrayed a scenario where all the birds had died due to pesticides, and began championing Earth Day to go along with all the experimental communes. Paul Ehrlich's *The Population Bomb* again put chills down the spines of a generation about the implications of uncurbed population. The late 1960s and early 1970s saw the first generation of Americans seriously wrestling with the fate of the earth.

The word "ecology," by the way, has the same origin as the words for "economy" and "ecumenism"; it means "house."

Ecology is a much more human word than environment. Ecology connotes everything fitting together and working smoothly and harmoniously. Ecology introduced a spiritual perspective on what we came to know as "environmentalism."

As hippies began to build communes and drop out of traditional society, they went back to the countryside in places like Santa Fe, Aspen, Boulder and Sedona. They began to espouse natural goods, such as Tom's of Maine toothpaste and Ben and Jerry's ice cream. There was a taste for natural goods that began to emerge in the 1970s, which would transform the tastes of America.

We now see groceries like Whole Foods, which are highly successful, where people are willing to pay a premium for authentic food and goods. For the first time in history, millions of people united around Earth Day to address the unparalleled threat to ecology, which at that time was seen primarily in terms of pesticides, pollution and smog. It was a little too early to anticipate the emergence of global warming. The concerns with smog, interestingly enough, were abated in Los Angeles when the region developed severe antismog laws and the air noticeably improved.

Environmental concerns characterized what became the "cultural creatives," now commonly referred to as the "greens." We saw the emergence of people who identified with alternative cultural perspectives, felt themselves one with creation and clearly identified themselves with ecology. In turn, the ecology movement ignited a green revolution that would spill over to all aspects of society. Today, even from the most conservative standpoint, industry complies with federal guidelines in providing environmental impact reports, and the Presidential Cabinet has held a Secretary of the Environment for decades.

Transvaluation of Values—
The Counterculture Goes Mainstream

In the 1970s, the Human Potential movement featured groups like Esalen as well as the whole transformational movement, with groups like TM and est. It went mainstream around the time of the women's movement and sexual liberation. The recent vice presidential candidacy of Hillary Clinton, and the actual presidency of Barack Obama, demonstrate the overall success of American society in absorbing many of the values of the 1960s and 1970s.

Under the past Clinton administration, "political correctness" was easily recognized, and the president often spoke of "a new paradigm." Transformation under the influence of movements like est was adopted into mainstream business and social vocabulary out of an earlier preoccupation with personal enlightenment alone.

"Unity in diversity" became more than just a slogan, due to a vastly more fluid society in North America as well as around the world. This global society enjoyed an increasingly complex communication infrastructure, with world travel readily available through extensive jets and supersonic transport. If we look back at this, we observe a transvaluation of all the values—the values of the hippies, of the Civil Rights movement, of the sexual revolution and of the PC hackers. All these people succeeded in overturning the main culture into an entirely new outlook, setting the stage for what would become the Planetary Age.

Why Does This Matter?

The world doesn't stand still and neither do our creative minds. This was a time in which a lot of sweeping events took place around the globe. In America, we realized that we had gotten sidetracked and became disillusioned with the whole materialistic approach to life. We started looking for something a bit more meaningful. Everything but rational thought was suddenly "in." We started critiquing the mechanical nature of modern society and questioning everything from the Western tradition itself to all its institutions, to any concept of authority; on the other hand, we were becoming more and more intrigued by global civilization, culture and philosophy.

Along with a new social consciousness, which included Women's Liberation, came a new cultural awareness that put a high value on alternative forms of spirituality over conventional religious traditions—all at the expense of the evolutionary rational humanism of the late Modern Age.

The space race between the United States and the Soviet Union resulted in an immense acceleration of advanced technology that would result in a transportation and communications revolution, along with the first truly planetary perspective of Earth.

The Industrial Revolution began a process of environmental degradation and increasingly sophisticated weaponry that would culminate in the nuclear arms race. We began to realize that there simply must be a better way.

Chapter Five:

What Brought Us Together

Late Transition—Integral Thought *(1980-2009)*

As the world became more and more pluralistic, the Cold War melted and cutting-edge technology was increasingly directed away from rockets to miniature components, introducing high technology. Globalization emerged in this period as an irresistible force as the Cold War wound down and budgets were freed up for commercial purposes. Starting with the microprocessor and PC, computer technology began to impact all of our lives in both the workplace and at home.

With the end of the Cold War, restrictions on travel and trade barriers loosened up. Audrone Wippich came to the United States from Lithuania during this time. With the commercialization of the Internet and broadband mobile communications, the infrastructure had been laid down for all humanity to come together.

High Technology—From PC to iPhone

The space race between the Soviet Union and America, along with America's commitment to land a man on the moon, inspired a great demand to compress electrical equipment that might be deployed in outer space—first with the transistor and then later with the microprocessor.

America successfully deployed a man on the moon because it focused its efforts on miniaturization, which inadvertently led to high technology. It is noteworthy that the National Aeronautics and Space Administration (NASA) was the only federal program to make a profit. The effort that went along with this transferred over into the birth of the high-technology industry. It is also interesting that Houston, along with Cape Canaveral, was the center of the space program, backed up by key corridors of high technology, such as Silicon Valley in northern California, Boston and the Raleigh-Durham area.

The invention of the transistor eventually led to the breakthrough of microprocessors in 1971, enabling the world's first PC in early 1975, initially created in Albuquerque, New Mexico, by a former U.S. Marine, Ed Roberts. With the user-friendly graphical interface, the PC revolutionized both business and media, starting with the printing industry. Initially, the PC was character-driven and quite primitive. Development of its memory went up 1,000 times, quite literally, and the sophistication of processing speed emerged like lightning, enabling it to have the graphical interface that made it compellingly attractive to users.

People became increasingly interested in using a PC for both business and personal reasons. The impact of this technology was to literally transform the printing industry through prepress. People could prepare their documents on the computer for publishing, including both layout and graphics, and then send them to large offset presses. Eventually, many of the presses themselves became digital.

With Moore's law, computer technology doubled in power every 18 months, enabling an exponential leap that would ultimately lead to the BlackBerry and iPhone. There was a magazine ad a few years back with a picture of an office on the moon, looking up at the blue Earth above. The copy maintained that, if the space program had kept up with the computer industry, this would now be your home office. If you double technology every 18 months, as has been the case in the computer industry, you would not have long to go in the doubling process before sparking a revolution.

There is an ancient Hindu story of an early entrepreneur who bartered with his king. "I only want a grain of rice but ask that you double that grain of rice every day for 30 days straight." Guess what? He ended up owning all the rice in the world! That's the power of doubling.

The Cold War Thaws

When President Ronald Reagan ventured upon his Strategic Defense Initiative called "Star Wars," trying to build a space shield that might protect the United States from Soviet missiles, he inadvertently led another round of technological development that nearly bankrupted both the Soviet Union and the United States. After the 1970s, American politics veered sharply toward the right. President Reagan initially took a hard-line position against the Soviet Union, which had invaded Afghanistan earlier.

The Star Wars initiative was a quick fix that sought to end the Cold War by achieving an overwhelming technological advantage. At that time, there was talk about a preemptive strike against the Soviet Union with the idea of knocking out the Soviet missiles before they could be delivered to the United States in retaliation. Fortunately, that strategy was rejected, but it took a little longer to realize that the whole Star Wars effort, which envisioned a protective antiballistic shield in outer space, was highly impractical because the lines of required code would go into the billions. The whole thing was far too problematical.

Mikhail Gorbachev, a superb negotiator, came to power in the Soviet Union during that time with a very practical background of working in Soviet agriculture and having a penchant for diplomacy. He introduced on a formal basis "glasnost" (free speech) and "perestroika" (restructuring) in the Soviet Union, expressing a keen intent to transform Soviet society. At that point, the Soviet's attempts to keep up with Star Wars were literally bankrupting their economy. Gorbachev had a clean slate to negotiate peace with the United States to maintain a reasonable standard of living in Russia.

Margaret Thatcher, Prime Minister of the United Kingdom at that time, along with President Reagan, agreed that they could work with Gorbachev who, interestingly enough, wore French suits. The rest was history.

It is important to realize that the superpowers collectively held over 50 times the firepower necessary to destroy the entire human race. At that time, one American Trident submarine had sufficient firepower to destroy every large and midsized city in North America.

There was also a development called "multiple independently targetable reentry vehicles" (MIRVs), which meant that a single ballistic missile could go out to a metropolitan area, such as Los Angeles. Each warhead on that missile would spread out like a display of fireworks, hitting a separate part of that region. Thus, one nuclear missile could turn all of Southern California into ashes. This was the kind of lethal technology available in the nuclear stockpile.

When the Berlin Wall fell in 1989, the world witnessed the Velvet Revolution of Eastern Europe, which would help bring the Soviet Union, as such, to an end. In this situation, we saw Poland pave the way with an increasing number of strikes. We saw a loss of morale in the Soviet Union and an interest in following rational policies, giving increasing attention to world opinion. It was very clear that, by the time the Berlin Wall fell, Soviet troops lacked the will to fight. This would eventually lead to the comparatively smooth revolution of Lithuania, Latvia and Estonia, which Audrone Wippich personally witnessed in Vilnius.

Globalization Commercializes the Internet

In the wake of "The Year of the Voter," William Jefferson Clinton became president and initiated a brilliant strategy, focused on Silicon Valley, to rebuild the American economy, which had been sharply trailing Japan. After President George H. W. Bush's Gulf War, the American economy was sputtering and voter satisfaction plunged to an all-time low, as that whole military exercise had cost the United States tens of billions of dollars and, all the while, the U.S. economy was trailing that of Japan.

President Clinton won on a plurality and introduced "the new paradigm," along with "political correctness." Albert Arnold "Al" Gore, Jr., became his running mate and Vice President, whose father had preceded him in the U.S. Senate, inaugurating the U.S. highway system. Gore picked up the earlier theme in helping to commercialize the Internet by dubbing it the "information superhighway." Clinton and Gore traveled to Silicon Valley in the San Francisco Bay Area on almost a weekly basis, being visibly supported by major computer companies like Apple, Hewlett Packard and SGI.

During that era, the Internet was able to play to America's superior telecommunication system. The Internet deployed telecommunications, which at that time were designed primarily for voice and had a rather narrow bandwidth. Nevertheless, the American network was sufficiently superior to other countries and gave the United States the lead of a generation ahead of Japan and at least half a generation ahead of Europe. The positive implications to the U.S. economy were staggering.

Clinton's enlightened perspective and policies towards small business led to a new economy with the dot-com phenomenon out of Silicon Valley. We saw the greatest infusion of cash ever in Silicon Valley, along with the emergence of a virtual economy that would result in the dot-com boom and bust.

China and India Emerge as Superpowers

As Japan began a sharp decline, China began its decisive ascendency to manufacturing superpower, and India found a hidden opportunity with the pending "Year 2000" (Y2K) crisis. With the end of the Cold War, China seized the strategic opportunity, despite the 1989 fiasco in Tiananmen Square, to more aggressively expand its trade through an enlightened capitalism masquerading as communism. During the previous decade, Japan had been building infrastructure in both China and Korea, so now China was in the position of developing a superior manufacturing capability.

India rapidly emerged as a viable world economy by playing a crucial role in resolving the Y2K crisis through its expertise in legacy computer programming. The Y2K crisis was a quirk in earlier programming where only two digits— rather than four digits— were assigned for any given year, which had been designed to save what was originally precious and a severely limited computer memory. It was thought that, when the year 2000 hit, mainframes would literally run out of time. This whole effort required an immense backlog of programming of the aging enterprise systems, of which India had the largest pool of Common Business-oriented Language (COBOL) programmers in the world. This resulted in a vastly stepped-up demand for Indian programmers. Fortunately, many Indians had already come to places like Silicon Valley that had world-class universities like Cal Berkeley and Stanford in which to study and gain advanced degrees in computer science.

In Silicon Valley, many of these software engineers, who had originally come for higher education, saw the strategic opportunity and played a decisive role in the formation of the dot-com companies. Over one-quarter of these new ventures was started by software engineers from India who would eventually gain the most from the Internet economy. This new economy eventually became so overheated that the stock market and telecommunications pricing plunged. With the dot-com boom and bust, the extensive oversupply of fiber optics resulted in ever shrinking prices for Internet access, resulting in the movement toward global outsourcing. Countries outside the United States, particularly such emerging economies as India, lit up the dark fiber. This brought about the "flat world," allowing for every professional service— not just computer programming or quality assurance—to be done offshore, including accounting, law and marketing. The implications of this would change the world economy forever.

9/11 as Grotesque Media Event

When Y2K was successfully averted, the newly liberated world felt that the turn-of-the-millennium doomsday scenarios were premature. The Internet Revolution in early 2000 appeared unstoppable, as the nightmare scenario surrounding Y2K never actually materialized. Many engineers thought we never saw a meltdown because they were successful in preventing the event.

An extremely well-staged terrorist event simultaneously destroyed New York's Twin Towers on September 11, 2001 and damaged the Pentagon. In retrospect, as horrifying as this event was, with several thousand people losing their lives, 9/11 was actually poised as a cunning world media play highlighting America's vulnerability to terrorism. America was shown to be a paper tiger, much more vulnerable than had ever been imagined in the new interdependent world order.

The literal cost of destroying the Twin Towers from the perpetrators' standpoint was no more than $250,000 and a handful of people. Under the combined impact of the dot-com implosion and 9/11, the world stock markets severely declined, losing $8 trillion in net worth. The enormous boom of the high-tech sector, which was touted as the next global economy, underwent a literal bust. This allowed emerging economies to catch up with that of the United States and, in some cases, temporarily surpass it.

Islam as the New Scapegoat

With the decline of official communism in the early 1990s, Russia could no longer be perceived as the ultimate enemy. The U.S. and European military-industrial complexes reached out for a new scapegoat to blame for its economic doldrums. The attack of 9/11 provided America with the very excuse it needed for all their economic and political woes, now that Russia was no longer a credible threat.

President George W. Bush seized the opportunity to unify America in a global campaign against terrorism, leading to overt wars in both Afghanistan and Iraq. America once again swung to the far right, becoming phobic of Muslims. Many Americans, after global warming and an unsuccessful war in Iraq that was clearly degenerating into a fiasco, were amazed that Bush was narrowly reelected in 2004. It is hard to realize just how fearful Americans had become, as the 9/11 event had exposed their vulnerability in an unprecedented way. They readily assumed a reactionary and defensive posture, being clearly on a warpath in an age that could not easily sustain military campaigns.

These new wars in Afghanistan and Iraq, unsanctioned by most of the world, proved extremely expensive, running into hundreds of billions of dollars and the cost of thousands of lives, with a sharp decline in U.S. international prestige. The price of oil went up just as the stock market sharply plunged in 2008, which escalated to the global monetary crisis when everything seemed to fall apart just before the election of President Barack Obama.

In all this, we see that America began pointing fingers in a completely different direction than it had during the Cold War. It formed the basis for a profound misunderstanding of the very Islamic countries on which it depended for its vital energy resources.

Global Warming Fuels Green Technology

George W. Bush drove American politics to utter obsession with the Middle East and its petroleum, utterly neglecting alternative energy. It is noteworthy that Bush had a significant background in the oil industry, along with strong political support out of Houston. After losing the presidency in 2000, Al Gore took the occasion to brilliantly lead an international crusade on global warming that captured the imagination of the public, most particularly through the runaway success of his film, *An Inconvenient Truth.*

Since the 1980s, Al Gore had been preaching global warming to the jeers of many affluent American citizens, who had winced at the far-out nature of his prophecies because the condition was less apparent and less documentation had been accumulated. However, his efforts to reverse the dangers of ozone did make a difference.

After becoming vice president in the 1990s, Gore was overshadowed by Bill Clinton. The Clinton administration superbly sold the "information superhighway" to the entire world while underplaying environmental issues. Concerns with the economy overshadowed those around the environment. Al Gore's movie gave him the exposure that helped catapult him to Nobel Prize-winning status and set a green economic agenda for the following administration. Gore could no longer be laughed off; his ideas would finally be instituted in the Obama administration.

President Barack Obama clearly saw the upside of making green or "clean" technology the economic focus of his administration. The Silicon Valley venture firm, Kleiner Perkins Caufield & Byers, estimated that green technology alone would produce a trillion dollar industry. The entire economic thrust of the United States would begin to shift to that technology. In opening his administration, President Obama instituted policies mandating that all federal government buildings would use smart technology and began focusing heavily on energy savings.

It had finally become self-evident that the entire ecosystem was in danger of collapse, demanding concerted action on an international level and on a scale never before seen or even imagined.

The Obama Era — Social Networking and Media Take the White House

With the resurgence of the commercial Internet, fueled by the spectacular rise of Google, cyber-savvy youth did for society in the early 2000s what they had done for the economy in the late 1990s.

Barack Obama was the first American president to win the election by capturing the imagination of youth, as well as leveraging to the hilt the new social media networks. Obama continued his campaign beyond his election and inauguration through an email campaign directed towards the public and voters, doing weekly speeches through YouTube and other digital media. When Obama entered the White House, he even attempted to call out directly with his BlackBerry.

When we look at Obama in his role with the Internet, he was clearly capitalizing on the online revolution set up for him by Bill Clinton and Al Gore, without which Obama never would have been elected. Obama was tackling the global monetary crisis by building a bridge directly between the American people and their government, attempting to reinvoke the spirit of volunteerism.

Obama demonstrated his international savvy by declaring himself a global citizen back in July 2008. Obama set the global stage for a profound appreciation of unity in diversity. When we look at President Obama, we see a watershed in American politics — not only in terms of racial issues but also an understanding of people's role in government. Obama represented a new generation of Democrats who were mobilizing direct democracy.

If we stepped away, we might almost say that he was a revolutionary in transforming American government, brilliantly leveraging the new social media. The full implications of this are just becoming apparent.

San Francisco: Ground Zero of the Consciousness Revolution

Since the Gold Rush, San Francisco has been a cultural stew of many different nations and races—a process intensified around Silicon Valley, where engineers from South Asia, East Asia, the Middle East and Russia led the development of Internet technology.

The greater San Francisco Bay Area is a microcosm of the whole world with every nation represented. For example, within the Mission District of San Francisco, every Latin country in Central and South America is represented. Free-spirited, open-minded and liberal since the Gold Rush, San Francisco has emerged as the epicenter of global innovation.

This region provides the ideal conditions for the emergence of a new planetary consciousness in the sense of being experimental and open, having representatives from every country, developing an advanced communications and transportation infrastructure and having repeatedly been in the world's eye through a continuous stream of innovation.

As northern California helped build out the World Wide Web itself, its social media in turn would provide a channel for this new collective consciousness. We have yet to see the full implication of the social media applied to spirituality in matters of consciousness itself.

String Theory and N-Dimensions: Rational Empiricism Defeated in the Laboratory

Along with the rise of India as a software giant, there was increasing interest in metaphysics, especially recent quantum and string theories, which had totally eclipsed the mechanistic Newtonian paradigm. As India emerged as an offshore super-power, a renewed fascination with all things Asian and Indian emerged, including increasing awareness of its mystical traditions. American women, for example, began wearing saris.

With Brian Greene's *The Elegant Universe: Superstrings, Hidden Dimensions, and the Quest for the Ultimate Theory* and the cult documentary, *What the Bleep Do We Know!?: Discovering the Endless Possibilities*, string theory with parallel universes and multiple dimensions seized the popular imagination. It became all too apparent that the Newtonian paradigm had been completely eclipsed. The Einsteinian paradigm of relativity was already aging and quantum mechanics was already 70 years old.

String theory attempted to unify both Einsteinian physics and quantum mechanics in a single theory of the Universe by postulating an order of magnitude smaller scale of strings that were purely energetic vibrations at the Planck scale, literally 10^{-37}, an area so small that people questioned if we would ever be able to experimentally test its findings.

Quantum theory undermined the mechanistic conception of the Universe by highlighting the primacy of consciousness— not only in experimentation but also in all experience. We would also go to the orbiting Hubble telescope, which recently disclosed the mysteries of "dark matter and energy." It is now postulated that 95 percent of the matter of the Universe —likewise for energy— may not be visible to our eyes.

It was becoming increasingly apparent that, as far as "reality" goes, either we know nothing or "reality" is infinitely stranger and more wonderful than we could possibly imagine.

Why Does This Matter?

During this time period, we saw globalization emerge. The new digital infrastructure, which enabled social media, literally shrank the world, making it possible for humanity to finally come together.

It seems like history has been orchestrated from the very beginning. The Traditional Age set the foundation for the Modern Age. Without the Modern Age, we would have never been exposed to nature's "secrets" through the steady progression of scientific experimentation; we would have never been able to see their limitations and arrive at this higher mystical realization.

With the commercialization of the Internet and the privatization of telecommunications, a vast global network of rich communications and media emerged, which gave people around the world a voice in an unprecedented way. Many-to-many communication was born.

China and India emerged as next-generation superpowers, as more and more of the workload of both products and services was deployed outside the United States and Europe, enabled by thousands of miles of cheap fiber optics and advanced satellite communications.

Speaking of all human beings, have you ever pondered why we are being brought back together in this rapidly changing world? It is because we are all inherently ONE. We are one vast energy field that has broken up into billions of individual bubbles, encapsulating each of us as individual beings. We have been so caught up in our own individuality that we forgot what it is like to be the entire field. We forgot that, once we reunite with our Source, and with each other, we are invincible. What is keeping us apart? Differences? Not really. Differences are what keep this world spinning and keep us entertained, creative and innovative. How boring it would be if we were all the same!

It is time that we awaken as The One and start embracing unity in diversity, as all the magic begins from there.

Part II
THE MEGADREAM (MYSTERY)

Let us jump from history to pure mystery and see how we can't have one without the other.

Both the secular and the religious materialist views are obsolete. All that we know is pure consciousness. The entire material Universe is simply the interplay of form within an infinite field of consciousness. While people keep seeing the world through their childhood conditioning, nothing stands still.

It might be more comfortable to keep on thinking, seeing and doing things the same old way. Then again, do we really want to play by the same old limiting rules that our ancestors set up way back when? Growing up in a totally different era, their outlook on life and science was not informed by the amazing discoveries of recent decades. No wonder some of us have had such a hard time adapting to today's environment! Unless we unlearn what we previously assumed to be true, we will find ourselves dysfunctional.

In past centuries, much of humanity saw the world as three dimensional and unquestioningly real. The world was not seen as an extension of their bodies but, rather, their bodies were seen as tiny, insignificant fragments of the world. This unexamined conviction hindered people from readily probing the implications of Christ's claim that "All things are possible." His followers began rationalizing the claim, treating it symbolically.

With the recent popularization of quantum and string theories, a critical mass of people is finally arriving at the ultimate implications. *Anything* is possible, because there is nothing to prevent it from being so. The recent feature, *The Secret*, brilliantly—if narcissistically—highlighted all this.

More and more people are insisting on nothing less than the full integration of science and spirituality. In the Middle Ages, the world was supersaturated by infinite spirit; we are again thrown into a very subjective world. In the Planetary Age, the observer creates that which he or she observes. Nothing is really fixed. Things are open ended. We create and play as we go, moment by moment. Not only is this very planet our sandbox—our playground—so also is the entire Universe. Like a giant simulation, instead of splashing our way through "quantum soup," it allows us to live inside our very own collective dream, which we call the Megadream.

Chapter Six:
WHY NOTHING LOOKS THE SAME
(Reality)

As we move through the 2000s, we find that we are in a transformed landscape where everything is somehow different, including a new sensibility, a new set of values, new priorities and a new set of rules yet to be written down. As we discover that we are living in a new planetary civilization, we begin to realize that all the rules have changed; quite simply, the old rules no longer apply.

As the long-standing war between science and religion finally comes to an end, we find ourselves captives within a mysterious universe no longer having all the answers. In this light, the definition of "being human" has suddenly and dramatically shifted. It is now apparent that both individual and collective enlightenment are closely interrelated.

Reality a Matter of Perception

Cutting-edge physics and neurology reveal how all that we take for "reality" is a mental construct. The objectivism of the Modern Age was quite simply a working set of assumptions that bypassed the ultimate issues. All of our perceptions are contained within our own experience and are, therefore, interpretations.

When we see something, we actually "construct" it from our very own neural impulses and associate it with concepts. In the early 18th century CE, the German philosopher, Immanuel Kant, showed the West that it could never truly know "the thing in itself." Kant postulated the basic categories of time and space, coming to realize that his entire experience was self-contained; that anything he could say about something, which appeared to be external or outside himself, was an assumption. He felt that the best he could do was to describe his own experience without pretending to know the thing in itself.

You might say that this was an agnostic position, not an atheistic one. An agnostic position is to hold that we don't really know and will probably never know. It is not a declaration of "yes" or "no." The realization of Kant in the 18th century CE mobilized the Romantic era, which introduced impressive innovations in art, music, literature and philosophy. Kant's realization temporarily paralyzed rationalism in the West because intellectuals there were uncertain what foundation science might have and how we could move forward if the world we inhabit is all self-constructed or imaginary.

Later, particularly in France and the United Kingdom, philosophy went back to business as usual, applying the scientific method to such emerging disciplines as sociology, psychology and anthropology. As Western philosophers increasingly became aware of this subjective element of human experience, it became too scary for them to tackle it head on. They thus retreated into a type of scientific philosophy or sociology, ignoring the larger questions.

Scientific Materialism Discredited

Just as Newtonian physics reached its apogee, where the entire physical Universe was looked at as a gigantic clock and matter was considered inert, Einstein set the stage for a universe of energy and information where everything was relative.

With the discovery of electricity, along with research on

light, energy became the focus of physics, leading to Einstein's famous "theory of relativity." If we look back at the 19th century CE, we realize that this century gave us the light bulb, electric power and the steam engine with trains and steamships, introducing a broad range of technologies that released energy for the service of human needs.

The most interesting was the study of optics and electricity, which led Einstein to his relativity theory. Einstein's thought experiments began to be popularized after he won the Nobel Prize. The detonation of the atomic bomb vividly demonstrated to all at the climax of World War II that matter is instantly convertible into energy. Therefore, matter itself began to seem a lot less solid. In other words, matter is a form of energy and energy is a type of matter. At the root of reality, we move from a definition of reality being matter to reality being energy.

As the quantum revolution got underway as early as the 1920s, Einstein's efforts to unify gravity with electromagnetism faltered. Quantum physics emerged with brilliant discovery after brilliant discovery—all bringing into question our most fundamental assumptions about reality. It was pointed out that, without an observer, there was nothing to be observed. The implication was that the observer and that which was observed, along with the very process of observing itself, were all one and the same thing.

Einstein did succeed in making the Newtonian conception of the Universe quaint and inapplicable at very large distances, such as that between stars and galaxies. Einstein proceeded by questioning all of our basic assumptions, paving the way for the quantum revolution that trailed his early work.

Observer/Process of Observing/Observed As One

The Hindu sages within the Advaita Vedanta tradition maintain that there is no "two"; that everything is "one." In fact, they maintain that it really isn't "one"; it is just "THAT," the indescribable. As particle physics emerged in the 20th century CE with high-energy experiments, all the classic rules of physics broke down within this new quantum mechanics.

Werner Heisenberg's "principle of uncertainty" upset the classical scientific method, which presupposed that the observer could be completely independent of that which he or she observed. In quantum measurement, it became clear that the "principle of indeterminacy" kicked in, where you couldn't control or predict reactions at the subatomic level. There was considerable doubt as to whether it was all particles or waves. Scientists kept going back and forth between the two.

Increasingly it was recognized that, without an observer, there was no observation; in fact, there was nothing to be observed. In the principle of uncertainty, it was a matter of increasing recognition that we could observe a given particle's direction but not its speed, or observe its speed but not the direction. We couldn't do both at the same time. As these experiments progressed, physicists were uncertain about whether we see waves, particles or both. Some people cleverly dubbed the phenomenon "wavicles." Technically, they were considered to be waves of probability amplitudes, meaning that the probability of a particle appearing in a certain place can be estimated but nothing beyond that; therefore, the particles move as though they are waves.

The classic model of the atom as a tiny solar system faded away as smaller and smaller subatomic particles were discovered with literally no end in sight. This has scaled down so

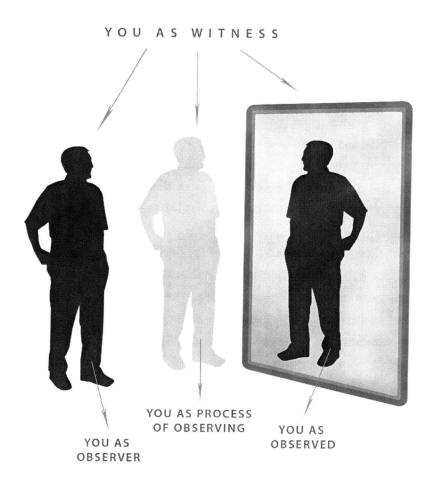

10: You are all of it: observer, the process of observing and observed.

minutely that string theory postulates strings at literally 10^{-37}, which is so infinitesimal an area that it dwarfs most people's conception, as it is trillions of times smaller than the smallest particle in an atom.

As these particles began to be referred to as "clouds" and "mathematical ghosts," it became apparent that there were no particles without an observer; that the interaction between observer and the observed was one. More mystical physicists began to entertain the thought that all this is but the interplay of our collective consciousness and that we create our own reality. These mystical physicists came from different schools of quantum thought, including the many-worlds interpretation and the Copenhagen interpretation of the collapse of superpositions.

Dualism Transcended

Einstein inseparably linked time and space in what he called "space/time," which he considered to be a "fabric," as in the fabric of space/time. If space and time are one or space/time, and particles and waves are one or "wavicles," then what is ultimately real? With ever-smaller particles and ever-larger expanses of space, such as clusters of galaxies measured in millions of light-years, can there be a smallest particle or a farthest star?

This is a serious question because every amount of experimentation reveals a new level of possibility. The Anglo-American philosopher, Alan Watts, joked that, if you have a more powerful telescope, you will keep seeing more and more stars emerge, because whatever you point at, you will see. If you have a smaller microscope, you will find smaller particles because, again, you will never perceive nothing; you will always perceive something. As the equipment becomes more refined and powerful, we literally create more particles and more galaxies, because they are not really "out there," which is the final realization.

It would appear that the very act of observation is an experiential construct that brings into the manifest Universe that which is not necessarily there. The Universe of opposites is the manifest realm, which is but the play of the unmanifest—that which we call "God" or to which physicists call the "field of infinite possibility." This field contains infinite possibilities, as is referred to in Buddhism as "the fertile void."

We often associate the word "void" with the color black; however, if you go to East Asia, black is a positive color and white is the color of death. We in America and in the West typically have a negative attitude towards the color black, and it is interesting that this response is culturally determined. The yin/yang symbol of East Asia illustrates the relationship of white and black and how they are interchangeable. Each circle is contained within its direct opposite, so you literally cannot have one without the other. You could think of the unmanifest as black, like black light, and the manifest Universe as pure white light; all is pure consciousness. Dualism is finally transcended.

Principle of Nonlocality (Bell's Theorem)

In 1965, John Bell discovered the "Principle of Nonlocality," where separate particles on opposite sides of the Universe that had originally been paired would continue to spin in parallel no matter how their spin changed and regardless of their distance apart, suggesting that consciousness might exceed the speed of light.

Nonlocality suggests that vast distances are not all that real but only a matter of appearance. Einstein, himself, expressed doubts about the independent reality of time and space, but this fact never got widely publicized in his lifetime. If all time is relative, and things do not have any fixed location, can there be such a thing as time or space? This principle is, therefore, referred to as "nonlocality," which is perhaps the greatest single discovery in physics to date.

Experimental particle physics decisively put an end to a strictly materialistic interpretation of the Universe. Not only is both the observer and the observed indispensable, you cannot have one without the other. Our notions of location are all relative. You can split yourself up into two people on opposite sides of the Universe, so to speak, and still maintain the same identity. The particles that initially appear are paired; they move in synch, no matter how far apart they might eventually go.

These implications are profound because, through actual experimental evidence, it has been determined that this functions independently of the speed of light, putting in question that the speed of light is the ultimate constant as Einstein had firmly maintained. It seems as though we might be in the early stages of moving beyond Einstein's relativity theory.

Indra's Net—Physical/Biological/Spiritual

Buddhists and Hindus share a mythological metaphor referred to as "Indra's net," which is a vast chain of pearls where each pearl reflects every other pearl, much like an infinite regression of mirror images. On the physical level, everyone and everything you observe is within your own field of awareness and, ultimately, your mirror reflection.

On the biological level, we are all part of a single web of life, such that what we do to each other, we are doing to ourselves

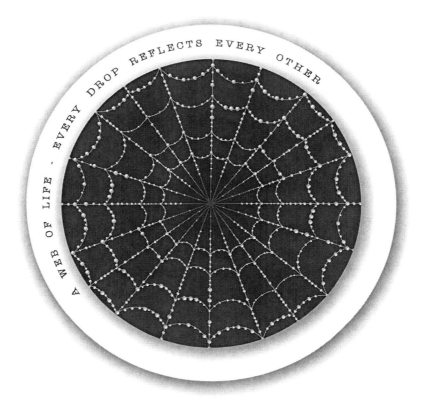

11: How we are all one after all.

as well. On a spiritual level, as separately appearing individuals, we share an interlocking set of consciousness, where each of our separate worlds intersects every other.

As in the movie, *The Matrix*, everything we see and interact with is a projection. Accepting this illusion for what it is constitutes our admission ticket to the game itself. The "matrix," called "Maya" in Hindu thought, is the manifest Universe, our very playground. As we look at Indra's net, it is actually a very sophisticated metaphor for how everything dovetails into everything else. It is apparently happening on a physical level, on an underlying biological level and even on a spiritual level. It is of interest that this corresponds directly with the most recent discoveries of quantum theory.

No One "Out There" to Blame— Letting Go of Judgment and Evaluation

As what was "out there" was reduced to probability waves and mathematical ghosts, it became totally absurd to think that you might find someone else to blame. All judgment and evaluation is based upon memory and appearances, where our mind automatically compares one event, situation or condition with another in a game of comparison and contrast.

All standards are mental constructs used typically to justify judgments and evaluations. While we all need a certain level of differentiation in order to function, we can easily take it way too far. In other words, we need a certain amount of contrast to tell one thing from another. We literally cannot function in this world without it. However, when we buy into those distinctions, we get fooled.

When you have a high "charge" on your judgments and evaluations, you come to "believe" that you are "right." You are setting yourself up in the process. If the observed and the observer are indeed one, then you are actually judging and evaluating yourself when you are judging and evaluating another. It is interesting that Christ admonished His disciples by saying, "Don't judge, unless you wish to be judged; for with what standards you measure others, those same standards will be applied to you." It seems like Jesus of Nazareth was subconsciously aware of this 2,000 years ago.

The way out is to stop taking your judgments and evaluations all that seriously; they are just more thoughts. A thought is a thought, a judgment is a judgment and an evaluation is an evaluation. When you cease to be preoccupied with your own thoughts, such as in meditation, you can begin to see what is already there without adding anything to it.

The ideal back in the early days of est in the 1970s was to allow that which is to BE, to give space for something, to observe it without commenting upon it or critiquing it.

Parallel Universes

String theory, which has sought to reconcile Einstein with quantum theory, has postulated 11 or more dimensions with parallel universes that might be only centimeters apart. Since quantum's early days, theoretical physics has opened up the envelope even further, postulating that there are an indefinite number of dimensions and possibly even an infinite number of separate universes.

String theory is a recent school of theoretical physics that was formed back in the 1970s. This school postulates that the smallest strands of energy might be shaped much like elastic strings. They have the ability to stretch and change their shape at will, being infinitely smaller than quarks, the smallest particles within the standard subatomic model. These strings would be at the Planck scale, the smallest currently conceivable size of 10^{-37} meters.

This discipline was developed to reconcile Einstein's relativity with quantum mechanics, which entailed two separate sets of laws operating on separate levels. In order to put these two together, we would need to arrive at a true "theory of everything." The upshot is that either the physicists know nothing or the Uni-

Four   Waves   of   Physics

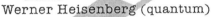

Brian Greene (string)

Werner Heisenberg (quantum)

Albert Einstein (relativity)

Isaac Newton (classical)

12: Reality is no longer the same.

verse is a lot stranger than any of us could possibly imagine—in which case, it is best understood from a mystical perspective.

With string theory and parallel universes, we are now in a stage of physics that is willing to venture on in speculation, beyond the furthest degree that the 20th century CE would allow. It seems indicative that we are indeed in a Planetary Age where a new type of science is emerging with a drastically different concept of what is real.

The Eternal Pulse

Hindus refer to "Spanda," the pulse of the Universe, throbbing trillions of times per second, creating the illusion of three dimensions. The entire Universe, what we call "reality," is continually blinking in and out of existence, never static even for a moment. Contemporary quantum theory shows how particles go from here to there without any intervening steps, known as the "quantum leap."

The human nervous system is actually wired such that it cannot possibly process these pulses fast enough. It thus inter-

prets things to be in continuous motion, just as you see pro-
jected frames on a strip of film that, when moved at 24 frames
per second, appear to be seamless with a silky smooth motion,
or like lights on a Christmas tree that appear to be blinking in
motion when they are actually blinking on and off in the proper
sequence and our eyes interpret it as motion.

Digital computers ultimately depend on a binary language
of on-and-off signals or tiny switches for all their most sophisticated processes. We are always going in and out of existence in
an infinite dance of energy. It would seem as though the pulse
of the Universe, vibrations if you will, is at the very heart of all
intelligence and what we consider to be God.

Infinite Possibilities

The upshot of quantum mechanics is a vision of the infinitesimally small as providing a context of unlimited possibility.
Unlike the determin-
istic framework of Sir
Isaac Newton, where
all interactions were
thought of as much
like billiard balls, quantum theory opened up
a whole new can of
worms: a universe of
infinite possibility.

If nothing is really
"out there," and our
true identity is that of
the Creator Himself or

*13: Infinite universes, infinite
possibilities lie within. Which
one will you play in today?*

Herself, then we can create anything at any time. If reality is ultimately an expression of separate points of consciousness, then it is only out of relationship that we create or recognize ourselves.

So, we end up with a whole discussion around the new physics with infinite possibility staring us in the face. We can no longer counter the claim that Jesus of Nazareth ascended into the sky with the argument that it is impossible for Him to have ever gotten to the center of the Universe because, even today, He would be in the Milky Way Galaxy. Space/time is a projection of our consciousness.

We can no longer be quite so certain about *anything*. With the added dimensions and parallel universes, we are now wide open in terms of possibility. It would be safe to say at this point that we know nothing, but it might also be safe to suggest that we are coming up with a dramatically different paradigm than ever existed before—a paradigm appropriate to the Planetary Age.

Why Does This Matter?

Have you ever questioned the external world and its supposedly "solid" existence? We have finally realized that science doesn't have all the answers and that we are living within a deeply mysterious universe. It all depends on how you look at things as to what you consider real. Let's keep in mind that all of our perceptions are actually contained within our own experience. Just by owning that very experience, and all the content within it, we can recreate and transform our future into something truly magical, as we are no longer dependent upon things happening "out there." We own what is happening right now while inviting and allowing new possibilities to emerge.

Quantum theory not only made the high-technology revolution possible, it also revealed that what we hold to be "reality" might not be all that "real"; that space/time is ultimately an illusion. People may find a cutting-edge quantum perspective initially intimidating, as it necessarily implies that there is really nothing "out there" in the normal sense of the word—only quantum soup or mathematical ghosts. If what we perceive to be "out there" are simply vibrations within our imagination, then we, ourselves, must be continually creating and composing everything that is in front of us every nanosecond of the day.

If that is the case, we are living in a field of infinite possibility because we create in conjunction with our Source—either consciously or unconsciously. You can guess which one is more entertaining! Entering our very creation requires that we forget Who we all are. We are about to remember that we deliberately chose to forget.

Since everyone and everything is literally interrelated in a continual dance of consciousness, we find no one to blame. We act out the Megastory within the Megadream as part of divine entertainment.

How wild is your imagination? How electrifying is your composition? Can you see it? The world is both your oyster and your pearl.

Chapter Seven:
HOW YOU MAKE A DIFFERENCE
(Individual)

Most of us were brought up in a culture dominated by a very mechanical sense of the Universe and humanity that English philosopher, Alan Watts, referred to as "the fully automatic model." It is only now that we are waking up to the complete implications of quantum theory, even though it was pioneered some 70 years ago.

The deeply spiritual nature of the Universe is finally becoming apparent, as the old mechanistic theory simply no longer plays well in the laboratory. Both outer and inner worlds continuously interact while you are ultimately beyond both. Now, transformation of your life and your world must begin within.

Yogic Theory (Animal/Human/Divine)

Yogic theory reveals that we all share three complementary identities—animal, human and divine—corresponding to the seven chakras, or centers of energy. This energy field underlies our central nervous system and corresponds with various points in the body. We can all feel this energy as we get excited. You can touch people from a distance and feel their presence as much as three to five inches away. Some people call this the "aura."

According to the yogis from India, there are seven major energy fields or psychic centers separated into lower, middle and higher. The first three logically equate with what we might consider the "animal" chakras. They focus on security, sensuality and power, centering initially in the abdominal area (rectum, genitals and navel—our power center). Humanity in the last several hundred years has been moving from a preoccupation with power, or our love of power, to the power of love.

The fourth chakra—the "human" chakra—is that of love, which is distinctly mammalian or human. So the human chakra is basically the first chakra where you can actually feel somebody else rather than looking at them strictly as an object. In the three lower chakras, people only exist as an object in relation to you. With the human chakra of love, there is actual identification with another being.

The higher chakras are the three "divine" chakras—one of cosmic consciousness, one of God consciousness and the other of unity. These chakras correspond with the throat, the dot between the eyes, which is often marked by Hindus, and just above the crown of our heads, which is called the "thousand-petal lotus."

In cosmic consciousness, you begin to identify the world as yourself and experience a consciousness within the world that unifies you and the world. In God consciousness, it is experienced between the eyes. You experience the identity of God and yourself as one, but there is a clear distinction. With unity consciousness, just above the crown of your head, you only experience The One beyond any categories of God and self.

We have all experienced the opening up of various chakras and, most likely, all the chakras at one time or another. We usually center upon just one. Meditational practice focuses on continuously raising one's habitual focus on the lower three chakras of security, sensuality and power, towards the higher chakras of love, cosmic consciousness, God consciousness and unity. The

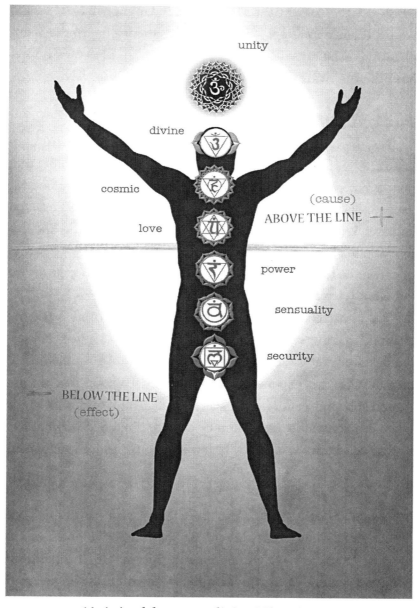

*14: Animal, human or divine: Where is your
psychic center: above or below the line?*

whole point is to elevate our energy to the higher chakras where we experience inherent perfection. This theory has endless implications. The masterful mind/body guru, Dr. Deepak Chopra, has built his entire work around these seven categories.

Creator/Creature—Living Above/Below the Line

Few people appreciate that Scientology made a major contribution to mysticism in suggesting a line of causality: that people either live below the line "at effect" or above the line "at cause." The line of causality directly corresponds to the seven chakras. With the animal chakras, which are below the line, we live at effect and are easily victimized. Our lives are a process of power relationships in which we use manipulation to try to get what we want.

The fourth chakra of love separates the animal from the divine chakras, making us distinctly human. With our higher chakras, we discover the world to be our own creation. Above the line of causality, we can experience life as divine, realizing that we are responsible and continuously cause it all. The world also aligns when our consciousness is literally centered in the lower chakras. In that condition, it is virtually impossible *not* to feel victimized one way or another.

Fake Self, Shadow Self, True Self

Any of us who struggle with an inauthentic life fails to appreciate that we have three separate selves: (1) Social Mask: who you pretend to be; (2) Shadow: who you fear you are; and (3) Divine Self: the real you.

On the surface is our social mask or whom we pretend to be. This is our social self at parties. While all of our close friends

THREE SELVES (MASK, SHADOW, DIVINE)

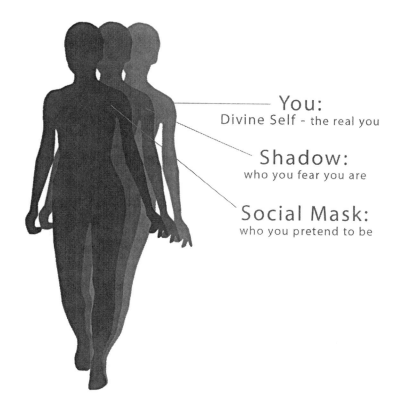

You:
Divine Self - the real you

Shadow:
who you fear you are

Social Mask:
who you pretend to be

15: Will the real you please stand up?

know better, we put our best face forward and, typically, we wear it subconsciously or unconsciously. Just below the surface is our petty, sometimes downright nasty, self from which we try to hide. Most of us are fairly convinced that this is our real Self; that underneath it all we are nasty, petty, selfish and mean.

This view is extremely damaging to our self-esteem, and yet it is held by most, if not all, of us. Very few people ever get down to their intuitive, innocent, divine Self. The premise here is that we are all essentially divine. We are all one with God. We put these social masks on out of defensiveness and protection. We have lost our original innocence—an innocence reflective of a lack of camouflage. The more camouflage, the more we buy our adult roles, the more we get sucked into our interpersonal dramas.

So, if we are basically going to be on the level of the fake self, our persona, our social mask and what we learn to do as a teenager, the point would be to enjoy using our fake mask while no longer taking it all that seriously. Rather than letting it unconsciously use us, we can have fun with it and play with it, much as we would in a costume party.

At the Speed of Thought
(The Galaxies Themselves Spin Within You)

The Principle of Nonlocality revealed that space/time was ultimately an illusion, like the Hindu conception of Maya, which can be thought of as the "matrix." The word "Maya" is related to "matrix," "mother," "meter" and "matter." It is very fundamental in the Indo-European languages, including English. Rooted in most of our concepts is the fixed notion that only that which can be measured is real.

The ultimate YOU is not only the Source of the Universe but contains the Universe itself. Contemporary quantum and string theories demonstrate how thought can transcend the speed of light itself, since the Universe is not really out there; with nonlocality, you could influence somebody across the planet instantaneously.

You can now get in vital touch with the Source within you, both infinite possibility and ultimate power. Our collective being is ultimately the Supreme Source in which the Universe spins. So, when we stop identifying with our body and our mind, we go back to being the context of all that is. In that sense, we can say that the galaxies spin within us.

Embracing Paradox and Contradiction

We are freed up to discover the ultimate mysteries only when we fully embrace paradox and contradiction—that what we think of as "reality" is riddled with inconsistencies. Life is inherently paradoxical and contradictory because it is not ultimately real.

Our mind sets us up to play in the illusion, the world of appearances. All spiritual progress requires an enthusiastic embrace of paradox to break through to the other side, to recognize the illusory nature of that which we experience on a daily basis.

The object is to be in the game, the wonderful playground of life, while knowing it is only a game, and yet still have a blast. So, all spiritual progress at this point in time depends upon our willingness to accept and embrace paradox and contradiction without assuming that we are stuck in a bunch of categories that make no sense whatsoever.

The Pyramid — Religion/Spirituality/Mysticism

If we step back from the great traditions, we gaze upon a giant pyramid where more than of one-third of it is externalized, one-third is internalized and the apex is the mystical core, dealing with pure Being, Consciousness and Bliss. You can actually visualize this huge pyramid with an eye at the top at the back of a dollar bill.

All the great religious traditions were originally inspired and are paths to realize God. The pyramid is like a mountain in which all of the individual paths lead to the top. Each path has three separate phases: (1) the base of the pyramid is external; (2) the middle of the pyramid is internal; and (3) the top of the pyramid is deeply inner, mystical and unitary. These phases may be compared to the three levels of the pyramid where: the first level (base) equates with what we know as "religion"; the second (middle) with "spirituality" and the third (top) with "mysticism."

Religion has to do with the externalities, with sociology, psychology, outward institutions — anything you can point to where you don't necessarily have to agree with it, accept it or get it. We are typically born into a given tradition without a conscious choice. The second level, which is spirituality, is your own relationship with the tradition, which you experience vividly. You own all the content and relate to it on a very personal level. You are working within a system for realization, and you take it very seriously as you are most definitely on the path.

On the third level, which is mysticism, you suddenly recognize the nature of this whole quest. It is no longer about external observation or spiritual appearances of being righteous and holy. Rather, it is all about Self-realization, the discovery of your ultimate Self and coming back into life dynamically informed with that awareness, which is often experienced as ecstasy and bliss.

Each of these three stages enables a deeper appreciation of "Who" and "What" we call "God." Any stage is okay. Any stage is right. Any stage is perfect *as it is*, but you need not stay stuck in that stage because you are always free to grow out of it.

16: Religion is the starting point in our quest
for unity leading to a higher truth.

Three Ways of Viewing Ultimate Reality
(Three Faces of God)

American author, Ken Wilber, recently gave the world a profound breakthrough by showing how different people experience God from three distinct perspectives. When God is experienced as first person ("I"), He is experienced as "I AM," which is our Ultimate Identity; to gain this experience, we meditate. When God is experienced as second person ("You" or "Thou"), He is experienced as our Creator; to reach our Creator, we pray. When God is experienced as third person ("It" or "Them"), He is experienced as a Sacred Presence beyond words.

We feel the presence, much like contemplating the overwhelming beauty of creation itself. What works for most of us is not necessarily one or the other, or even a mix of all three views. What works is to dynamically appreciate God from various vantage points, rather than being stuck in just one; each one has its unique advantages in facilitating spiritual development.

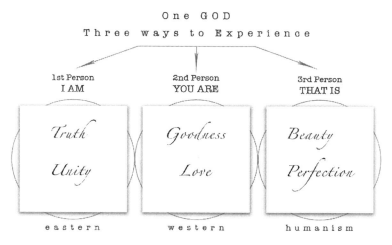

17: Any way you worship is the right way!

Four Spiritual Paths

In late 19th century CE Calcutta, Sri Ramakrishna Parama-hamsa set the stage for the unification of all faiths in the disclosure of four distinct spiritual paths found in every tradition. The first path is devotion to God, God as our Source and Ultimate Reality. This is a love relationship that is very often associated with immense awe and respect to a Higher Power. You preoccupy yourself with that Higher Power so that you merge with the Higher Power. In a sense, the ultimate payoff is to become God as you finally realize that God is all there is. Your individual ego is blown.

The second path is loving service to humanity, as God is in everyone. This is the path of Karma yoga or service, in which you act without attachment to results. You gladly act in the interest of others, whom you see as an embodiment of God.

The third path is contemplation, where you experience God as your ultimate Self, very often alone. This experience is often known as the yoga of knowledge or Self-realization. This path is often facilitated by continuously asking yourself, "Who am I?" and "Who is the one asking the question?" It is a process of going ever deeper into your ultimate Self.

The fourth path is channeling sacred energy up the chakras through tantric and yogic discipline. If you remember the seven stages of yoga, the seven chakras, each chakra leads to a higher one. In this type of yoga, through Hatha postures, meditation and breathing, and other exercises, you attempt to take the sacred energy—"the Kundalini"—and drive it up the chakras one by one until, when it hits the bell at the top of the thousand-petal lotus, you experience absolute enlightenment.

In India, all four of these spiritual paths are equally honored and recognized. The two most popular ways are the path of devotion and the path of service, together known as the "right-handed path." The people on the left-handed, tantric path prefer contemplation and channeling energy. While most of us relate to more than one path, we almost all have a favorite, which shapes our whole orientation to spirituality.

Discovering Your Gift

Everyone in this Megastory and Megadream is endowed with a uniquely precious gift to offer all humanity. Within the greater story, each of us has a definite role to play that contributes to the plot as a whole, where we are actually in a play, a drama, in a theater or in a movie. All of us have chosen to enter the dance and have forgotten who we are.

Each character that occupies this drama is endowed with a special gift that distinguishes him or her. Until a character wakes up to his or her own unique mission, vision and message, his or her gift remains under wraps and unexpressed. The faster that gift is discovered, the faster it can be put to work to make the show a real hit.

Most all of us, at one time or another, disparage our hidden talents and abilities, thinking that they are trite or ordinary, short-changing ourselves in life. The fastest way to discover this gift, other than having people explicitly tell you, is to listen to other people's compliments. Also, you lose all sense of time when you are exercising your gift.

You ARE Love

All along, the hidden secret of the Christian tradition has been that God is not merely "loving" but that God IS Love, and so are you—that is, your divine Self. When we look at the word "God" in the English language, we find that it is a very over-used word, which doesn't really define anything. It is literally a three-letter word freighted with connotations and a lot of baggage. In many cases, people have a difficult time associating what you mean when you say "God." Very rarely do people equate God with love.

When you open up from your heart, you will discover that very love that God, the Supreme Identity, IS. When you get in touch with that love, you can then pass it on, sharing it with others. The point is not that you become loving, but that love is within you; that love is God and that you already possess it as part of your very nature. There is nothing you have to do to become more loving; there is something you have to discover.

As you pass that love on, you begin to make a profound difference in the world. You finally come to realize that this very love you are experiencing and sharing with others is Whom not only God is, but whom you, yourself, truly are.

Why Does This Matter?

As creators living within our own creation, we are limited in our ability to consciously create our "outer world" when we are out of touch with our own true identity. Awakening from involution has to start deeply within each one of us. So where do we begin? First of all, there must be this hunger to explore and continually question our surroundings. Once our curious mind builds up enough steam to lift itself out of its self-imposed box, only then can we begin seeing the true colors of our entire composition and how much of ourselves lies in what we create.

We have been underestimating our power for many years because authorities and institutions have suppressed it. However, in this information-driven age, we realize that outward institutions and organized religions tend to focus on appearances. While they helped us immeasurably by preserving the eternal truths, they simply cannot keep up with all the rapid changes. The great spiritual traditions helped us recognize that God can be experienced in many different ways and realized through many different paths, but it became more and more challenging to access those hidden truths.

For a moment, let us put aside those masks and roles that we play in the outer world. Let us connect with that ultimate Source and Its energy, or whatever you may call it, and experience the love vibrating through every cell of your body. Go ahead and identify the world as yourself. You are its co-creator, so start taking the credit for everything out there, both the good *and* the bad. No more pointing fingers and distributing the blame. *It's all you!*

Our mind sets us up to play in the world of illusion and appearances, much like the gorgeous wrapping paper that conceals the precious gift. Our very love is what will guide us in the right direction. Always!

On the other hand, many of us are puzzled by paradox and contradiction, even though they are the very spice of life. In order to go beyond them, we have to accept and embrace them. Now that we are living in the Planetary Age, things are doubly paradoxical and contradictory. Even in so-called "normal" times, life is just that way, as it is not ultimately "real." We create our own comedy or drama while we continuously star in it, day in and day out. Stop and start noticing all of the special effects. View it as pure entertainment. As Werner Erhard once put it, "The truth doesn't fit. If you experience it, it's the truth. The same thing believed is a lie. In life, understanding is the booby prize." Alan Watts and Deepak Chopra have also suggested that we need to learn to embrace uncertainty, which offers infinite creativity.

As we awaken to our divine nature, we see that it has been there, deep within us, all along. We are all animal, human *and* divine. The "Who" and "What" of God, each legitimate, can be experienced from multiple perspectives. The common ground is love. Once you truly open up to it and tune into your innermost being, you will find that unique gift and talent you have to offer the world is largely overlooked.

Chapter Eight:
HOW YOU FIT INTO THE BIG PICTURE
(Collective)

When you look at fulfilling your individual destiny in the new Planetary Age, it readily becomes apparent that you cannot do this without regard to the collective self. We never live in isolation; we always live in relationship to one other. Given today's advanced global infrastructure, relationship is more important than ever before. We are who and what we identify with the most. In the Planetary Age, our individual identity dovetails with our collective identity. Whether you know it or not, you are a part of the collective enlightenment of humanity.

"We are the world!"

In the wake of est's "The Hunger Project," there was a lot of passion in the 1980s around the song, "We Are the World." Your ultimate Self goes way beyond your individual self to include everyone and everything. When you love the world, you identify with it. To enlighten humanity, you must start with yourself; to enlighten yourself, you must also enlighten the world along with it. It's a magic circle.

The fastest way to wake up the world is for each of us to wake up within. We recognize the interdependence between the world and us and between humanity and us. Some people say that the world is our extended body; that every person we meet is our reflection in the mirror. We are moving as a civilization and as humanity out of a perspective that we are our bod-

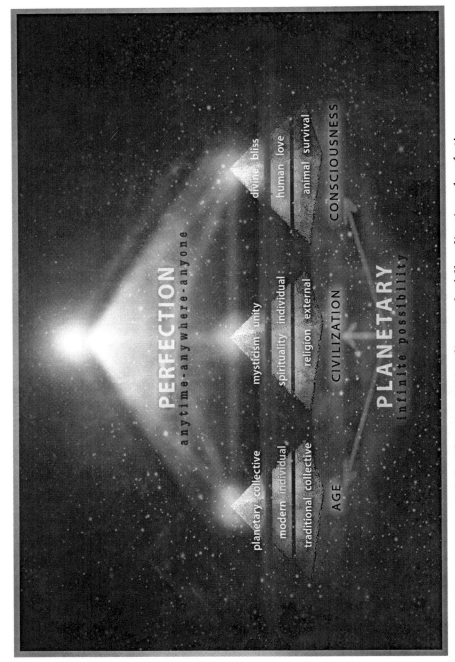

18: It took the Planetary Age to discover the full realization of perfection.

ies, minds and name tags. Most certainly, we are not our clothes or costumes. We are both the play and the playground.

Our ultimate self is playing all the time. The song, "We are the World," which was designed to commiserate with our fellow human beings and identify with them, has profound metaphysical implications.

Unity in Diversity

Since 9/11, it has become increasingly apparent that the only way for all of us to move forward is to honor, even relish, unity in diversity. Tolerance alone is no longer sufficient to turn the world around. We move from tolerance to acceptance, from acceptance to appreciation and from appreciation to embracing.

When we look at how different religions "get along," progress is often simply defined as "not killing each other." In our current era, we have to go way beyond that limited standard. Mere acceptance simply allows someone else to be. For example, I am a Buddhist and someone else is a Muslim. I accept the Muslim, that he or she is Muslim and always will be a Muslim. There is not much I can do except allow him or her to be a Muslim and honor that.

From acceptance, you come to the point of appreciation—that there is something interesting about Islam that you would like to discover and explore. You are no longer simply neutral towards Muslims; you are actually positive and want to know more about their views and faith. You can then go from appreciation to embracing, where you actually get excited about Islam, wanting to actively delve into it, to explore and extend it into your own consciousness and into your own being. All the while, your own faith is so unshakable that you are not threat-

19: Embracing diversity: Our true wealth lies in one another.

ened by other people's faiths but are stimulated to explore them out of interest and appreciation of diversity.

Diversity truly is the spice of life. The more we embrace, the richer we become. The deeper we go, the more we appreciate one another as conscious beings. We can no longer afford to be ignorant of one another's religious traditions. Simply moving from tolerance to acceptance is a start, but we can do much better than that. We see with the emergence of a biracial president and the defeat of a rigid, authoritarian and fundamentalist perspective that we now need to open up in new ways that before might have been uncomfortable.

East/West Convergence

Ever since President Clinton toured India, and China emerged as a manufacturing superpower, it became apparent that East and West were colliding at high speed. As the geopolitical power balance shifted, the United States found that it could no longer dominate other nations and cultures in quite the way in which it did before. Their economies, capabilities in manufacturing and even services were going up dramatically. The world was becoming interdependent with its resources, and people from every region were increasingly scattered throughout the world. Thus, every culture became increasingly multiracial and multinational. As each year passed, it made less and less sense to continue to operate on a strictly national basis.

As the superpowers emerged, such as China and India, they began to exert strong cultural and social influence around the world, including an interest and a preference for their own cuisines, their own movies and even for their own apparel or dress. This also extends to more fundamental aspects of life, including religion and spirituality.

The Western world is becoming increasingly exposed to various Eastern religions, and vice versa. If we look at the United States over the past 50 years, we now find people of every religion in metropolitan areas like St. Louis, let alone San Francisco, Boston and New York. This whole process is accelerating, resulting in a truly new planetary society and worldview.

We can imagine a new planetary spirituality emerging that incorporates all of these great traditions while transcending them. The whole challenge is to include every view while extending the possibilities beyond each of the views to include and transcend them. This is becoming increasingly urgent as East and West collide economically and politically.

The Puzzle Snaps Together

The unification of the East and West will also result in the unification of the North and South, allowing a truly planetary picture of the divine to emerge for the very first time. From a mystical perspective, we have the Eastern and Western Hemispheres as well as the Northern and Southern ones. Western mysticism is devotional in nature, while Eastern is primarily wisdom-based. Northern mysticism entails humanistic science, which recently has emerged around quantum theory; Southern mysticism reflects the creation consciousness of Earth's indigenous people.

All four directions are rapidly converging into a whole new planetary consciousness. Each tradition has a unique piece of the puzzle that only it can fulfill. As all the pieces snap together, we now have a much clearer picture of the Universe as our

20: A global brain for a planetary consciousness.

Source. Literally, the time has come for a much fuller appreciation and conception of God than was ever before possible.

Planetary Consciousness — Bucky Fuller

In the 1960s and 1970s, Richard Buckminster "Bucky" Fuller introduced humanity to Marshall McLuhan's *The Global Village: Transformations in World Life and Media in the 21st Century*, postulating that we would all share a new consciousness, which might be referred to as "omniperspectival," that which incorporates every possible perspective.

Fuller provided a critical insight into the space race between the United States and the Soviet Union in conjunction with McLuhan's vision of a global village. Fuller saw that we were clearly orienting ourselves to outer space; that space is really our home and we are already in outer space, which the ancients referred to as "Heaven." Thus, Heaven and Earth could actually converge. Fuller claimed that humanity was about to undergo its final examination, anticipating planetary citizenship in surmounting the immense environmental, geopolitical and economic problems that plagued humanity even then.

Back in 1969, American astronaut Russell Louis "Rusty" Schweickart floated in near space on a rocket-powered chair, which was tethered just outside his spaceship. Floating at thousands of miles per hour, he noticed the Earth below him without any frames or boundaries, a gorgeous blue/green sphere. Schweickart tuned into the unified whole of creation and had a profoundly religious experience that shaped the direction of his life.

Environmentalists have suggested with the Gaia theory that the Earth itself acts and behaves like a conscious being, as though it is an independent identity. True planetary consciousness incorporates every one of these perspectives and allows for any and all perspectives. This is the context that can subsume all the different religious faiths in a higher one, being informed by these faiths while still going beyond them.

Interbeing

The Vietnamese Nobel Laureate, Thich Nhat Hanh, introduced a new conception of reality when he spoke of "interbeing," interlinking our Source, our world and our fellow human beings. Buddha realized that there are no independent things and that everything mutually co-arises.

Appearances are regarded as just that—appearances—whereas the underlying reality might be considered Being,

Consciousness and Bliss or, as a Buddhist might put it, *sunyata*, the fertile void. The entire phenomenal world is an expression of the very same Being, including plants, animals and people.

Eckhart Tolle recently wrote of "The One Life" that we all share, so "interbeing" could potentially be the next big concept, the next big idea into which humanity tunes, where all of us as plants, animals and human beings divinely share participation in the same Supreme Identity.

Gaia—Loving Our Mother

In the Age of Aquarius of the 1960s and 1970s, such as was portrayed in the movie *Hair*, a new conception of the planet emerged: Gaia, our ultimate Mother. Gaia was the ancient Greek name for the Earth, in that the Earth was considered to be a goddess.

As indigenous people have realized all along, the Earth is indeed alive. It truly is conscious, even its very rocks. From outer space, we can clearly see the entire planet as a single living system. In much of ancient mythology, the Earth was considered feminine and the sky masculine, foreseeing the marriage of Heaven and Earth.

As the Western traditions stressed the masculine over the feminine, we soon neglected and eventually forgot that the Earth is our mother, considering it something to be manipulated, exploited or taken for granted. Today, we will save the planet and ourselves only insofar as we once again learn how to truly love our Mother and appreciate the environment and its ecology, plants, animals and fellow human beings. It is time that we honor and cherish the very ground that supports us.

Communitarianism: Economics Goes Collective

In the late 1980s, the economist from the University of Texas, Raveendra "Ravi" N. Batra, influenced by the work of Indian nationalist and freedom fighter, Sri Aurobindo, predicted the timely collapse of both communism and capitalism. "Communitarianism" is a placeholder for the idea that we are merging capitalism and communism in a new economic order.

To some degree, an actual political theory integrates the two economic systems. Batra pointed out in his book, *The Great Depression of 1990*, that the ideal in his Indian ashram at Pondicherry was that no one person should make more than 10 times any other person and that there should be definite limits. By contrast, on Wall Street recently, the most highly compensated person made thousands of times more than the least paid person. Surely there must be some ethical issues around this level of disparity!

Influenced by ancient Hindu thought, Batra accurately envisioned the collapse of first communism and then capitalism. When an economic system disappears, it does not mean that human beings suddenly vanish. We saw a transition from communism into a type of market capitalism, but then Batra predicted the end of capitalism itself. Certainly, we see the end of capitalism as we know it. We are looking at a whole new concept of capitalism as we recover from the global monetary crisis.

A new planetary economy is undeniably emerging. All the old rules are now obsolete and the new ones have yet to be written. All so-called "economic experts" must be questioned as to how accurately they predicted what happened in the fall of 2008. In order for this new emerging economy to work, we must all share a new collective consciousness. We are all in this together. None of us can stand apart. Even the wealthiest person alive is in danger of losing much of his or her wealth in a rapid fall of market conditions. Our true strength lies not in bleeding each other or trying to get even, but in pulling together out of mutual compassion.

Alternative Spirituality

In the wake of the Internet Revolution, the proliferation of mobile interactive communications and media, we can now go online for true spiritual community—many-to-many rather than many-to-one.

In the face of a revolution in digital communications, which started in the 1980s and is now moving into high gear with the BlackBerry and iPhone, our religious institutions can hardly keep up with the increasing demand for alternative spirituality. So many people think that religious institutions were deliberately obstructing us; that they were just trying to be impossible and mess us up. We don't think this is the case. Because we are at a pivotal point in history, the world is shifting into high gear, and things spontaneously happen.

We now have increasing demand for alternative spirituality because the institutions have a hard time keeping up with these changes despite their best efforts. Spirituality can now be found as much online as offline. For example, we found that the National Methodist Church had a brilliant website. New forms of communal expression now present themselves continuously. As these various forms of community express themselves, spirituality and consciousness become increasingly widespread in discussions. This online sharing of communities will have a transformative impact on mainstream traditions.

At this point in time, it is difficult to look at any institution without regard to its equivalent in cyberspace. Each of these institutions will pave the way for all faiths to merge into the new planetary consciousness.

Transforming the Past

In the 1970s, Werner Erhard, creator of est, suggested that enlightenment reaches back into the past and transforms that past, which was recently confirmed by quantum theory. We all live in the eternal now moment; the past and future are mere constructs. Perhaps this is the real meaning of 2012.

When we are enlightened, our relationship with the past and the future is transformed. We recognize that our true identity lies beyond time and space. Recent quantum experiments demonstrate how particles can move into the past from the future, bringing into question the physical foundation of what we consider to be time. If time cannot be pinned down, is it really "time"?

As we learn how to forgive everyone and everything, we will transform history as we know it. The quantum world suddenly emerged and introduced the possibility that we are transcending the concept of space and time, both of which are actually mental constructs—not all that "real" and not very convincing in the laboratory. If time is a construct, or construction, then our ability to move into the past or future is unlimited. We hold the past in our minds and continue to reinterpret it as our relationship with the future, so we can build an empowering relationship with our past and future.

There is nothing out there that is imposing a negative definition of our past or future. The past and future are not really "out there"; they are continually being created in the present tense. They are continually in the eternal now moment.

Why Does This Matter?

We are at the point where individual and collective consciousness matter equally. We have entered an exciting era where the world is no longer about "you *or* me" but about "you *and* me." This deeply spiritual age is collective in its nature; it needs you, me and everyone else as never before. The magnitude of the crises we collectively face requires all of us to pull together.

What we can do together, we cannot do apart. When the U.S. economy plunged, other countries got pulled down with it. It's a chain reaction demonstrating how everything is interlinked. It is an ongoing interplay of our collective consciousness, of which we are becoming more and more aware.

Everything that ever happened *had* to happen to bring us to this climax in the screenplay where everything is about to be revealed. The East and West convergence has helped us to merge the two core spiritual aspects: wisdom and love. The new consciousness is neither Eastern nor Western, neither Northern nor Southern; it is all of them. We see all of the pieces of the puzzle suddenly snapping together to form a perfect image of God.

Why collective? We can look at it from a different perspective. We form a single, vast cloud of energy. We share the very same energy with each other, including God, Who is experiencing the world's existence directly through us. While we are all one to begin with, we are all so different … with distinct values, religious traditions and beliefs. The more you think about it, the more complex it all gets, and the more entertaining and exciting it becomes. However, we took this game a bit too far. Do we really need to bomb and destroy each other because of divergent views of the same

God? In the midst of this insanity, God IS Love, but this realization got lost in translation. When does love ever need to kill?

The time has come to appreciate God within us and His various vantage points. It is time we began embracing unity in diversity. It is diversity that keeps us in this continuous play and showers us with fresh perspectives.

Are we hungry enough to see a transformation in our world today? At the end, the outer is a reflection of the inner. When we engage in interbeing, we tune into our collective identity with each other and with God, discovering a miraculous power that no one and nothing can overcome.

Chapter Nine:

HOW TO BRING ALL THE MAGIC BACK
(Practice)

If the Planetary Age means anything, it is the re-enchantment of the entire Universe, bringing all the magic back, just like it was meant to be. The Modern Age, with its rational humanism, drained all the magic out of life. Life was meant to be a playful adventure packed with mystery. When our consciousness is transformed, we can experience this life in a whole new way.

As we own our world as an expression of infinite possibility, we discover the ability to keep creating it newly.

The Perfection Process

It is possible for any of us at any time to realize perfection as a living experience with a very simple process. Our very being is perfect; it always has been and always will be. It is appearances that get us into trouble. Our mind is active most of the time with comparison and contrast, so we get into judgments and evaluations, which camouflage the inherent perfection of everyone and everything.

On the individual level, each of us is perfect just as he or she is, but not as someone else, such as a preconceived ideal. So Audrone is perfect as Audrone, but she may or may not be a perfect woman. Phil is a perfect Phil at any given moment, but most definitely is not the perfect man. Just like a mirror, we can observe everyone and everything around us without judgment or evaluation.

A thought is just a thought and a feeling is just a feeling. They do not have to mean anything. We give it the meaning. In meditation, we watch our thoughts and feelings drift right past us like clouds in the sky. When we start witnessing life, and start moving into our daily experience from the point of view of observation, we can experience it on a much deeper level. That experience eventually expands to include the past and the future.

We begin to see that life itself is a continuous process of discovering perfection in its myriad aspects. This is a bold premise. Most of us do not consider ourselves *ever* perfect. Even the very possibility of perfection is seen as infinitely remote because we equate perfection with some arbitrary ideal. An ideal is only an ideal, whereas our behavior is our behavior, our perceptions are our perceptions and our being is our being.

When you tell the truth and come from your experience directly into life, you experience this inherent perfection. Perfection always dwells within the being level. Each of us at any time can access the divine experience of perfection at a moment's notice, as long as we get in touch with just what that perfection actually is.

Life is a continual process of experiencing perfection, losing touch with it and experiencing it all over again. Losing touch with perfection is inherent in the process itself. The challenge of the game in which we find ourselves is to accelerate the process so that we spend more of our life experiencing perfection and less experiencing the reverse. This is not possible unless we can go beyond our mind. We quite literally have to "lose" our mind.

Read more in the section called "The Perfection Process."

Our Manifestation Manifesto

Our Manifestation Manifesto states that, "You can create anything you truly want as long as you choose things exactly the way they are." The trick is in realizing what you *truly* want, as opposed to what you only *think* you want, as well as choosing things *exactly* as you find them, not as you hope they might be. We are always manifesting whether we are conscious of it or not. Every one of us, and all of us collectively, are constantly manifesting as the outer world reflects the inner world. What we are thinking inside has a way of making itself known outside.

Until we own and appreciate what we have already created—the world we inhabit—we unwillingly block ourselves from creating it all newly. What you want is what you want and what you have is what you have ... no need to confuse the two. Choose that which you want to transform to be perfect *just as it is*. For example, it is perfect that Phil is heavy; it is also perfect that Phil loses weight. Both are possibilities, and both possibilities are perfect. When you hold one against the other, you run into trouble.

Take what is already there, discover and then bring out all of its hidden possibilities. Our Manifestation Manifesto suggests that, in order to produce miracles, we need to start with what we have all around us. If you analyze the work of consummate miracle workers, including Jesus of Nazareth, you will find that they always work with what is in front of them. For example, Jesus met a man who was born blind. When Jesus initially tried to heal him, the man could only partially see. Jesus then got some soil, spit upon it and massaged the man's eyes until the man saw perfectly.

Typically, miracles don't entail money dropping out of the

sky although, in weird circumstances, that might actually happen. The opportunity lies in seeing what you have right in front of you, discovering its hidden possibilities and making those possibilities visible rather than taking some arbitrary attitude.

Awaken/Create/Play/Celebrate

Four being values comprise all there ever really is to do in life as we move from sudden awakening to conscious creation to daily play to ultimate celebration. As any spiritual practice leads to these four "being" values, why not start with them? Is there anything more that you would want out of life other than to awaken, create, play and celebrate?

True, most of us struggle with their direct opposites of endarkenment, destruction, struggle and despair, but we need not stay that way. All of these are a perversion of our basic being, characterized by awakening, creation, play and celebration. When we get in touch with who we ultimately are on the being level, we discover and hang out in these precious states. These states are the whole point of life; the clearer we are about that, the freer we become.

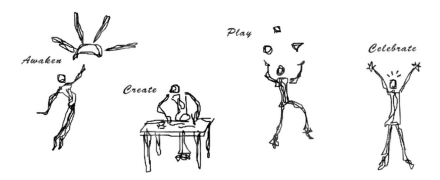

21: What life is all about.

"Awaken" is the sudden realization of our ultimate self expressed both individually and collectively. We stop taking appearances as anything more than appearances and tune into our inner reality.

"Create" implies that we create in communion with the Source, that we were created to create. Creation is our very nature. One famous yogi, Paramahansa Yogananda, suggested that the divine characteristic of human beings is our imagination and that this is what makes us like God. God has imagination and so do we. It is out of that very imagination that we create.

"Play" is an attitude, a state of consciousness, which is an ability to immerse ourselves in everyday activity with clear joy and lightheartedness. The essence of play is to be unattached to the results of what we do. Whenever you do something, you do it without regard to or preoccupation with the consequences; the activity itself is the whole point. In addition, when we consciously create, we can truly play within our own creation.

"Celebrate" suggests that life itself is a blast. Our ultimate purpose in this entire playground is nothing less than Being, Consciousness and Bliss. We are celebrating God. We are celebrating life. We are celebrating our Ultimate Being because there is literally nothing to do. Celebration, interestingly enough, is associated with worship. In many progressive churches, you will find worship services presented as a special kind of celebration. When we realize that we were created to create, we can start celebrating our very own creation as the only thing left to do.

Divine Love

Whenever we get in vital touch with divine nature residing in our upper chakras, we are free to love as God loves, to express the ultimate "true love," beyond, but including, romantic love. When we get in touch with our innermost being, we discover that we are pure love. This is not something that we have to put on. It is not something that we have to go out of our way to feel. It is something that we discover for ourselves by getting in touch.

This love is an experience completely independent of any circumstances and is unconditional in nature. If we extrapolate the ultimate meaning of the New Testament and the Gospel, God IS Love. Love, itself, IS God. Once we open ourselves up, we find that that very love is our ultimate joy and fulfillment.

Play God or Be God—The Choice Is Yours

Our ultimate choice, moment by moment, is to let go and truly experience God, or try and pretend that we are God, totally autonomous and unaccountable. While it might sound like blasphemy to suggest that we either "Play God or Be God," it is really the choice we face at every moment. Whenever we cater to our ego, whenever we assert our own humanity against that of someone else, we are playing God. We are taking a prerogative that belongs only to God.

Whenever we surrender to the moment, we enter life with acceptance and allow that which is to be. We then realize that we are, in truth, God. We are one with the Creator, and we are consciously experiencing that which we see before us. To play God is to interact with the world through our own ego and most superficial self. All of us are vulnerable at one time or another to control dramas, which usually backfire in a futile attempt to get our own way at all costs. All efforts to play God, whether politically or on an individual level, come out of a mistaken sense of self-righteousness, our attachment to our own viewpoint.

As Baba Ram Dass put it, "Our ego is our cognitive frame

of reality." Our ego is nothing more or less than how we hold things. If we hold things in a very narrow way, we continue to bump into other people. While being God, we have no need whatsoever to prove anything, as we realize we are united with everyone and everything. Why would the Creator need to prove Himself? That is patently absurd!

We move from our pretense to our shadow to our ultimate self. The more we are caught up in our pretense, the more apt we are to play God—unless we use our pretense in a playful way, not taking ourselves quite so seriously. It is perfect that we play God. It is also perfect that we BE God. The choice is ours, along with the consequences.

In the whole realm of perfection, any possibility is perfect. You cannot have perfection if only a certain set of conditions is perfect. By definition, you will almost always fail. Perfection is when *any* possibility is perfect so, when all things are perfect, and you are in a condition of acceptance, you allow them to be, and you find yourself the Creator.

Dance with Your Monsters

Don't go looking for the monster under your bed; he's hiding right inside your head! Our monsters are our greatest fears. Our fear materializes through a natural tendency to project. How do we dance with our monsters? If we think of Pixar's movie, *Monsters Inc.*, we see a group of monsters who are more afraid of the children they scare than the children are afraid of them. We are all afraid of our ghosts and of our own shadows. Until we overcome our fears, anyone or anything can be a monster.

We typically resist monsters in our life, refusing to see the lighter side of them; that they are simply there to ensure the game stays interesting. For example, the meltdown of the global monetary system could be pretty scary for most of us; in fact, it could be viewed as a nightmare and most certainly as a monster. By the same token, it allows us to create an entirely new global monetary system from scratch, which would be possible in no other way.

When we truly face ourselves, we can then begin to actually play with our own monsters. The whole idea is not to kill or destroy our monsters. The challenge is to own our monsters and then transcend them to the point where we can actually dance with them.

A State of Grace

Everyone has experienced rare, magical moments when everything seems to flow effortlessly to his or her ultimate satisfaction. Is it possible to increase or extend these experiences? This is a state of grace where we just happen to tune into a higher frequency or Higher Power, being guided by coincidences. We typically want to hold on to this state. It is very natural to do this, all very human. However, the harder we try to hold on to that state where everything flows, the faster it all seems to slip away from us.

The secret seems to lie in our willingness to let go of the experience and recreate it a little further down the road. It seems as though the faster we surrender, the sooner it is likely to return. The state of grace is noticeable to anybody in athletics, to anyone involved in the performance of anything, to any artist, even to anyone in sales. It has many names and meanings, but it entails the idea of being in the flow when everything just happens to work, where everything is play and effortless, where somehow our ego is out of the way. A state of grace is not unique to the Christian tradition; it is available and integral to people in every tradition.

Instant Enlightenment

If you want to get enlightened in 60 seconds or less, seek no further than your own immediate experience. This can happen in either 60 seconds or 60 years; for many of us, it may take a lifetime. While it all sounds so simple, people typically find it extremely difficult.

Here's an experiment: Notice that anything of which you are aware at this very moment, YOU are aware of it. No one else. Anything you can *ever* imagine is contained within the framework of *your very own experience*. As Kant put it, you can never know the thing in itself; you only *assume* that people and things are really out there. The self we just described—the self that witnesses this present moment—is who we all ultimately are; in other words, *there is only God, and God is our only true self.*

This is a very profound experiment and could literally lead you to "satori," the Zen term for a "flash of enlightenment." It is probably the scariest experiment upon which you might ever embark. We all know that we experience and know from our experience; anything else is conjecture. If you think this through, you will find yourself right on the edge of enlightenment.

Cyber-Spirituality

Social networking and media are impacting all of society—from government to corporations to people's spiritual communities. The new social media are changing all of our institutions, including religion and spirituality. Broadband Internet and mobile communications are sparking a revolution in consciousness. They have already elected an American president … *What can't they do?* We can now instantly access people of every possible path and tradition right on the Internet.

Just as the new social media made the election of President Obama possible, so will they bring people together spiritually in stunning new ways never before imagined. When we look at computerization and its myriad applications, we realize that it moved in a vector from computational machines where computer technology was all about computing to processing—as in processing words and data—to communication itself.

With the communication revolution, computers are finally demonstrating their true potential. This has been extended through networking, ultimately through the Internet and now through wireless technology, where there is a whole new realm for people to show up in cyberspace and for spiritual expression, community and communion.

Planetary Sourcebook and Temple

We are moving toward the ultimate expression of collective celebration, culminating in a truly planetary sourcebook and temple, which unites every tradition and ethnic group with a dazzling presence in virtual space. As an opportunity, we can build an online interfaith temple with world scriptures, which is truly planetary in scope.

Much like that used in Second Life—the Internet's largest, user-created, three-dimensional, virtual world community—technology now makes possible this 3D environment, which includes rich media such as video, animation and high-definition sound. The sky is literally limited at this point in time but very few people see it yet. Right now, we can access a spiritual archive of American Standard Code for Information Interchange (ASCII) text, pooling scriptures from all the major religions. As simply ASCII text, very few people would find it all that appetizing.

The planetary sourcebook and temple will allow us to instantaneously explore how each faith interrelates with dynamic links from religion to religion and from topic to topic. Thus, we will begin to have a truly planetary perspective on all faiths.

Much like Second Life, we can create a spiritual city or temple of digital environments where people of every faith intermingle, expanding their boundaries. This virtual playground will fulfill our ultimate purpose in being a communal celebration with our Ultimate Being. It could be a planetary sourcebook and temple much like a spiritual Disneyland, except online, where it could be sponsored by a broad array of religious groups encompassing a unifying planetary perspective.

Why Does This Matter?

We all long for a truly magical life where we relish every moment and everything just seems to flow without effort. While, on the surface, we must do something; our actions can flow like a warm summer breeze caressing our hair in just the "right" direction.

Perfection is our true foundation. Can we create a solid house on a weak foundation? Most likely it will not hold. The same thing applies to our creation and manifestation process. How can you create or transform your current moment when you are hanging out below the line? You need to come up for breath because perfection can only be realized at the level of creation.

When we attune ourselves to our divine nature, we begin to consciously create our experience rather than feel the effect of everything that transpires. As discussed in Chapter Seven, "below the line" is the world of survival; "above the line" is the world of being, where you are in charge of your own creation. On that level, your entire life is experienced as celebration. When you realize how precious this dance is, you give up your attachment to suffering.

As you choose your experience, it flows, while remembering your divine nature, allowing whatever is to be without any interference on your part. You begin to realize that there is nothing to do in life but to awaken, create, play and celebrate. We always have the mutually exclusive choice to *play* God or *be* God. We can make our point of view "right" or allow all points of view to be right. While we are God all the time, playing God sabotages the living experience of God. That is why all the great traditions espouse profound humility.

You live while being in full charge, directing your very own movie wherein you play multiple roles and celebrate the entire cast. Then you look at your worst problems as a chance to befriend your shadow monsters and dance with them. They are there to add spice to the scene of the day. As you are aware of the illusory nature of your problems showing up at your door, you find it easier and easier to dance with them.

At this point, you can awaken from "reality" any time you want by simply noticing that everything you are aware of, YOU are aware of. You and your field of awareness are ONE. All else is an assumption.

Collectively, we can re-enchant the world by sharing our spirituality and pooling our wisdom traditions. When this effort reaches critical mass, a new vision of God will emerge that will continually inspire, empower and enlighten us. In this context, we can create a planetary sourcebook and temple, honoring every faith and wisdom tradition. We will eventually all come together in cyberspace to celebrate planetary consciousness, community and communion, or interbeing.

22: How planetary consciousness is bringing us all together.

Chapter Ten:

WHERE WE ARE HEADED

Future—Planetary (*Beyond 2012 CE*)

As we come to terms with the Planetary Age, we realize that we are heading towards a stunning culmination of history, much like the grand finale of a fireworks display. Everything that ever happened in the Megastory *had* to happen in order to bring us to this exact moment. We are already swept up in a process leading to a culmination that seems as if it were out of our hands. We are living in the most exciting time in history:

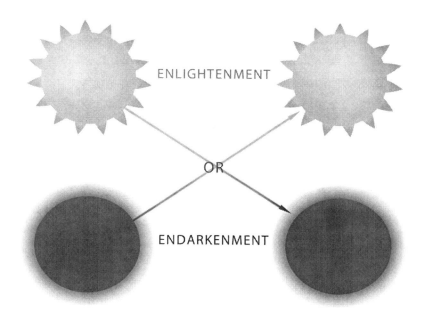

23: From endarkenment to enlightenment:
the only path that makes any sense.

when all of humanity finally awakens from the dream.

The Omega Point

Much as people in the 2012 movement suggest, the 20th century CE French archeologist and theologian, Pierre Teilhard de Chardin, envisioned the ultimate transformation of humanity as it enters eternity. The Omega Point is held to be the culmination of all consciousness on Earth, with humanity itself being an expression of the divine and merging with it. This is when Planet Earth becomes conscious of itself as planet and humanity becomes conscious of itself as humanity. We come to realize that consciousness is all there ever is.

Time, as we know it, is about to end because humanity will see time only as a function of the collective mind—almost as if it were merely a convention. Humanity will come to realize that we have always been living in eternity but never before realized it. We will smile when we fully realize that, all along, we have been the Creator hidden within His creation. We chose to forget who He is. We are all playing the ultimate game of hide-and-go-seek.

With the Omega Point, humanity is coming together into an ultimate fusion of consciousness. It looks like this is the entire thrust of creation and all of history, the Megastory and the Megadream. It could happen in our very lifetime.

From Integral to Transpersonal

The integral movement has correctly seen the shift from the pluralism of the green movement, which acknowledges many realities, to everyone and everything coming together in a higher order. The Planetary Age will shortly reveal itself to be profoundly transpersonal in nature. The transpersonal is a realization that God is both personal and impersonal; that while God includes personality, God clearly goes beyond it.

After a generation of pluralism, Ken Wilber, who inspired the integral thought of today, successfully introduced integral consciousness as the next big thing, offering humanity a true "theory of everything." We feel that integral thought is a warm-up for a truly transpersonal perspective. It is not *we* who are dreaming God; it is, rather, God who is dreaming *us*.

We postulate that the ultimate reality is pure consciousness itself, which is also known as God. To know that reality is to know ourselves. All there is IS consciousness itself. There is nothing to which we can really point.

The Impossible Becomes Possible

A further trend in the new era in which we occupy is that both quantum and string theories are capturing the popular imagination and will unleash a frank recognition that nothing is "impossible," echoing what has been declared all along in the scriptures. It was not the movie *The Secret* that first publicized this. The great masters of every tradition have declared that, with God, "nothing is impossible"; their practitioners have largely ignored that realization.

The world, due to appearances, has had a tough time accepting this at face value. Ancient physics, like that of the Modern Age, assumed that whatever was solid was real. From the modern materialistic perspective, this view that nothing is impossible was totally absurd. As the new physics emerged, there was no conflict with the ancient understanding that quantum theory is really a physics of possibility.

Since there is really no one and nothing "out there," we

are ultimately free to create anything in the matrix, the canvas and ultimate screen of our lives. As we consciously realize that we are divine, and that divinity is all there is, we can draw on Higher Power—or our higher nature, if you will—to accomplish what was earlier inconceivable. Thus, the implications of quantum and string theories are in a blowout of all self-imposed limits, possibly within our very lifetime.

All Faiths Converge into a Higher Truth

As every tradition goes planetary in scope and encounters the truth within all the others, every tradition (whether Christian, Muslim, Buddhist, Hindu, Jewish, humanist or shamanic) will begin to discover the missing pieces of the puzzle, leading to the collective realization of a higher truth, hinted by the ancient prophets but never before disclosed.

The time has come for humanity to bring an end to all its religious wars as we witness everyone and everything converging. The Modern Age has really been the setup for the world to come together, even if it accomplished it with a very heavy hand. Before our new age, no single tradition—not even Buddhism, Christianity or Islam, which are considered world religions—could become truly planetary in scope.

It is now much easier to see that every great tradition holds unique missing pieces of the puzzle. Every tradition was sufficient for individual enlightenment, but no one tradition could be sufficiently complete to allow for collective enlightenment. The promised millennium, symbolized in the Old Testament prophecy of *Isaiah* with the vision of the lion lying with the lamb, points to the emergence of a single planetary faith that, in the voice of Werner Erhard's The Hunger Project, will include

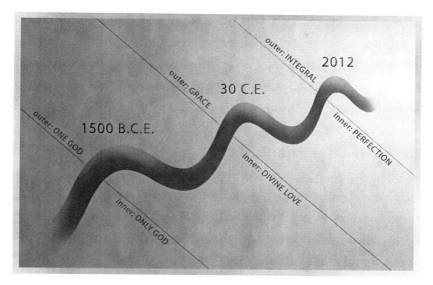

24: Three waves of revelation leading to an ultimate realization.

"everyone, with no one and nothing left out."

Spiritual Literacy and Intelligence

It will very soon be realized that the greatest educational imperative will not simply be financial literacy but spiritual literacy and intelligence, one's ability to connect with and interface a higher order of being.

On account of the historic divorce between science and religion, many people developed a deep suspicion of all forms of religion. In academic circles, religion was more or less marginalized. As a consequence, we literally had no sufficient vocabulary with which to discuss religious differences. In fact, in that environment, ignorance was bliss.

Undergoing a profound reversal of values in the last 50 years, educational institutions will now begin placing a premium on the domain that they formally despised. Once we succeed in developing a deep language of spiritual expression that can interlink all faiths, the divisive spiritual differences that tore us up will harmonize in stunning new ways.

Open-Source Spirituality

The open-source movement, spawned by the spectacular success of Linux, and being adopted by such leading computer companies as Hewlett-Packard, IBM and Oracle, will catalyze open-source spirituality; all the great spiritual truths will become readily available online, sparking a new generation of creativity.

As people from all around the world collaborate on spiritual projects, they will introduce new inclusive paradigms of faith. The planetary sourcebook and temple can become a focal point that will demand an open-source approach to build it, where people everywhere have the opportunity to contribute.

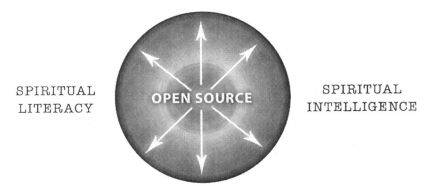

SPIRITUAL LITERACY   OPEN SOURCE   SPIRITUAL INTELLIGENCE

25: In our deeply spiritual age, new
intelligence and literacy are required.

Intercontinental spiritual forums will allow people to probe the farthest reaches of consciousness in the most remote spiritual disciplines. Individual and spiritual mentors will be instantly available on a 24/7 basis. We will see something like the equivalent of the United Nations in religion—or United Religions—emerge, growing beyond the current world crisis, which will be easily accessible to all citizens of the Earth.

The collaborative space in developing software code has extended to a wide range of possibilities. In Don Tapscott's *Wikinomics: How Mass Collaboration Changes Everything*, open source is seen as a key to further economic expansion as people collaborate. In the case of Boeing Airlines, some 60 countries collaborated, where Boeing, the parent corporation, actually shared their schematics with their partner companies.

We are now in an environment where collaboration and open source are both viable and profitable. As we use this approach to spirituality, we will witness a transformation of spirituality itself.

Web of Life

As people increasingly recognize "The One Life" expressing itself in everyone and everything, a profound respect for the sacredness of all life will most certainly emerge. As the movie, *The Lion King*, celebrated the Circle of Life, humanity will join indigenous people everywhere in reverencing every species.

In his book, *A New Earth: Awakening to Your Life's Purpose*, Eckhart Tolle introduced various processes of observation through which we can directly discover that all life, and the world itself, is one. As we cherish this fragile web that we inhabit, this biosphere will spontaneously begin to heal. As the prominent holistic medicine pioneer, Dr. Andrew Weil, noted, long-term environmental studies have demonstrated how a regional ecosystem with extremely contaminated rivers and streams began to spontaneously heal in just 30 years as the pollutants were eliminated. We maintain that the same thing will happen with Planet Earth. As humanity becomes conscious, our environment will become conscious and undergo a transformation.

From Realization to Revelation

The distinct traditions of mystical realization and divine revelation—in other words, the East and the West—will merge into a common understanding. When a fresh wave of revelation sweeps the Earth with a magnitude greater than anything ever seen before, all will be made clear to humanity.

The three Persons of God will unite, and people will experience Source, Itself, through multiple channels of communication. The first-person experience of God is that of our ultimate Self, and the third-person experience of God as Sacred Presence will fuse with the second-person experience of God as Absolute Other. As we learn how to experience God in every possible way, we will experience our Source as being equally within us and without us.

We are looking at the most fascinating period of spirituality ever to emerge. All the means are now at our disposable for collective realization on a higher order than ever before imaginable. With fresh revelation, whole new scriptures can emerge virtually out of nowhere. We are now at a point where the time has come for Source to reveal its ultimate nature.

Democracy Meets Theocracy

As the fundamentalists unwittingly have proven, we are now in a deeply spiritual age that suggests government will become a combination of human and divine, democratic and theocratic, at one and the same time.

Recently, America has been torn apart between religious activists, such as the Moral Majority, and liberal-minded evolutionists who bitterly opposed the wars in Iraq and Afghanistan and insist upon a more humane and compassionate society. The continuous struggle between Democrats and Republicans reflects a passionate disagreement about the best way to incorporate spirituality in the political sphere. Is it a private or public matter? While both sides—liberal Democrat and conservative Republican—have a legitimate case, the greater truth lies in a synthesis of their respective viewpoints. We feel they have both made important points that need to be heard.

As a truly planetary faith emerges, a profound respect for every tradition will be universal and no longer narrowly sectarian, and the role of religion will no longer be disputed. Democracy is based on the assertion of human rights and the resolution of conflict through pointed discussion and consensus. Theocracy has traditionally been based upon revelation and divine authority around a finite religious institution.

In the new environment, where divine love is realized to be the very heart of all true religion, that love will finally fulfill the demands of both democracy and theocracy, and the arbitrary division between religion and government will begin to fade.

If we look at the Dalai Lama, who early on became both the temporal and spiritual leader of Tibet, we see how it might be possible to combine theocracy with democracy. While he is historically considered a sovereign monarch, he is also a highly educated and disciplined monk. While he follows Vajrayana Buddhism, he is a spokesman—not only for all forms of Buddhism but for all the great religious traditions. When meeting Westerners, he makes a point of encouraging them to stay with their childhood religion; that to think like him doesn't require them to change their faiths.

One of the important marks of enlightenment is to see every point of view, not just our own. His Holiness has been praised by highly distinguished Western scholars and scientists on numerous occasions for the immense breadth and depth of his thinking. In his book, *The Universe in a Single Atom: The Convergence of Science and Spirituality*, the Dalai Lama suggests that we might create an inner science to complement the outwardly focused science of the West. In all of this, he has demonstrated incomparable humility and compassion. The very name "Dalai Lama" means "oceanic master" because his lineage has been characterized by spiritual masters of extraordinarily comprehensive thought and magnificent heart. With the demise of Pope John Paul II, few would deny that His Holiness has become the preeminent spokesman—not only for the East but for all of humanity.

The Culmination of History—God Behind the Wheel

As we enter the culmination where everyone and everything comes together at once, we will suddenly realize that *there never has been any real accident, that it was divinely orchestrated all the time.*

As we see it all come together at once, we discern a continuous inner thread woven throughout the story of humanity, which we call the Megastory. We often envision God as apart from us, imagining God arbitrarily judging and even condemning us. In Western religions, we often come across the idea that it would all come to a "Judgment Day" and subsequent condemnation.

Rarely did it occur to most of us that God has never been sitting idly on the sidelines but, rather, *God has been with us all the time, experiencing every single thing that we are going through. It is as though the Universe is experiencing the Universe through us as the Universe.*

Very often, orthodox believers are bitterly opposed to the cynical viewpoint that God is playing with us as if we were merely a bunch of toys, much like the Greek gods playing with humans for recreation. This is an inaccurate perspective. This whole spectacle has been set up and orchestrated by our Source to have a blast *with* us, not as a joke *on* us, but in order to have a supremely rich experience *with* us and *through* us. God is experiencing every single one of our pains and sorrows. As we collectively wake up to this possibility, we will find that the whole Universe awakens along with us to the divine Presence. Nothing will ever be the same. For those of us who heed this vision, our lives will be utterly transformed.

Three Ages/Three World views:

	Traditional	Modern	Planetary
Nature of Cosmos	Magical	Matter and Energy	Conscious Playground
Origin of Cosmos	Divine Will	Evolutionary	Supreme Being's Play Of Consciousness
Nature of God	Arbitrary/Patriarchal	Rational, But Far Removed	Absolute Love/Our Supreme Identity
Nature of Humanity	Center of Sacred Circle of Life	Intelligent, Resourceful Species	Inherently, Unalterably Divine
Nature of Life	Reincarnation/Enlightenment/Salvation	Evolutionary Mechanism	Source Experiencing Its Own Creation As Itself; Each Life Uniquely Precious
Purpose of Life	Creation Glorifies Creator	Self-Determined	Perfect Game of Enlightenment
Humanity's Role in World Order	Center of Sacred Web of Life	All Species at Humanity's Disposal	All Life Forms Share Single Consciousness
Problem of Evil	Ignorance/Active Rebellion	Ill-Adaptive Survival Mechanism	Self-Chosen Limitation To Ensure Enlightenment Game Stays Interesting
Human Destiny	Collective Salvation/Realization	Emerge As Higher Life Form	Create New Cosmos In Communion With Source
Highest Value	Prosperity and Longevity	Individual Fulfilment	Transformation

26: *Why it all HAD to happen.*

Why Does This Matter?

Is the world changing for the worse? Quite the contrary! It is perfect that the world is in such turmoil today because we are at the culmination of a centuries-long process of bringing everyone and everything together.

Time seems to be accelerating because change has become exponential. We are fast approaching the Omega Point when the world becomes conscious of itself as pure being, and humanity becomes conscious of its own divinity. As we begin to experience God in everyone and everything, we will begin to realize that all there is IS God.

We are all collectively about to jump into a whole new level as all the sacred traditions are pooled together and fresh revelation streams through each one of us. We will find ourselves in sync with this profoundly spiritual age. As the materialist paradigm becomes increasingly obsolete, people will feel at home integrating spirituality into every aspect of their lives.

As the conventional notion of time ends, we will find ourselves already in eternity exploring other planets and galaxies. Time has been a human construct to account for apparent change in the world. In truth, there is just Being, Consciousness and Bliss—the space where truly anything is possible. As we collectively commune with our Source, we will find that we are truly divine.

Our ultimate destiny as divinity is to consciously create a whole new Megadream and Megastory, a whole new universe. We will discover that any dream we come up with is perfect, and we can choose to play in it anytime we want.

CONCLUSION
A Transformed Life Needs No Justification

Can you feel the massive shift in energy throughout the planet today? How could we have moved forward if we had stayed stuck in the past, playing by old rules that no longer apply? How many of us have stepped back far enough to relish the full panorama?

Every age has had something major to contribute in order for us to get to the one in which we now find ourselves. We had to go through all of them to fully blossom. We had to plunge into the unknown so we could discover and tap into its underlying truth. If we look at our most recent past—the Modern Age—we see how we lost ourselves in the production of material goods at the cost of our environment. Gluttons for power, we utterly identified with our egos, cutting ourselves off from each other and from all of creation. In the Modern Age, our analytical mind reigned supreme. We were never paid to *be*, only to *do*. Being busy was a mark of godliness. Feeling inadequate after divorcing ourselves from our Source, we could never do enough to prove ourselves. We found that we could never get enough of what we didn't really want. Play was relegated to children and the senile. Our challenge was to get ahead at any cost, not to grow or celebrate life.

We dove into our historical narrative to offer you a perspective on our present era as being distinctly different from the Modern Age, an era with a dramatically different sensibility, set of challenges and possibilities. With access to digital devices like the iPhone, people now have many times the power of communication that they enjoyed even 50 years ago. We live in an age of instant information that allows us to learn about and respond to any subject, making the issues of global community our own. We are actually looking at a totally new civilization, which no longer glorifies the individual at the price of the collective. Transformation leads to unity in diversity, equally honoring both. Our collective global brain, if you will, is more powerful than that of any of us, especially given the magnitude of crises we face today.

The Whole Point of Awakening

We are back to a very spiritual age; this time more than ever. When you clearly appreciate life for the journey of enlightenment that it is, you suddenly realize that it is all perfect, always has been and always will be. Looking back, we could not relate to perfection as we can today. Only now we can see the big picture well enough to understand and appreciate it.

Our whole sensibility and perspective have vastly expanded. Our story is what we mistook for reality. This story focused on "doing" at the expense of "being," driven by fear of loss, survival of the fittest. It all seemed very real until we awoke to our true identity, realizing that there could be no story without a storyteller. There is no dream without a dreamer, and there can be no doing without being ... "being human," that is.

Being is our divine home. When we distance ourselves from it, we become weak and get sucked into the world of process, which seems so real but is ultimately only an illusion. We can't drive a car from the passenger's seat. We were meant to be creators, and the whole process of creation happens only from the being Universe. We cannot create from the doing Universe, since it is perpetually a world of appearances. Whenever we buy into these appearances, we lose out.

When we don't come from creation, we lose the sense of magic and miss out on the true meaning of our existence. Awakening to perfection within and without opens wide the gate to infinite possibility and abundance. Being aspirations—awaken, create, play and celebrate —are the bridge that unites both the being and doing worlds. Once we awaken to our "divine Self," the whole game changes. We were created for something far bigger than ourselves. We were created to create in conscious communion with one other and with our Creator. When we forgot that we were divine, we soon lost touch with our own humanity. We even relegated animals to machines, losing any sense of soul. Preserving the status quo meant selling out, void of any scruples.

This awakening turns everything inside out. The entire Universe is within each of us. *I am you, and you are me.* Source is everyone and everything while being beyond everyone and everything. Divine love alone is sufficient, and divine love is everywhere, once you open your eyes. Life is inherently a celebration, yet all we have seemed to do is manage to survive, even while accumulating a mountain of goods.

Even our spirituality was seen in terms of instant gratification. We forgot that love is surrender, letting go and letting God. In opening up, we transform others, the world and ourselves. We awaken to the eternal now, which has always been here and always will be here. The present moment is a precious gift in which we create and experience our own being. When we look at time, it is just a way to measure the play of Being, Consciousness and Bliss. We already create on a daily basis, largely doing it unconsciously, losing out on the immense play and celebration that is out there, up for grabs. If we don't take responsibility for our own creation, how can we consciously play in it? How can we enjoy the drama or comedy of the day? When we lose that sense of play, we definitely forget that our whole purpose in living is to celebrate life itself.

Does life have to be "serious" for it to be important? All burdened down to do the right thing, we cherish a propensity toward mischief that undoes our best efforts. Just try to kick a bad habit. In the West, we have interpreted the consequences in terms of Heaven and Hell. In the East, we have interpreted them in terms of inadvertently being chained to an endless wheel of *samsara* for yet another *karmically* unfavorable birth. The traditional assumption was that we were up to no good and needed to be chained in place to stay out of mischief; however, when we realize that life is but a dream, an illusion, we challenge its seriousness. If it is only a dream, then why does it matter? If we are not really punished in Hell, or if we don't actually undergo a karmic regression, then why not play all out and aim for excellence while remembering what truly matters: Life, Light and Love?

We live in a dream of dreams. Our nightly dreams vary greatly, while our daily dream has a certain consistency about it, largely maintaining the same circumstances and point of view day in and day out. Yet, it is intermittent. We are going in and out of the same daydream as the earth spins. It is a little bit like a soap opera, with new episodes constantly being rolled out, including complications, intrigue, conflict and resolution. Always, there is something slightly different to maintain audience interest.

The dream is for the sake of the Self, who both transcends us while including each of us. We are both on and off the stage. We are both the actors on the film set and the audience munching the popcorn while watching ourselves in the film. And, if our life is much like a movie, a 3D simulation, the last thing we want is for it to seem dull and fake. We want it to be thoroughly convincing. It is a far greater show when the actors and actresses enjoy themselves while making a movie. When we truly play, as opposed to merely survive, we are not preoccupied with being serious. We simply enjoy the experience. The prerequisite of play is to do something for its own sake with a very experimental attitude. You are no longer all wrapped up in the outcome. The journey itself is the reward.

Going for the Illusion

To grasp life, it is essential to realize that there is always far more than meets the eye. The opportunity and challenge in the Planetary Age are to consciously go for the illusion itself, *knowing that it is only play*. Of course, we will forget about it in the midst of the action, but there will always be a reminiscent awareness that this is not ultimately real.

We realize that illusion typically has bad connotations. We usually speak of illusions being shattered, of dreams being broken. It places the stress on appearances, contrasting it with "reality." What is the point if appearances are only appearances? Can't you see? We can simply play with them. We are all illusionists or magicians as well as the audience that likes to observe the act. We deliberately want to pretend and see what the magician can accomplish on stage when the spotlight is lowered. The feeling of surprise and amazement meets a deep human need. More than one quantum physicist has been drawn into his discipline through this preoccupation with magic.

So, the matrix, or illusion, seduces us all into buying appearances. Some of us get the nature of the game: that it is a truly educational process whose whole point is to turn endarkenment into awakening, self-preoccupation into creation, survival into play and dread into pure celebration. Alan Watts wrote on "the taboo against knowing who you are." So often, who we really are remains unspoken, at best read between the lines. When the whole world culture shifts, when people from wildly disparate parts of the world meet and share their sensibilities, when people in developing countries stop buying into the myth that the modern world is better or even any longer relevant, and start honoring their own culture and civilization, magic can happen.

We discover that the entire Megastory has been a long growth process or divine school, if you will, for everyone to awaken to their divinity. It is challenging for us to get our arms around the idea that this collective illusion is the most precious thing we have; that it is deliberate, tacitly agreed upon and a divine celebration. If we step back and look at the Megadream and the Megastory, we see, as did Dante Alighieri, that it is far more a divine comedy than a diabolical tragedy. Some might think that life is a cruel joke that God has played on us. However, God is playing *with* us, in the sense that He is experiencing what every one of the characters is experiencing. He is engaging in the entire action from every point of view. There is always an undercurrent of infinite love for the asking.

When we think of Heaven, it is most often construed to be a place where you go when you die … if you were "good" or, more correctly, *if you are saved*. Popular conception entails clouds with angels and harps perched on top of Mount Olympus. The most radical conception of all is that *this very earth*, and *this very life*, ARE paradise. If one takes a tour of the solar system, one readily appreciates the uniquely favorable conditions of this planet for life. The astronauts, who went to the Moon and back, were profoundly moved by the sheer beauty and immensity of Planet Earth as a unified whole, with "no frames, no boundaries." They saw it as the greatest miracle imaginable.

So, should we live as we were meant to, this would indeed be paradise. From this, we might suppose that paradise is a state of being in the eternal now, where each creature is one with the Creator, where each individualized consciousness rests in absolute harmony with the Supreme Consciousness.

Plotting Your Destiny

When we look at the possibility that each of us is authoring our own life in concert with our Source, we might wonder why we have such spectacularly bad taste. We don't seem to be able to put onto the paper what we truly want. The plot seems so convoluted. We hold ourselves to impossible standards without even once wondering just how we came up with those same standards. Of course, if we thought about it, we would each have an entrée and an exit. However, this doesn't answer the deeper question of where we came from. Why would we kill something that we, ourselves, created?

When we come at our life from cause, we give up looking outside ourselves for final explanations. We recognize ourselves as neither the body nor the mind. We mirror everyone and everything who reflect us. Everything is contained within the circle of our experience, right in the center of the eternal present.

We are Source and Source is us. Source is both immanent and transcendent. We have been granted the power to create and translate. The past and future are not really "out there"; they never were. Thus, we are given the ability to reinterpret them in the light of divine love. Whom we forgive IS forgiven. When we forgive the past, we release the past to be the foundation of a glorious whole.

Life is a precious gift. As we appreciate it for what it is, we can enrich it. As we let it go, we can get it right back again. Since we have all collectively conceived a supreme love story, we need not be overly concerned about how it all ends. We simply need to come back home, remembering our divine origin. In order to participate in this vast dream, each of us has had to embark on a hero's journey, starting from our very birth. We are the ones who survived, who continued to press forward. We now lean upon the grace of God, no longer pretending that we must do it all ourselves.

We have the power to remember and invoke that sacred presence anytime we want. When we "let go and let God," we start to play all over again. Whatever happens, happens. When we interpret our lives as an interwoven tapestry of divine love, we can start to dance. Each of us is unique, yet each of us shares the same Supreme Self. We are one humanity and one divinity. When we interpret our lives as a glorious process of awakening, of realizing perfection, of moving forward, now on, now off, we realize that there is absolutely no rush. Our task is just to BE. As we ARE, we begin to act and interact consciously. We are not only our individual roles but also the entire cast of characters.

Your Role as Co-creator

If we look back at history and the three major ages from a spiritual standpoint, we find that the Traditional Age was all about unity, shifting from the belief in many gods to The One (monotheism), while the Modern Age was more about realizing that God is loving and merciful, not preoccupied with keeping points. The Planetary Age has discovered interbeing, disclosing that all there is IS God. God is the Supreme Being, pure consciousness, a consciousness of absolute unity, love and perfection. The Planetary Age becomes more and more transpersonal, with everything and everyone translucent.

This new consciousness is going to totally transform everyone and everything in its wake. The agenda for this stunning new era is now fully in place. To move forward, we must all get with it. Our opportunity as individuals is to unite in this new consciousness and accelerate the pace of its adoption. We have run into an absolute dead end with the modern consciousness, which drove us all into spiritual destitution. The ancient traditions of East, West, North and South are breathing life into us once again. While we will likely learn to travel through space and time, we can never really go back to the traditional or modern eras. It is just that the post-modern era—the Planetary Age—will bear a very strange resemblance to the Traditional Age. We will see theocracy once again; however, this time, it will be a democratic theocracy.

When you look at your own life, you will find that it doesn't make any sense *not* to join this revolution and revelation. All you need to do at this point is discover your destined role within it. The greatest single contribution you, or any of us, can make is to live from the center of this new planetary consciousness. Empower everyone in your world to recognize his or her divinity; that the very fact that we are human also means that we are divine. We are all citizens of the planet, citizens of the Universe. The Universe belongs to us as much as we belong to it. Even more important, our Source belongs as much to us as we belong to Him. There is only God and God IS Love, which means it is all perfect, always has been and always will be.

Only until the past few decades was it even imaginable that humanity had the power to destroy the earth. While the planet could theoretically spit us out and vomit all forms of higher life, we, as humanity, are endowed with the unique capacity to re-frame our worldview. It is paradoxical that, to survive, we must go back to the consciousness of primal people and literally see Earth as our divine Mother. We must see God in every rock, in every tree, in every animal and in every stream. Most of all, we must go back to *being*, surrender to Higher Power and cherish our role as co-creators.

For us to stubbornly refuse to get it would be to destroy life as we know it. Yet, there is no limit to the power of meditation and prayer. What will happen this time, which has never happened before, is that a new collective consciousness—via the Internet, our matrix and global brain—will overwhelm humanity. It will be supersaturated with divine love, overpowering every petty impulse. Our very perception of reality—self-identification, val-ues, priorities and sensibilities—will flip-flop and be utterly trans-formed in this glorious new Planetary Age. Suddenly, everything and everyone will come together, not at all through premedita-tion but through divine intervention. We will come to see that ev-erything that every happened *had* to happen. It was all ordained. God's hand has never even for a moment left the celestial wheel.

Starting right now, as a divine being, you can now access bliss, independent of your current circumstances. You need merely step up to who you already are and let that character glow and grow. As you keep your eyes and ears on all the avatars and paths that speak to your inner self, you will find yourself in magical places. Live with both passion and grace. Reach out to the stars and reach into your innermost being. Play and celebrate in every way imaginable!

The new paradigm is fast upon us. The transformed communication infrastructure will catalyze a conscious planetary community where, in communion with Source, we can transform any crisis ahead of us. By joining heads and hearts, we can harmonize every tradition with every other one. We are about to discover a greater God ... a greater Being, Consciousness and Bliss. *The time has finally come!*

THE PERFECTION PROCESS

Perfection is the ultimate realization of life, in concert with unity and love. Whenever you have a peak experience or a satori—a sudden flash of enlightenment—you will find that everything has its place, and no one and nothing appears by mistake. You are ineradicably divine, and pure being is your ultimate nature, with the complex dance of life your exquisite expression.

There is really no way that you are supposed to be. You are what you are. You do what you do. Whatever happens, happens.

The following steps make available the direct experience of perfection:

Step 1:   We are all part of a cosmic drama, without which it would be rather tasteless. Part of the rollercoaster of life is getting upset, based upon disappointed expectations, thwarted intentions and undelivered communications. The truth is that you simply get upset, but you almost always associate your upset with someone or something.

• *Suppose that it is perfect to be upset, and that whatever or whomever made you upset was the perfect vehicle to help you further expand and open up.*

Step 2:   To calm your mind, you must first notice what is going on with your body.

- *Choose to feel any sensations that come up for you. You can start from your neck down. Invite each part to relax.*

Step 3:   Let's give attention to the chatter inside your head. It is perfect that you have thoughts. You don't have to be them until and unless you choose to.
- *Notice the thoughts streaming across your head, just like cirrus clouds in the sky.*
- *Notice how seductive it is to listen to them.*
- *Realize that you don't have to listen to each thought as it babbles away, much like a mountain stream.*

Step 4:   Let's look at your emotions.
- *If you find yourself upset right now, choose to be upset. The moment you choose an emotion, you gain perspective.*
- *Distance your feeling from whatever it is that you think provoked it. Remember, YOU caused it.*
- *Realize that it is perfect that you are upset. You can choose to be upset any time you want to, and you can likewise choose to let go.*

Step 5:   Let's look at your relationships. Keep in mind that everyone you meet is your mirror.
- *Think of the person who is on the bottom of your list right now. Get off your cloud and forgive him or her! When you forgive anyone else, you are actually forgiving yourself. Why make this life more miserable than it already is?*

In summary, realize that whatever comes up within your space, it is all within *your space*. You can experience *being* anytime you choose since you already are perfect. However, it is perfect that you also *do*. Whatever you are doing right now, go right ahead and do it, but only do it consciously. Live all out; holding back is a real pain. Then you will also experience perfection.

KEY CONCEPTS

(Italic words generally refer to other entries in this section.)

Advaita Vedanta: This is the supreme Hindu philosophical school of monism or nondualism *(see dualism)*. "Advaita" literally means "without two" and "Vedanta" means "end of the Vedas." All that we take for real is seen as ultimately an illusion, and all that we take for illusion is held to be the only thing that is truly real. What we consider to be *reality* is considered to be simply name and form. We mistakenly assume that form has an underlying material reality, and so conceptualize it, where *Being, Consciousness and Bliss* are the only true reality.

Affirmative action: In this official policy of American federal and state government, ethnic and/or religious minorities are given preference in job and school placement over the majority ethnic or religious group. It was instituted under President Lyndon B. Johnson's administration in the 1960s to ensure that equal opportunity for African Americans became a reality, and was soon extended to other racial and ethnic minorities as well as women in general. Corporations and universities as government contractors were required to maintain quotas.

Age of Aquarius: In the late 1960s and early 1970s, there was an active interest in astrology throughout the United States and much of the world. The Age of Aquarius was equated with the *New Age*, as the age of Pisces, begun around the time of Christ, was passing into the Age of Aquarius.

Age of Enlightenment: After the religious wars following the Reformation, Europe was ready for a more rational outlook on life while preserving the independence from authority initiated by the Renaissance and Reformation. While the Renaissance allowed freedom of expression within boundaries, the Reformation encouraged freedom of conscience. This would move into freedom of thought, as prized by the "Free Masons." Freedom of thinking would lead to freedom of speech and the press. This would be followed by a series of revolutions, with the American Revolution by far the most successful, and the French Revolution the least, suffering setbacks for decades. Key to this age within the *Modern Age* was the emergence of publishing, with newspapers, periodicals, books and an ever-increasing rate of literacy, including some women.

This would lead to public education and the initiation of the world's first secular universities—first in Germany and then in the United States. The scientific method was prized, and the Industrial Revolution began in earnest, which would sweep everything in its path. The downside was a vicious attack on all forms of *religion* and most forms of *spirituality*. A strong secular bias emerged in Western culture that suppressed emotions and intuition. As early as the 19th century CE, we would see a sharp reaction in the Romantic Rebellion, a period offering stunning poetry and art. Late in the 19th century CE, we would see the emergence of fundamentalism in reaction to *evolution* and excessive rationalism. Faith was prized for itself without the need for justification by reason.

Age of exploration: Beginning with the discovery of the Americas by Christopher Columbus, this age was a subset of—and actually began—the *Modern Age*, which set the stage for a truly global civilization and society. Europeans discovered the Americas, systematically exploring them, while also beginning to explore Sub-Saharan Africa and, ultimately, remote parts of Asia, including Indonesia and Australia. It was set off by the Crusades and an attempt to find a more efficient way to reach India, which was prized for its silks and spices. Discovered by accident, the "New World" became the source of huge deposits of gold and silver, which greatly stimulated the European economy. It resulted in humanity becoming conscious of inhabiting a vast sphere for the very first time, and for mass migrations of people, such as the European colonialists and settlers to North America, to remote areas, and later by the millions to the United States. By the 18th century CE, we would see the emergence of the *European Age of Enlightenment,* just before the emergence of nationalism in the late Modern period.

Agnostic: This word describes one who is uncertain whether or not there is a "God." He may either be open to the possibility of knowing, or doubt that such a possibility exists. He could take the posture that "I don't know if God exists, and I will never know."

Allah: This Arabic name for God in the *Qur'an* literally means "*The* God."

Atheist: As one who actively maintains the belief that there is no God, he is not even open to the possibility that God exists.

Aura: This field of energy surrounding our bodies can actual be felt a few inches away as body heat. Many people claim to actually see it, interpreting the various colors to reveal states of health or *spirituality*. Kirlian high-voltage photography actually attempts to photograph auras based on the emission of heat or energy. Most interesting is the realization that the haloes common to saints and sages in religious iconography is actually an attempt to depict their auras, with the implication that they are projecting great energy, or an inner light.

Awakening: This core meaning of *enlightenment* describes waking up to another *reality* and to the truth of being, no longer taking appearances at face value. Buddha, as a title means, "awakened one." Hindus refer to "turiya," or the "fourth state," where you awaken from your normal state to experience yourself as pure consciousness.

Being/doing universes: When we stop time and profoundly enter the present moment, we discover perfection. When we are tied up with action and forget about being, we lose all sense of perfection and even deny its very possibility. The experiences are so startlingly different that we might as well be living in completely separate universes.

Being, Consciousness and Bliss: This core concept of God in the East, referred to as "Sat-cit- ananda," brilliantly speaks to *what* God is, and characterizes it on the physical level ("Being"), the biological level ("Consciousness") and the psychospiritual level ("Bliss"). Hindu masters maintain that the three are inseparable; whenever you experience one, you experience all the others. These three attributes correspond with *Light, Life and Love,* found in the first chapter of the Gospel of John, and refer to God in more personalistic terms as *Who* God is. These two sets of terms interlock and comprise a planetary code spiritually linking East and West.

Being values/doing values: Being values contrast with the survival values of conventional society: awaken, create, play and celebrate. One finds that, other than concerns of survival, there is nothing else to do. The secret is to come from awakening, creation, play and celebration with every activity. It is a little like dancing on the razor's edge. As Jesus of Nazareth put it, "Be *in* the world, but not *of* the world."

Bell's theorem: The physicist, John S. Bell, postulated that, when two particles are entangled such that their spins are correlated, they maintain that correlation no matter how far apart they may go, even to opposite sides of the Universe. This is referred to as *quantum entanglement* and *nonlocality*. The implication is that the speed of light is no longer an absolute barrier, suggesting that space and time are ultimately illusory. This was formulated as a response to Albert Einstein's thought experiment, called the *Einstein-Podolsky-Rosen (EPR) paradox*, designed to disprove *quantum mechanics*. Bell's theorem was later experimentally demonstrated in the early 1980s by Alain Aspect in France. Bell's theorem has been considered by some as the most important breakthrough ever made in science. In effect, it suggests that the entire Universe is subjective in nature.

Bhagavad Gita: This is the classic devotional discourse of Lord Krishna within the great Hindu epic, the *Mahabharata*. The title can be loosely translated as "The Song of God." It advocates religious devotion while doing your duty with no attachment whatsoever to the result. It reveals numerous approaches to *enlightenment* and points to a very exalted conception of God as the Supreme Self.

Bhakti yoga: This Hindu *yoga* of devotion to God is considered the most efficient way for busy people to eventually come to a full *realization* of God. It is complementary to *Karma yoga*, the yoga of action, which entails loving service to others whom you see as uniquely precious expressions of God.

Binary: Considered the core language of computers, the digits "1" and "0" represent the states of "on" and "off."

Born Again: This term expresses different ideas specific to each religious tradition. In *Christianity*, it refers to a spiritual rebirth in which one joins a new humanity in union with Christ. It is a more radical notion than *awakening*, although the ideas are similar. In *Hinduism*, it can refer to reincarnation, or taking on another body after you pass away. In that tradition, it can also refer to a higher birth, corresponding with the higher *chakras*, where you come closer to *enlightenment*. In Pure Land *Buddhism*, it ties in with *Sukhavati*, where you are born into a lotus paradise where enlightenment is accomplished with great ease and elegance.

Brahman: This is the supreme underlying *reality* conceived in impersonal terms. It is the context of the entire cosmos, that which contains it, and is formless and immaterial. One might think of the black matter and energy underlying the visible Universe as an analogy, or the field of consciousness. "Brahma" is considered the first person of the Godhead, comparable to the "Father" in Christianity. It is supposed that this ground of all being is the medium in which the Universe is experienced and contains all phenomena. The root meaning emphasizes expansion and so connotes infinite possibility. It corresponds to the "Atman," which is the internal equivalent, the very nucleus of our being infinitesimally small at the center of our being.

Buddhism: This is considered one of the world's great religions, with over 350 million contemporary adherents. Estimates are that it was the world's dominant *religion* in the 19th century CE before the advent of communism, as well as the zealous efforts of colonial missionaries to convert all the people in subjugated lands to *Christianity*. Given probable censorship in China, the number of Buddhist adherents may be far greater than supposed. The *religion* originally began in India with Gautama Siddhartha, Prince of Kapilavastu, who left his kingdom to find *enlightenment*. The path to waking up was originally conveyed systematically with great simplicity, as the culture was mostly oral, and the principles could more easily be remembered.

Celebration: In this book, life on the being level is all about *awakening, creation, play* and *celebration*, as opposed to a preoccupation with survival. In essence, life is a pure celebration of being by being. It is occasion for joy and remembrance of all the good that one receives with gratitude and appreciation. This requires getting off of an overly serious attitude for oneself. Awakening, creation, play and celebration are ends unto themselves. They need no further justification. They are ultimately satisfying. *Planetary consciousness* is one where these functions predominate. If we think of the essence of *religion* from both Buddhist and Christian standpoints, it is *divine consciousness, community and communion*. Communion is the living experience of unity between The One and the Many. It is the ultimate celebration. Think of an endless party. Think of God "having a ball."

Chakras: These are the seven ascending energy centers in one's subtle body. The term means "wheels" or "circles." They correspond with key parts of the lower, middle and upper body. As the *Kundalini* energy rises to the top, one undergoes or experiences *enlightenment*.

Christianity: Named after Jesus of Nazareth, this is the world's largest *religion*, with 2.3 billion adherents. Christ is a title meaning "anointed one" or "king." The term literally means "Christ in you." The focal point of the entire religion is *divine love* and a transformational relationship with Jesus Christ leading to a new humanity, or divinity.

Circle of Life: The movie, *The Lion King,* portrayed this circle that encompasses all plants and animals in a common *ecosystem.* No one species, and no one individual, stands alone. It encapsulates the notion of *interbeing.*

Civil Rights movement: This is an adaptation of Mohandas Karamchand "Mahatma" Gandhi's sustained campaign to liberate India from British colonialism, which toppled the British Empire and was followed by a wave of nationalism throughout what was referred to as the "Third World" of the disenfranchised. Martin Luther King, Jr., from the Montgomery/Alabama bus boycott, applied this term to an extensive campaign that lasted well over a decade, featuring most of the civil disobedience tactics that Gandhi employed, such as marches, sit-downs and demonstrations. In the United States, the emphasis was on ending racial and ethnic discrimination. Under President Jimmy Carter in the 1970s, the term was extended to human rights around the world, such as freeing Soviet dissidents imprisoned in Siberia. The Civil Rights movement became the model for Women's Liberation and a variety of ethnic campaigns in the United States, culminating in the Gay Rights movement and the rights of so-called "handicapped" people.

Collective enlightenment: From the time of *Siddhartha Gautama,* the possibility of collective enlightenment has been raised. The Bodhisattva tradition emphasized the refusal to enter Nirvana until all sentient beings were enlightened. *Christianity* introduced *enlightenment* of the heart over the head and sought to build what Saint Augustine called "the City of God." Tibetan *Buddhism* introduced *Vajrayana* to accelerate the pace of enlightenment and create a widespread monastic society that was freely accessible to all. With the emergence of the press, publishing, widespread media and the *Internet Revolution,* it is now conceivable to transform large percentages of humanity simultaneously. The evangelist Billy Graham spoke directly to almost 500 million people with his Crusades, amplified by television, radio and movies. Over seven million people directly responded to his alter calls. Werner Erhard, with *The Hunger Project,* challenged his generation to create "a world that works for everyone with no one and nothing left out." This book introduces the possibility that, in the *Planetary Age,* enlightenment and empowerment will be the birthright of every human being and that we will all come to a full *realization* of our inherent divinity and perfection.

Communion: This describes communal participation in *sacred* rites with the implication of an interchange of being, where many become One. For Protestants, it connotes what Catholics refer to as the "Mass." In *Christianity*, the implication is that the community of followers becomes one with Christ, with God and with each other.

Communitarianism: This recent term suggests a combination of socialism and capitalism in a new economic order. The word resembles both communism and libertarianism. Open-source economics points towards its potential in the midst of the *global monetary crisis.*

Conscious revelation: We are now in a crucial period of our collective story where everything seems to be coming together as if it were predestined. As we put together our religious and wisdom traditions, thanks to the Internet and globalization, the whole seems greater than the parts. We find a vastly greater God than we had before imagined. We discover a hidden perfection that few of us thought possible, endowing our lives with a sense of the miraculous. The great religious and philosophical riddles are resolved only when the time has come, and we can accept and appreciate the role of paradox and contradiction. As we collectively open up, we all achieve a stunning clarity never before available.

Conscious revolution: Nonviolent revolution in one's own consciousness, and of the planetary community, through a paradigm shift. This concept maintains that which was once considered real is no longer accepted as real, and that which was previously regarded as illusion is now accepted as real. Rather than being the content of our experience, we now recognize ourselves to be the context of our own experience, or that which contains it all.

Copenhagen interpretation: By Niels Bohr and Werner Heisenberg, this interpretation of *quantum mechanics* emphasizes uncertainty; that the actual process of observing impacts whatever is observed. It refers to the "wave function" collapse where a particle is seen in terms of probability that it will appear at a certain place. It was realized that one could estimate the position, but not the trajectory, of a particle, or the contrary (the trajectory but not the position). It has been characterized as reducing what we take to be "matter" to mathematical ghosts. It ended forever the naïve assumption that an experimenter can be absolutely certain about the results of his or her experiment because the process of experimentation necessarily interferes with the end result. The observer is now seen as a necessary part of the equation of whatever happened.

Copernican Revolution: Nicolaus Copernicus was the first physicist to postulate that the Earth actually revolved around the sun, contrary to appearances. This amounted to a paradigm shift, a whole new perspective on the Universe. At the time, the Catholic Church dominated intellectual life, and rigidly and uncritically held to the view of Ptolemy, the ancient Greek philosopher, that what was apparent to the eye was in fact the truth. Eventually, Copernicus was vindicated through the efforts of Galileo Galilei, with his telescope, and enshrined in Sir Isaac Newton's elaborate calculus of the movements of the solar system.

Cosmic consciousness: This identification with the world and the Universe as being continuous with the body corresponds with the fifth, or throat, *chakra*. One experiences unity with flowers, trees and mountains while recognizing a difference among them.

Creation (see creationism): This process, generated by being, brings something out of nothing by making distinctions such as "This is not that." The basic concept is to draw a line and give it a name. In the *Advaita Vedanta* tradition, name and form are the basic characteristics of the apparent world, with the full *realization* that nothing is actually there. *Quantum theory* and the mystical traditions emphasize the importance of vibration and impulses of on and off, most readily identified with speech, "And God said, 'Let there be light, and there was light.'" If all is reducible to vibration within infinite consciousness, then the vibrations themselves might be considered as the act of creation. It is highly empowering to realize that human beings were created to create; that creation itself is an attribute of being.

Creationism: This is a belief that the Universe was created by the *Supreme Being*, rather than having merely evolved by blind chance. In the West, it has been closely identified with a literal interpretation of the Bible, especially the first two chapters of Genesis. *Intelligent design* is a popular school of thought that recognizes stages of development as the fulfillment of a *divine* plan.

Creative visualization: Drawing upon affirmations and visualization and evoking positive emotions, this is a process of consciously creating one's life and experience the way one would like it to be.

Culmination: This is the point in the *Megastory* that corresponds to the climax of a plot in a movie, play or story; the point in history where all the pieces come together in a grand finale, revealing the ultimate theme and dramatic objective of the story.

Cyber-spirituality: This new online frontier of planetary *spirituality* enables humanity to converge, transcending the apparent limitations of space and time. The new social media and networks have opened up immense possibilities for the spiritual community—to allow even the smallest of faiths, such as Bahá'í, to enjoy a worldwide presence and be easily accessible, and to offer illuminating dialogue between faiths and real-time comparison among all aspects. It can accommodate a truly *planetary sourcebook and temple,* which will enable simultaneous *celebration* in a vast number of languages with rich media and visual hyperlinks to instantly transport the participant from one tradition to the next. Substantial studies have been done by the practitioners of Transcendental Meditation about the impact of thousands and even millions of people meditating at the same time for the same purpose. It is conceivable that all of humanity could thus enjoy true *communion.*

Daoism: This ancient Chinese philosophy, also called "Taoism," refers to "the WAY" and going with the flow of creation. It is based on the masterful *Dao De Jing* (or *Tao Te Ching*), a long poem of some 80 "chapters," which characterize how it is when in utter harmony with the way things are. It is a major force-feeding into *Zen,* with an emphasis on spontaneous *enlightenment.* Both offer a pressure valve from the rigors of Confucianism, the Chinese social philosophy that permeated China and most of East Asia. This philosophy is unique with its rich sense of humor and playfulness.

Democracy: Virtually every government on the planet is theoretically held to be a democracy, with kings and queens as puppet figures and military dictators and demagogues all acting in the name of the people. Direct democracy was pioneered in Athens, Greece, in the 6th century BCE, and was rediscovered during the Renaissance. Representative forms of democracy emerged from the English Revolution onward. With the American Revolution, basic concepts of freedom, equality, majority rule, protection of minority rights, free speech and free press were firmly established. Core to democracy is the notion of opposition, such as the prosecution and the defense in the legal system. The notion is that the truth will always rise to the top when thoroughly debated. As the environmental crisis emerged, the weaknesses of democratic institutions became apparent. We might succeed at economic and political systems that proceed to destroy the Earth as we know it. The interests of the majority only matched those of the natural environment when the population is truly enlightened. All too often, no one spoke for the Earth, and economic prosperity has lead to environmental ruin.

Democratic theocracy: This is the social and political order postulated for the *Omega Point,* when both the planet and humanity become conscious. It is supposed that a critical mass of awareness and love will flood the world, and a planetary society guided by profound love will emerge. *Theocracy* has actually been attempted in select times and places, such as ancient Israel, much of the Islamic world and John Calvin's Geneva during the early days of the Reformation. The problem has always been the question of who leads the theocracy and who speaks in the name of God? This perspective integrates the best of *democracy* and theocracy. To be effective, it mandates universal *enlightenment* and transformation. It is interesting how far the U.S. Republican Party has moved in this direction. (One might also think of Orthodox *Judaism* in contemporary Israel and many of the proposals advanced by the late Maharishi Mahesh Yogi.) The problem lies in *Christianity,* or in any other great tradition, not yet being a truly planetary faith. For this to work, all faiths must be equally represented and incorporated, and a new planetary perspective must emerge that is profoundly spiritual and mystical. Hence, this book!

Dharma: This term, both Hindu and Buddhist, has many meanings, including "law," "rule," "principle," "duty," "role" and "teaching." The most promising interpretation is that everyone has a unique purpose and destiny, equipped with a unique gift to offer the world.

Dialectic: A convergence of thesis and antithesis into a whole new synthesis. The process of realizing the truth was pioneered by Plato, then picked up by Georg Wilhelm Friedrich Hegel and popularized by Karl Marx. When an idea, or thesis, is clearly established, it inadvertently generates its direct opposite, or antithesis. The competition of ideas then leads to a synthesis yielding elements of both. The process then continues iteration after iteration to infinity. More interestingly, the term suggests the reconciliation of opposites; that opposites are necessary and part of a higher purpose.

Divine: Not just human, we share the attributes of God. This has been referred to as "being a son or daughter of God." If one takes the Greek, Roman and Hindu gods as examples, they appear immortal, omniscient and omnipotent. They don't suffer from human limitations. In *Christianity*, one is *born again* into a *divine* nature, which shares in eternal life via a spiritual rebirth and resurrection. The implication is that every human is inherently divine, as he or she embodies animal, human and divine attributes. The destiny of humanity is to fully realize its divinity and union with The One.

Divine love: The ultimate justification of existence lies in the *realization* of unconditional love. God can most easily and delightfully be realized through the direct experience of love. It is the grand theme of the *Megastory* within the *Megadream*. In movies, love stories are always the most popular. Merging with another who is regarded as altogether beautiful is highly appealing. Even more moving is the experience of absolute love that won't let you go, that won't ever give up on you. This is the core of the Bhakti tradition in India. We realize God in the most delightful way through heartfelt devotion and loving service to humanity. With the crucifixion, *Christianity* enshrined *divine love* and upheld Jesus of Nazareth as the supreme embodiment of absolute love. In this book, the Glorious News, as opposed to the Good News, reveals God's love as absolute, infinite, eternal, omnipotent, such that no one and nothing can possibly overcome it. The corollary to that experience is the realization that we are all divine with deeply moving destinies. While this sounds wildly optimistic to most, it is the mystical core of the original Gospel, only recently becoming fully apparent.

Divine plan (*see* divine, divine love *and* divine play): Within the *Megastory* of our *Megadream*, this is the notion of a destined sequence or plan that encompasses the smallest details. Everything that ever happens is orchestrated by the Creator. Life itself is seen to be a divine work of art designed to be enjoyed and appreciated by God within us and God "outside" us.

Divine play: This is the highest conception of life and the Universe, the *Supreme Being*, pure consciousness, playing with Himself. *Play* is a *being value* and, when you are in the flow, coming from the *being Universe*, you no longer experience it all as a struggle. The Hindus have the term "Lila" for this, connoting a song, a dance or a drama. We are a *divine* sport, a game, and the ultimate form of entertainment for God. This does not at all imply that God is making fun of us, as God is playing *in* us, *with* us and *as* us. This comes out of the *realization* that there is ONLY God. Thus, each of us is a uniquely precious expression of God. *Religion* perennially suffers from a tendency to be overly serious about everything, partly because humanity has had to contend with survival issues from the very beginning, as symbolized by the Fall in the Garden of Eden. Western religion, in particular, finds it hard to realize that God has a profound sense of humor, partly because it is so attuned to the drama we play out, as if this particular movie were the ultimate. The greatest realization is that paradise is here and now, as our lives are pure *celebration.*

Domino theory: During the Cold War between the United States and its allies, and the Soviet Union and its allies, political and military power were closely balanced. Concern was widespread that the balance could easily be destabilized if enough strategically important nations fell to the opposing side. In the case of the United States, Vietnam was considered such a nation. The thought was that, if Vietnam fell to the communists, every neighboring state would as well, just like a row of dominoes. This initially served as a convenient justification for what ultimately became an unacceptable loss on the part of the United States.

Dualism: This philosophical stance maintains that there is an inner world and an outer world fundamentally in opposition to one another. René Descartes, the founder of dualism, identified himself with the thinker and held everything else as being other than him. The "I" is seen as being housed within the body but utterly immeasurable. With the emergence of *rational empiricism,* only that which was susceptible to measurement was considered "real." Thus, the inner "I" became irrelevant from a scientific perspective. The extreme expression of this viewpoint was that we are all machines that emerged out of nowhere purely by accident in a pointless universe.

Ecology: This is the interrelationship of every element of the environment viewed organically, as though Planet Earth were a living being. "Eco" means "house" and is the root word of "economy" and "ecumenism." We are all aboard the same spaceship and must care tenderly for her and all her occupants.

Ecosystem: *Ecology* can be seen as a giant system of life support on our fragile biosphere. The layer of life on the surface of our planet is a small fraction of the total density, equivalent to a firm layer of varnish on a globe. If we work and *play* in harmony with the system, it has a tendency over time to heal itself.

El Shaddai: This early name for God in the Hebrew Bible connotes "God of the Mountains." In many instances in the Bible, God is simply referred to as "the Lord." There are numerous names in the Hebrew Bible, but The Supreme One was revealed first to Moses in the flaming bush, "Yahweh" or "YHWH," which means "I AM" or "I AM THAT I AM" or the Self-existent One.

Empowerment: The process whereby we come to a realization of our infinite potential through opening up to our deeper identity and coming clean and clear with people such that we are not as attracted to manipulation or as easily manipulated as before. The transcendent realization that we are all one, and that our only true identity lies in Who and What we regard as "God," greatly accelerates this whole process. If we are truly divine, and we get fully in touch with it, like avatars, bodhisattvas and messiahs, we can make a profound difference. One need only review the life of Mahatma Gandhi to see a perfect model. It helps to realize that enlightenment and empowerment go together. Where you find one, the other is sure to follow. Ironically, power for the sake of power is refuted. Power is appreciated in terms of loving and compassionate service. The notion would be to give power, not just to yourself, but to all humanity, and by extension, to all sentient beings.

Endarkenment: This is the direct opposite of *enlightenment* where the nature of *reality* lights up as well as the seriousness with which you take your ego and sense of individuality. Practically speaking, it refers to what most people consider to be evil, increasing people's preoccupation with survival, their attachment to transitory conditions, their taking physical forms to be their only self. The irony is that endarkenment was necessary to have a game in the first place. When Siddhartha Gautama, Jesus of Nazareth and all the other avatars, bodhisattvas, saints and sages entered history, they shifted the whole emphasis from things getter darker and darker to things getting lighter and lighter. Today, endarkenment never leads to true satisfaction and fulfillment. In short, it doesn't work anymore, if it ever truly did.

Enlightened realization: *Realization* and *revelation* are two sides of the same coin. A realization is experienced as coming from within and a revelation as coming from without. *Enlightenment* has to do with a growing awareness that our true Self is the space in which our life unfolds. The content of our life is the *play* of our consciousness, and we are the consciousness itself. We are not the light bulb but the light within it.

Enlightenment: Along with *transformation* and being *born again,* this term refers to intellectually or spiritually achieving illumination. It is the broadest generic term for *awakening* or Self-realization. In the 18th century CE Western *European Age of Enlightenment,* this was seen in terms of the triumph of rationalism over dogma, which was needed at that time to overcome the religious wars. This overlooked the fundamental role of intuition and insight, which assumed a much larger scope in the late 20th century CE.

Environmentalism: This is a social and political movement that places humanity's environment at the forefront of concern. In any conflict, the ultimate victim is the environment itself. However, since humanity is utterly dependent upon its environment, the planet has the potential to snuff out the life of humanity. We experience an interdependent relationship where we are the flowering of our environment, and our environment is the physical foundation of our life. In the decision-making process, it is no longer a strictly human equation. The environmental impact must always be weighed.

Esalen: This highly innovative educational center for the *Human Potential movement* was set in the exquisite grounds of Big Sur in northern California. Many of the key figures, such as Joseph Campbell, Alan Watts and Timothy Leary, were featured there. It continues as a nonprofit institution with extensive seminars and workshops, featuring its famous hot baths.

Esoteric/exoteric: These two words describe the inner and outer aspects of a religious tradition. "Esoteric" refers to inner mystical truths realized and disclosed by a very few; "exoteric" truths tend to be the standard orthodox view held by many. The mystical core is the beginning of any great tradition but gets further and further removed as that tradition undergoes institutionalization. The danger is to end up totally forgetting the ultimate purpose of the institution. Often mere ethics replace any interest in spiritual illumination.

est: "Erhard Seminars Training," which lasted over two weekends, was a breakthrough *enlightenment* intensive started in the 1970s. It was picked up by prominent people in the media and had broad appeal to mainstream America. Werner Erhard was a master packager of various disciplines within the emerging Human Potential movement. He had a critical exposure to *Zen,* catalyzing an enlightenment experience in which Erhard knew that he knew nothing. He realized that all his thought processes were contained in a mechanism, which, in his words, "precluded the possibility of aliveness." Graduates of the training and its successor, Landmark Education with its Forum, number in the millions and are characterized by crispness, clarity, a broad sense of responsibility and the ability to live comfortably in the present time.

Establishment: The countercultural view of institutional America, especially what they referred to as the "military-industrial complex," which was sending youth unwillingly to a hopeless war in Vietnam. At that time, there was widespread hope in creating a new society. Many actually did "drop out" to create communes and artistic colonies.

Event horizon: This is a boundary around a black hole in which light cannot escape, such that the object entering it appears infinitely suspended.

Evolution: This highly sophisticated but mechanistic approach to the question of how life came about was made famous by Charles Darwin's classic, *On the Origin of Species.* An impressive mass of evidence in terms of the fossil record has emerged over the last century. It is noteworthy that the progression of life in evolutionary theory closely corresponds with that of the Genesis account. As a scientific theory, God was purposely taken out of the equation. The theory answers *how*, but NOT *who* or *why*. The fossil record makes it a strain to conceive of creation in six actual days, as is maintained by fundamentalists. Shall we use Greenwich Meridian time? However, if the Genesis flood actually happened as narrated, it would explain a lot of the evidence. The theory brilliantly accounts for the complexification of life in adapting to radically varying environments, which cannot be denied. Who did the adapting? Was it God or genetics? The subject became volatile when Charles Darwin applied it to humanity in *The Descent of Man, and Selection in Relation to Sex.* If humanity descended from apes, how could it be *divine*? The real problem is that evolution is often taught as a fact rather than the brilliant theory that it is. It is difficult to witness genetic adaptation in real time due to the phenomenally long periods required for it to come into effect. It doesn't even consider *involution*, the theory that God has literally become the Universe, which would explain its conscious nature. Deeper still is the issue that it might be technically considered a "mythology" in modern scientific language. The fact that so many people "believe" in it indicates its status as a myth. People don't tend to believe in actual facts. Deeper still is the issue of the mystical nature of the Universe and the powerful evidence in the new physics that nothing is really "out there." How then can we account for evolution without coming to terms with our own metaphysics? The most honest response would appear to be that we simply don't know. Since we are in the new *Planetary Age*, we might suppose that a new organic approach to explaining the origin and nature of life might arise in the face of the green revolution, with its emphasis on the phenomenon of consciousness itself.

Fertile void: In *Hinduism, Buddhism* and *Daoism,* black is not a negative color. As in contemporary physics with dark matter and energy, a void implies infinite possibilities. We can't create without emptiness. As the Buddhists eventually maintained, form is emptiness and emptiness is form. One is always resolving into the other. Thus, the void is seen as "fertile," the matrix of creation.

Field: This is an expanse of consciousness, as well as energy, out of which *reality* emerges. It was originally inspired by Maharishi Mahesh Yogi's depiction of God as a "field of infinite possibility." With increasing recognition of *quantum physics* and *string theory*, along with dark matter and energy, space is no longer viewed as truly empty but housing vast, invisible energy.

Flower Children: An idealized view of the San Francisco hippies surrounding Golden Gate Park in the *Summer of Love* in 1967, they gave flowers to strangers and encouraged people to wear them in their hair. This was closely tied into the slogan, "Make Love, Not War." It also connoted "Flower Power," which referred to marijuana and other psychedelic substances. The message was to literally stop and smell the flowers. Stop and enjoy life. What is the point of running about trying to make money as a cog in the machine? Given that the United States was caught up at that time in an unwinnable war in Vietnam, people were encouraged in the words of the immortal Professor Timothy Leary to "Turn on, tune in, drop out."

Four directions: North, South, East and West symbolize four broad cultural and spiritual trends that correspond with different civilizations and are based on geographic considerations. Each tradition has its own version of the mystical experience. North stands for the humanistic tradition of Western civilization that emerged out of ancient Greece; South stands for the indigenous tradition of *shamanism*, which today is found to the greatest extent in the Southern Hemisphere; East stands for the tradition of Self-realization that came out of South and East Asia; West stands for the Judeo-Christian-Muslim tradition of the Near East, with the influence of both Babylon and Egypt.

Four revolutions: The Greater San Francisco Bay Area has been the epicenter of four separate revolutions that shaped this free-spirited region, endowing it with extraordinary openness to new thoughts and ideas and exceptional innovation. The first was the Gold Rush of 1849, which attracted people from all over the world, including the Chinese, who called it "Golden Mountain." The second was the Love Generation of 1967, which was influenced by psychedelics to try to make over global society. The third was the dot-com boom of 1994, which triggered a vast infusion of capital and shaped the emerging Internet economy. The fourth, which began in the wake of the events of September 11, 2001 and the dot-com bust, is a new planetary perspective, placing a premium on consciousness with attention to a flat, institutional structure and green technology.

Gaia theory: James Lovelock in the 1970s came up with the Gaia hypothesis that the Earth is a giant organism, much like a green goddess. All its systems are living and have the capability of regenerating themselves when not interrupted. Complementary recent theories suggest that the entire Universe is conscious.

Glasnost: In the mid-to-late 1980s, this public policy of Mikhail Gorbachev instituted a Soviet era of free speech, openness and transparency in affairs. It was paired with the term *Perestroika* or restructuring. It would eventually set the conditions for the breakup of the Communist Bloc and the transition of the Soviet Union into the Commonwealth of Independent States.

Global citizen: Due to the revolution in advanced transportation and communications, people everywhere are waking up to the possibility that we owe allegiance to our own country and our own "God" as well as to the planet itself and all humanity with its *divine* vision and emerging *planetary consciousness*. Barack Obama successfully acknowledged his global citizenship in Berlin during his presidential campaign. If the President of the United States of America can, why can't we all do so? It all began with the League of Nations after World War I and the United Nations after World War II. Jesse Jackson in the 1980s achieved some amazing things as a "citizen diplomat." With the deepening of the environmental movement, it has become apparent that, unless a critical mass of people world-wide awakens to the implications of *global warming,* we will inadvertently make the Earth uninhabitable. Finally, *globalization,* with its flattening effect on social structures and the mobility of the Internet and wireless devices, has made the "unthinkable" practical.

Global infrastructure: In order for all of humanity to come together in a mean-ingful way, this had to be built out for both transportation and communica-tions. Fiber optics, satellite transmission and wireless technology had to con-verge to make the Internet a reality.

Globalization: This is the process where *planetary civilization* is emerging with a shared culture worldwide and a common unifying language, such as English, backed by a *global infrastructure.* Fiber-optic oceanic cables lit up nations, such as India and China, to provide professional services worldwide on a 24/7 basis.

Global monetary crisis: As a consequence of easy lending for real estate, a crash in the global markets was precipitated as consumers began to default on their loans and the notes went bad. America had gone through an intense period of extreme financial deregulation. This ricocheted around the world and threat-ened the value of currencies. With the collapse of the Soviet Union, most coun-tries had standardized on some form of capitalism. Capitalism as an economic system was thus thrown into question.

Global village: In conjunction with the space race, Marshall McLuhan in the 1960s coined this term to stress that Planet Earth is much like a satellite streaming through space. The revolution in transportation and communications had the ef-fect of collapsing space and time. We now sink or swim together.

Global warming: Albert Arnold "Al" Gore, Jr., popularized the rising average temperatures around the world with the subsequent melting of the arctic zones, which results in the disruption of weather patterns. Left unchecked, it could re-sult in massive flooding of the coastal areas, along with desertification of once-fertile lands. It is estimated that temperatures could rise as high as 140 degrees Fahrenheit, leaving much of the planet uninhabitable.

Good News/Glorious News: The traditional word "Gospel" means "good news." Given that it was interpreted in terms of Heaven and Hell, it had a negative edge: "You must believe or else ..." The *realization* of universal redemption and salvation is deeply transformative and is truly glorious news. If the love of God is absolute, and God is the Creator and our Source, then our challenge is to simply come to a full realization of that Love.

Great Spirit: Native Americans had a sense of God being a great spirit. Thus, the Christian concept of God the Father could resonate to their indigenous traditions as "the Great Spirit."

Hellenism: This cultural orientation, favoring the civilization of Greece, was extended to much of the known world through the conquests of Alexander the Great. For Greeks, a barbarian was anyone untutored in their language. It is closely linked with *humanism* in a very high culture of philosophy, history, literature and theater. Hellenism would serve as the foundation of the values of the Greco-Roman civilization, which would closely complement those of the Judeo-Christian tradition to form Western civilization. It also played a crucial early role in the emergence of science.

Higher Power: Like *Supreme Being,* this is a very useful term for God that is not freighted with connotations. It suggests that God is the *Source* of empowerment in our lives.

Hinduism: The word "Hindu" originally referred to people who dwelt on the eastern side of the Indus River and came to represent a complex of *religions* united in a concept of *karma* and *dharma* or duty and reincarnation. Two epics, the *Ramayana* and the *Mahabharata,* dominate the region. Even today, it would seem as though all of India lives inside these great stories. While there are as many as 330 million gods, most of them are considered demigods, analogous to angels in the Catholic Church. It is widely recognized that there is one ultimate *reality,* "Brahman," thought of in impersonal terms, with infinite *manifestations.*

Humanism: In the Renaissance, Western thinkers construed that "Man is the measure of all things." In the Western *Age of Enlightenment,* the philosophers insisted that "the proper study of Man is Mankind." By implication, with the emergence of *rational empiricism,* concerns about God were marginalized. With extreme humanism, concerns with the environment were suppressed for the sake of expediency, and long-term thinking was lost.

Humanistic mysticism: Humanism is not especially known for *mysticism*, and the *rational empiricism* of modern philosophy places supreme importance on logic and measurable observation. Nevertheless, from Classical Greece onward, mystical schools grew. It is interesting that *Christianity* initially was viewed as a mystery cult. This tradition continued with the hermetic tradition, the alchemical tradition and masonry. Early on, the Greeks held numbers to have mystical importance, as well as the ideals of *the True, the Good and the Beautiful.* Plato postulated an ideal world that transcended the apparent world. He felt the "real" world was only a crude approximation of the ideal world. This mysticism continued through the Renaissance. Most significantly, many great scientists, such as Albert Einstein, Werner Heisenberg and the modern physicists, became deeply mystical because they could no longer reduce natural phenomena to the old rational categories. It is widely held that anyone, whether explicitly religious or not, can have an experience of *cosmic consciousness* that will render him or her a lifetime mystic.

Humanistic psychology (see humanism *and* mystical humanism*):* Called the "Third Force" in psychology (after psychotherapy and behaviorism) and inspired by Abraham Maslow, it departs from the presupposition that human beings are psychologically deranged, in desperate need to get well and adapt, or from the preoccupation with a very narrowly defined "learning acquisition," to the standpoint that humanity progressively experiences higher and higher needs ultimately leading to transcendence. This opened up what became the *Human Potential movement* and the *Transformational movement.* The discipline of psychology finally became relevant to "normal" people seeking *empowerment* and *enlightenment.*

Human Potential movement: In the 1960s, Abraham Maslow came up with the idea of peak experience in a hierarchy of needs and values. He introduced *humanistic psychology* as a study of possibility. He led a shift away from a narrow clinical psychology focused on treating sick people to a psychology that might help seemingly normal people to truly excel. Many people, such as his student, Wayne Dyer, took this into a deep spiritual focus on transcendence.

Hunger Project: Werner Erhard launched this extraordinary movement and organization in October 1977 to establish a deep and lasting commitment to the end of hunger and starvation as a chronic condition, likening the effort to the American space program, which achieved the seemingly impossible objective of deploying a man on the moon in less than a decade. Recently, Albert Arnold "Al" Gore, Jr., echoed this view in his feature film, *An Inconvenient Truth*, in which he maintained that what prevents us from stopping *global warming* and beginning to heal the Earth is a lack of political will. Most significant about the project is the emergence of the vision in Werner Erhard's words of "a world that works for everyone with no one and nothing left out."

Indra's net: This is a metaphor within *Mahayana Buddhism* of the interdependence of all phenomena. No one and nothing exists in isolation. Every object and person reflects every other object and person. The picture is of one vast string of pearls or dewdrops where every pearl reflects all of the others. Technically, it is referred to as "dependent origination" or "mutual co-arising." Thich Nhat Hanh brilliantly phrased it *"interbeing"*.

Infinite Intelligence: The word for "God" that Napoleon Hill used in his inspirational prosperity classic, *Think and Grow Rich*. The author may have derived the term from the *New Thought movement*. It beautifully combines the personal and the impersonal in a *transpersonal* perspective. The Universe is not looked upon as accidental, and prayer actually makes sense, as Infinite Intelligence is "there" to answer the person. It would fit well with the *creationists'* of *intelligent design*.

Integral: This approach, which unifies disparate elements into a coherent whole, is often seen in terms of a developmental hierarchy fulfilling the possibilities of *evolution*. It bears certain similarities to the holistic, with a focus on the whole over the parts. It is usually associated with *Spiral Dynamics theory*, which views individual and cultural development through history as a progression of increasing complexity and sophistication.

Integral Theory: Spearheaded by Ken Wilber, this new discipline comprises a *theory of everything* based on consciousness, explicitly postmodern, and even beyond the pluralism of the hippies and the greens. It takes an evolutionary approach to stages of development, embracing earlier stages, such as modern and traditional, as necessary to bring us to where we are today. It implies, but rarely states, the notion of inherent perfection with its strong developmental approach. The emphasis is upon the future, or the next stage, rather than the eternal present. Many brilliant distinctions are made that enable extraordinary philosophical clarity to discourse, such as "Three Faces of God"; how different parts of human speech—"I," "You/We" and "It/Them"—impact our whole experience and understanding of the *Sacred*.

Intelligent design: In recent years, scientists who accept the Bible's account of creation have taken a new tact by introducing the study of design into biology to demonstrate the necessity of a designer. To maintain the idea that the Universe occurred by blind chance and is, therefore, fundamentally indifferent to all human concerns is abhorrent to all but the most tough-minded intellectuals. How do we account for human values and sensibility, let alone the *divine*? The six days in Genesis could be symbolic. Six discrete eras certainly makes sense. Why couldn't God have used processes and still be God? Humanity as a special creation could be disputed, but it is hard to dispute the birth of a special consciousness we identify with humanity as well as an appreciation of the divine. The harder we look, the less random chaos makes sense. Certainly, there is a higher intelligence, if only in the Universe itself. However, if the new physics is correct, the Universe isn't really "out there." We and it dwell within the Mind of God. The choice is ours. We can either identify with the dream or the dreamer, himself. Should we identify with the dreamer, we will suddenly discover our own divinity. Perhaps the problem has been in the anthropomorphic conception of God in the Bible and other *sacred* texts. This is a problem of cultural symbolism and is readily resolved by sophisticated scholarship, philosophy and theology.

Interbeing: Popularized by Nobel Laureate, Thich Nhat Hanh, it is synonymous with the Buddhist doctrine of dependent origination, which emphasizes that everything and everyone is related to everything and everyone else. Buddhists think in terms of every "sentient being" and include plants and animals. The implications for both *ecology* and ecumenism are profound. This concept could best describe the Christian rite of the mass, or *Holy Communion*.

Internet Revolution: The commercialization of the World Wide Web was the final step in *globalization* that would lead to a unified *planetary civilization*. Even in the 1960s, and 1970s, we enjoyed travel by jet, televisions and radios with satellite transmission of broadcasts and widespread telephones. However, telephones were still relatively expensive, for voice only, and international calls were unthinkable. The early Internet was only for large institutions, such as government, defense and education. With a user-friendly interface, more and more emphasis was placed on data transmission with flat rates. Publishing became the metaphor and, with broadband and wireless, it emerged as rich mobile media with ubiquitous voice. Suddenly, everyone was theoretically linked with everyone else in real time. One could finally develop relationships across the ocean without even thinking of the expanse. Within 20 years, much of the world's supply of knowledge went online and was instantaneously accessible. The world has never been the same.

Involution: This is the opposite of *evolution*, in that God is seen as literally becoming the Universe, hiding out within the Universe or even posing as the Universe. This could happen over eons of time. Nevertheless, it could account for the progression described in Genesis as well as the *theory of evolution* itself. God is eventually seen as God by all creation as the creatures wake up to their own *divine* nature. The ultimate *realization* is that there is nothing but God.

Islam: The world's second largest religion, next to *Christianity*, is the fastest growing with nearly 1.6 billion adherents. It is the third of the Abrahamic religions, starting with *Judaism*, and features the world's purest form of monotheism, taking exception to the Christian doctrine of the Trinity and the divinity of Jesus Christ. Its mystical version, *Sufism*, is profoundly ecumenical and seeks to unite people everywhere through a direct experience of God in the heart. It is based on the *revelations* received by the Prophet Muhammad, who received the Word of the *Qur'an* directly from the angel Gabriel over a 20-year period, starting when he was in a cave at the age of 40. As a faith, it features many benefits and is, in truth, the world's most democratic religion, early on giving exceptional recognition to female rights, which were not matched in the West until the late *Modern Age*. The word "Islam" means "surrender to God." It is noteworthy that all forms of *enlightenment* entail a process of some sort of letting go. It is also important than Islam, at its core, refutes the notion that God is an old, grey-bearded man in the sky. Although He is considered personal with attributes of justice and mercy, He is without any kind of form. The concept could properly be considered *transpersonal.* Largely through profound ignorance and rivalry, the West has been reluctant to give Islam the recognition it deserves. A great breakthrough is the *realization* that all three faiths—Judaism, Christianity and Islam—form monotheism and ultimately comprise a single faith.

Jnana yoga: Considered the *yoga* of knowledge or Self-realization, one continually asks the question, "Who am I?" It eventually begins to dawn on the questioner that the "I" is not the one he thinks he is. He, as a separate person, doesn't actually exist. There is only the *Supreme Identity* and the *Transcendent Mystery.*

Judaism: The people of ancient Israel and Judah—through Abraham, Moses, David, Isaiah and the other prophets—gave birth to monotheism, which was picked up by both *Christianity* and *Islam.* They also gave birth to the concept of destiny, as opposed to fate, where God is seen as actively at work within history to communicate with humanity through *revelation* and to accomplish His perfect will. This basic *religion* has survived intact, despite the destruction of the temple and the 20th century CE Holocaust, which resulted in the systematic destruction of over six million Jewish people. Estimates are that just 13.5 million Jewish people remain, although those estimates may be highly conservative.

Judgment Day: In the Western religions, this is seen as the decisive moment in history when God personally returns to Planet Earth to judge the nations and the people, establishing permanent order and peace. It implies severe moral judgment, often tied in with the resurrection, that people are brought back to life only to be condemned. In Christianity, provision is made through the redemption of Christ to escape the "Wrath of God," of being thrown in Hell. It is often seen as brutal and unnecessary, a doctrine concocted by the Medieval Church to ensure religious conformity. This book sees it in symbolic terms only, maintaining that Jesus of Nazareth, in the Megastory, voluntarily took on the karma of the human race, suffering the immense pain and suffering of the Passion. He is thus accorded a supreme status, making him a true "superstar" in the plot. It also has a deeper meaning of a life review and assessment, which is certain on the deathbed but also possible every moment. The ultimate answer to the dilemma posed by this strange doctrine is a growing appreciation of the absolute nature of the Love of God, that no one and nothing can possibly overcome it.

Karma (*see* Karma yoga): In this Hindu word for "action," with implications of a chain of causality, every single choice we make has a consequence that can ricochet back upon us. This appeals to the common-sense biblical notion that what we sew, we reap. The notion is that whatever you get you deserve. In the West, it typically has negative connotations. In Buddhism, it can be thought of in terms of accumulating merit or de-merit. In the Abrahamic tradition, and others, such as the Krishna movement or the Bodhisattva of Mahayana Buddhism, grace can override an indefinite amount of negative actions. *Divine love*, as expressed in the cross of Christianity, burns through and transcends all notions of karma. The implication is the Savior or Enlightened One already took the rap on our behalf.

Karma yoga: Yoga implies unity with the *Supreme Being*, and Karma, which literally means "action," suggests realizing union through devotional service to the world without any attachment to the results. In the *Bhagavad Gita*, Lord Krishna enjoins Arjuna, his disciple and companion, to give the fruits to him. The implication is that God is responsible for what ultimately happens; you need merely do your duty and fulfill your role in the *divine play*.

Kundalini: This divine energy, which arises through the spine and reaches its highest expression at the top, or crown *chakra*, results in God consciousness and unity. It is compared to a slumbering serpent that awakens. It represents the path of *yoga* as contemplation and the transmutation of energy, often associated with Lord Siva in India.

Left-Handed Path: Both left-handedness and right-handedness have meaning beyond their literal definitions. As more people are right-handed than left, it often refers to the creative and dangerous path. Right-handedness suggests being straight; left-handedness suggests being hip. In magic, left-handedness suggests grey or black magic in which people actually get hurt. In *Tantra*, left-handedness suggests an unconventional approach to *enlightenment* where you deliberately re-activate yourself to accelerate moving through barriers, such as eating meat in a vegetarian community or having sex without a formal relationship. More broadly, left-handedness refers to the entire tradition of Jnana yoga, the way of knowledge, and Raja yoga, the way of energy. In India, this corresponds with worship of the god, Lord Shiva, as opposed to Lord Vishnu.

Light, Life and Love: In the first chapter of The Gospel of John, these three terms are interlinked into a kind of code. Curiously, they tightly correspond with one of the supreme Sanskrit designations for God: "Sat, Chit and Ananda." Light, like "Sat" or being, is physical; Life, like "Chit" or consciousness, is biological; "Love, like 'Ananda' or bliss, is peculiarly human, is spiritual. In *Christianity*, Jesus of Nazareth is considered the supreme expression of God, and these are his attributes. The term is very useful in decoding religious symbolism to arrive at the inner experience. In essence, when you are purely being, totally conscious and at bliss, you are truly *divine* and an inspiration to everyone around you. The spiritual objectives of East and West are thus united.

Line of causality: A very useful notion drawn originally from *Scientology*, this describes a line that corresponds roughly with the fourth *chakra*. Below the line in the lower chakras, you experience the world in effect as separate objects with which you must interact and over which you try to prevail. At the line, you begin to have a heartfelt feeling for others. You have a willingness to see things from their viewpoints. Above the line, in the higher chakras, you experience *divine* consciousness and experience unity with everyone and everything in your world, including the Supreme.

Mahabharata: This is one of the two great classic epics around which Indian civilization has been built. It is the story of the *playful* avatar, Lord Krishna, most particularly around a civil war, the Battle of Kurukshetra. Just before this gruesome battle, the good king, Arjuna, feels qualms about killing all his relatives. Lord Krishna *plays* the role of his chariot driver and counsels him on the meaning of life and death.

Manifestation: This is the process of making visible and tangible that which already exists in the world of ideas. It is the underlying principle behind all magic and miracles. It is also the underlying principle of creation itself. Our ultimate Self is a *field* of infinite possibilities. What is absolutely real is invisible and unmanifest. Illusion is all that appears real and manifest. In order to create a new "*reality,*" one must master the art of making that, which is invisible, visible.

Manifestation Manifesto: *Manifestation* entails making that which is invisible, visible. The underlying idea in the New Thought movement is that ideas have a "*reality*" unto themselves and entail form. The idea of a sports car is directly related to a "real" sports car apparently "out there." One can transmute consciousness into physical reality. That is the basis of the medieval art of alchemy, which directly preceded modern science. The principles of manifestation have to do with intense focus, a profound acceptance of things as they are, along with a total openness that they be different. Metaphysics reveals that all form involves making distinctions. When we make new distinctions, we are on our way to enjoying a new "reality."

Many-worlds interpretation (quantum mechanics): Quantum mechanics is a theory of possibility. When particles appear, they are measured in terms of probability amplitudes or mathematical ghosts. They appear and then disappear. In a game, such as basketball, there are an indefinite number of possibilities as to what to do with the ball and where to put it. In the "many-worlds interpretation," each separate possibility comprises a separate world. This ties in with the parallel-universe interpretation of *string theory*, where there might be an entirely different universe from you a millimeter away.

Matrix: The movie, *The Matrix,* portrayed people living entirely within a simulation in isolated pods, never even glimpsing the real world, similar to a caterpillar in a cocoon. Those living in the real world had to find a way of *awakening* them from within the simulation to a radically different world. Otherwise, those living in the pod could never improve their condition. It was a profound metaphor for *enlightenment.* The word "matrix" is associated through Sanskrit with "mother" and "meter." The Sanskrit word for illusion is "Maya," which connotes magical powers. This all goes with the idea that the real is the opposite of illusion.

Megadream: We live in a vast dream of many dreams, each of us dreaming everyone else, and every dream strangely interlocking every other. It is what we normally consider to be *reality*. Ultimately, there is but one dreamer dreaming each of us and posing as each of us in the glorious game of life. Core to this is the Hindu notion that God is at *play*.

Megastory: Within a dream, you always find a story, as strangely as it may appear. This story can be construed in terms of literature, theater or movies. What we call "history" is a great story, encompassing a seemingly endless number of other stories, where all the *players* intersect each other, all within one great dream of dreams. This is the story of our lives, of humanity and of *divine* redemption. It is the key to integrating Eastern and Western *religions*. The East emphasizes the dream; the West the story.

Modern Age: This is a period of history from Columbus's discovery of America in 1492 up until September 11, 2001. Many people alive still consider themselves to be living in that age, because they grew up with it and assumed that things would always stay "modern," as progress was conceived to be inevitable. Western imperialism and colonization of the entire planet enabled the creation of the very transportation and communication infrastructures that would unite all humanity. In the process, a new *planetary civilization* was created that would be neither East nor West but instead comprised of all parts of the globe. Unprecedented innovation emerged across the board, including printing and publishing, widespread literacy, democratic institutions, the scientific method, the Industrial Revolution, vast improvements in medicine and the early emergence of high technology. After World War II, contradictions within Western-dominated politics and society would lead to a transitional period from the late 1960s to the late 1990s, when the commercialization of the Internet would lead *globalization* to a high pitch. Of great importance in this book is the secular nature of the Modern Age and the unprecedented neglect and damage to the environment, which ended up directly threatening the survival of humanity. A new *planetary consciousness* that is profoundly spiritual and inclusive is suggested as the way out, bringing together the marriage of Heaven and Earth, the full recognition that God, in whatever way we conceive Him, is our "Father" and the Earth is our "Mother." We are all precious strands in the fabric of life participating in the *cosmic consciousness*.

Monism: In this notion, there is typically a single reality, the apparent Universe is not ultimately real and there is only Who and What we call "God." This is classically poised against the dualism of the *Modern Age*, which supposed there was both matter and spirit with separate laws, and that they were equally real. The mystical quest strongly leans toward monism, as does *religion* as a whole, which is preoccupied with *unity* (*see* unity in diversity), particularly that there is a substratum of the apparent Universe that is more "real" than anything one can physically sense.

Moore's law: This is a long-term trend in computing where the number of transistors that can be placed on a microchip doubles every two years or so. This produces an exponential curve in computer processing speed and memory capacity. Due to the pervasiveness of high technology, the implications are vast. With every doubling, a new class of human problems can be addressed. For example, early on, computers were just that: number crunchers. Then they became information processors for words, spreadsheets and databases. Then, largely due to the influence of Apple Inc., they became communications devices, ultimately enabling the iPhone and the iPad. It is amazing to realize that they both contain the full Macintosh operating system.

Multiple dimensions: In classic physics, we have just three dimensions (length, width and depth). The theory of the *Modern Age* is the period of history from the Renaissance and the discovery of the Americas by Christopher Columbus in the late 15th century CE to the late 20th century CE with the space program and the development of high technology. It is essentially the period when Western Europe, and later the United States, gained global domination through colonization and exploitation. In the process, a truly planetary transportation and communication infrastructure was established, enabling supersonic jets, rocketry, the World Wide Web and rich mobile media and communications. For people born in the 20th century CE, it is easy to confound the new *Planetary Age* with the Modern Age, as the operating assumption was that "Modern" would last forever and never be overturned. This age brought humanity many wonderful things, such as publishing, literacy, democratic institutions, prolific scientific understanding, religious tolerance, advanced medicine, and industrial-powered prosperity on a scale never before imagined. It made it possible for humanity to literally come together, which has already happened in our early Planetary Age. The price was pervasive materialism and a profound secular bias that was caustic to all religious and spiritual expressions. This was not unique to the Soviet Union and Communist China but was applicable to every continent and nation in the world. Even the spiritual forms became materialistic in expression, such as the various forms of fundamentalism. *Mysticism* and contemplation were largely lost. In addition, the planetary *ecology* was profoundly disrupted, driving it very nearly to collapse. To use a dialectic perspective, the Modern Age came to contradict itself and lay the foundation for its own demise. A cultural analysis of the transition from "Modern" to "Planetary" would start the process with the space program and the birth of high technology to the effective commercialization of the Internet and the events of September 11, 2001. The destruction of the Twin Towers marked the official end of the Modern Age, but the process had already begun in the 1960s. The Planetary Age centers on the *reality* of the convergence of all humanity and where we go from here.

Mysticism: This is the inner *reality* of *religion* and *spirituality*, realized through deeply intuitive processes. It is the *realization* of ultimate unity of the Creator and creation. God is all, and all is God. Yet, God transcends that all. Hindus see God in terms of *Being, Consciousness and Bliss,* and Christians in terms of *Light, Life and Love.* Ultimately, there is just "THAT," the inexpressible. One can simply see that there is just The One. From there, the *Advaita Vedanta* tradition of *Hinduism* insists that The One is not two. In other words, ultimately, there is no differentiation.

Natural revelation: From the standpoint of Western *religion,* especially the Abrahamic family of faith, creation itself discloses much about the nature of the Creator. If God is Infinite Intelligence, it makes sense that He would become evident from the Universe he created. One can see exquisite beauty and detail in the smallest to the largest forms of life, from the cell of a mosquito to an elephant or whale. From the indigenous perspective, all of life is imbued with consciousness, even the very rocks and elements. From the mystical humanistic perspective, consciousness is inherent in the Universe itself. From the Eastern perspective, God became the Universe as a form of *play,* setting up Self-realization and *revelation* as the whole point of God. In other words, it is all about hide and seek—God hiding from Himself as a form of *play.*

N-Dimensions: In *string theory,* the physical Universe is explained through extra dimensions beyond the conventional three dimensions of space and the fourth dimension of time. Recent speculation requires a total of 11 dimensions. The additional dimensions are often referred to as "higher dimensions." Because the exact number has been variously determined, and because their very existence is speculative, it is referred to with the "N" to represent a variable number. Extra dimensions may be necessary to effectively integrate quantum theory with classical physics with Einstein's relativity theory. Relativity adds time as a fourth. However, to explain the behavior of subatomic particles, we must add other dimensions. Currently, string theory favors 11 dimensions. This is frequently expressed as *N-dimensions;* for now, the precise number is indefinite.

Neo-evangelicalism: Under Billy Graham, this movement became an inclusionary proclamation of the Gospel that overlooked denominational and doctrinal differences and worked with any and all churches to gather people together in mass evangelism for a born-again experience. The stress was on the individual's personal relationship with Jesus Christ. Hell was no longer depicted as much in terms of the "flames of judgment" but in terms of the absence of Christ and separation from God. This deeply resonated with modern people's sense of isolation and increasing alienation, referred to in sociology as "the lonely crowd."

Neo-orthodoxy: This is an attempt to bring *Christianity* into the late *Modern Age,* taking a mid-position between the extremes of fundamentalism and liberalism. It advocated an emphasis on the Gospel while being socially active in making a difference in the world. It stressed unity while maintaining the uniqueness of the Christian *revelation,* both individually and collectively.

New Age: This term emerged in the 1960s and 1970s as many American and Europeans, concerned about racism, the war in Vietnam and environmental destruction, looked away from the Western tradition and began focusing on the present and consciously creating a new society on the communal level. Loosely identified with the astrological *Age of Aquarius,* the hippies—like the French postmodern philosophers that would shortly follow them—saw that the *Modern Age* had run its course. Progress was not inevitable and technology was no longer regarded as the cure-all for every human malady. Due to the space program and real-time satellite transmission, as well America's increasing involvement in world affairs, *globalization* was emerging, but only later would it be seen as the defining characteristic.

New Thought movement: Beginning in America in the 19th century, this movement unites various liberal churches focused on positive thinking and faith healing. They look toward a loving God, and tend to regard Jesus of Nazareth as an inspirational guide. They have acted as a major force in the new age movement, which helped bring an end to the modern age. It is clear from its practitioners, writers and speakers that there is an absorption of Eastern thought, *Hinduism* and *Buddhism,* as well as elements of philosophic idealism. A practical difference from the transformational movement is its reliance on maintaining positive thoughts at all costs, rather than observing and transcending the thought process to arrive at pure being. *Noble Eightfold Path: Buddhism* offers a prescription for human suffering in the Four Noble Truths, with a methodology that is social, psychological and spiritual. In essence, suffering is seen as an attachment to conditions over which one has no ultimate control. The key to letting go of attachment is moderation and contemplation, avoiding extremes at all costs. The body is not to be punished. Asceticism, *per se*, doesn't really facilitate spiritual liberation. The object is *awakening* through the direct *realization* that the human "self" is an illusion. Buddhism puts a premium on the direct experience of *Being, Consciousness and Bliss*, the Hindu notion of the *Supreme Being*, rather than on philosophy or *spirituality*. At its best, the tradition is profoundly experiential and existential.

Nonlocality: In quantum physics, this is the notion that paired particles maintain their common orientation, no matter how far apart they may actually be separated. The implication is that such relationships transcend the speed of light. It presses physicists toward the conclusion that the *space/time matrix* is not ultimately real but a convenient construct. Spiritually, the implication is that our true Self resides beyond our bodies in yet another dimension.

Objectivism: Termed by the Russian-American philosopher, Ayn Rand, the world is viewed in strictly rational terms as having an *objective reality*. This philosophy ties in with the whole *rational empirical* tradition and *European Age of Enlightenment* tradition. The task of humanity is to adjust to a preexisting external reality such that they can get what they truly want and find happiness. From this perspective, the world is very much "out there."

Omega Point: The French anthropologist and theologian, Pierre Teilhard de Chardin, envisioned a point in history where the entire process culminates with Planet Earth becoming conscious of itself as planet and humanity as humanity. This has been also referred to as the "noosphere," or sphere of being. God consciousness reaches a critical mass and becomes the new norm. People see and experience God everywhere, in everyone and in everything.

Open-source spirituality: The Internet, along with the revolution in rich, real-time mobile media, allows for a many-to-many exchange of views and perspectives. When directed to the great wisdom and spiritual traditions, this can result in a vast expansion of Whom and What we construe to be God. Open source has transformed much of the development in high technology and is beginning to revolutionize commerce and economics. While myriad *sacred* texts are online, they have yet to be organized and correlated into what might be called a *planetary sourcebook and temple*. This is now feasible and wide open to our imagination.

Paradox: This word refers to that which appears impossible and yet, nonetheless, is true. It is closely associated with contradiction. To realize the ultimate truth, one must move through paradox after paradox. This is likened to two lions at the gate that guard the inner sanctum. To get through, you must overcome fear and reluctance. It helps to realize that life is inherently paradoxical. This is because we live in a glorious illusion: the *Megadream* and the *Megastory*. Full *realization* allows one to see that even this is perfect. We inhabit God's *playground*.

Parallel universes: In *quantum mechanics* and *string theory*, it is recognized that there may be an infinite number of universes, covering every possibility. What happens is based on which one we choose. This is closely related to higher dimensions, beyond time as the fourth dimension. Physicists have been driven to such a radical perspective due to the many *paradoxes* discovered in high-energy particle experiments.

Peace movement: In the late Modern period, it became increasingly apparent that total war exacted an unacceptable price on humanity with extensive civilian casualties. With the detonation of atomic weapons at the end of World War II, the search for peace became urgent and the United Nations was soon formed. When one thinks about it, it is amazing that, with the planet's fragile *ecosystem*, so few international laws are intact. Apart from empires and military alliances, anarchy seems to have defined international relations. In the United States, two unsuccessful wars in a row—the Korean War, followed by the war in Vietnam—catalyzed an intense antiwar movement led by the youth, who were systematically drafted into a hopeless war by well-meaning but unconscious adults. Along with civil rights, this fueled the counterculture of the 1960s and 1970s. In the 1980s, the peace movement became more sophisticated and less partisan in protesting the nuclear arms race. As it was conducted on high ground, the Republican Party under Ronald Reagan saw the advantages of détente with the Soviet Union and moved to end the Cold War. Under President George W. Bush, recent military campaigns have maintained a degree of censorship in the press and media, even though the campaigns were largely unsuccessful. President Barack Obama has led the way in organizing the nation through the new social media and networks, which seem to defy effective suppression.

Pentateuch: This is the Greek name for the books of Moses, the first five books of the Bible, which Jewish people refer to as the *Torah.* This is the foundation of the Western understanding of God as creator revealing Himself to His creation. God is seen as personal, with infinite wisdom, power and glory. The implication is that this *divine* spectacle is not so much about us as human beings as it is about God, Himself. Where one draws the line of development determines whether he or she is Jewish, Christian or Muslim.

Perestroika: In Russian, this means "restructuring," which corresponds with *glasnost.* Mikhail Gorbachev instituted a movement in the mid- to late 1980s in the Soviet Union toward liberalization, democratization of the political structure and a new pragmatism over economic matters that minimized the importance of the communist ideology. This brought him unparalleled appeal and capabilities in negotiating with the American President Ronald Reagan and the British Prime Minister Margaret Thatcher. The rest was history.

Persona: Originally, this was the megaphone mask that Greek actors used to *play* a specific role within a tragedy or comedy. Acting was seen to be a process of impersonation. The term in modern times came to mean that which individuals identified themselves. The implication is that this is never our real Self.

Persons of God: Intellectual honesty requires that anyone seriously addressing the nature of "God" recognize that we are entering into irreversible mystery. God has been variously called "the *Transcendent Mystery* and "the *Supreme Identity."* Distinct in *Christianity,* but echoed in *Hinduism* as well, is the notion that the *Supreme Being* is comprised of three "Persons" who are likened to states. The idea is that three persons comprise a single Godhead. In Christianity, it is the Father, the Son and the Holy Spirit, with "Mother" conspicuously missing. Since "mother" in mystical thought is often synonymous with the universe of form, she is commonly identified with our Planet Earth, or Gaia, the Greek goddess. Clearly, the Father implies our *Source* and the Son proceeds from the Source, or the living word, or *revelation.* In Christianity, this is considered the *divine* aspect of Jesus of Nazareth, the Christ Principle. The Holy Spirit is in neuter form in Greek. "Spirit" is associated with presence and life. One could take the Holy Spirit to actually be the divine consciousness of perfection. The whole point of *mysticism* is to realize and abide in that divine consciousness. In Hinduism, there are three "persons" of the Supreme God—Brahma, the Creator; Vishnu, the Preserver; and Shiva, the Destroyer, who also prepares the way for the Creator. In Hinduism, creation is viewed as cyclical rather than a once-and-forever event. One of the most compelling implications of divine persons is the notion of *interbeing*, where the heart of reality is relationship.

Planck scale: Max Planck, a Nobel Prize recipient, speculated that the smallest possible space would be something like 10^{-37} meters. This is so small that even subatomic particles might, in comparison, be seen to be as large as planets.

Planetary Age: This is a designation of the *New Age* as the *culmination* of the gradual process of humanity coming together through a revolution in transportation and communications, with the *global infrastructure* to support it. A *planetary civilization* and consciousness have emerged along with it in sharp contrast to the *Modern Age* before it. This New Age is profoundly spiritual in outlook— a *spirituality* that is also profoundly inclusive. There has been a decisive shift away from a narrow preoccupation with humanity to the cosmos itself, seen as *Being, Consciousness and Bliss.* Humanity is finally *awakening* to its own inherent divinity. God consciousness is no longer a matter of embarrassment but a condition that is highly prized. While it is tempting to suggest that it all began on September 11, 2001, it is increasingly clear that the transition from Modern to Planetary began in the late 1960s with the space race and satellite broadcast.

Planetary citizenship: With advanced globalization and the commercialization of the Internet, a new *planetary civilization* is emerging that has decisive breaks with the *Modern Age.* If we are living in a *Planetary Age,* with a planetary civilization with a new *planetary consciousness,* then our highest allegiance must go beyond our town or city, state or province, nation or territory. It must go to Planet Earth itself, and ultimately to the entire cosmos and to our *Source.* Before being elected, President Barack Obama in Berlin, Germany, referred to "world citizenship." The United Nations was constructed to that end, influenced by the Bahá'í movement, stemming from the 19th century CE, with the vision of one language, one country and one God. In late modern times, this was referred to as "the fatherhood of God and the brotherhood of man." When planetary citizenship becomes our lowest common denominator, our individual and collective birthright, we will have arrived, and humanity will finally come to realize its inherent divinity.

Planetary civilization: The emergence of the Industrial Revolution, followed by high technology, has changed the face of the Earth. The Earth has shrunken for many people due to supersonic transportation, space probes and advanced electronics, such as the World Wide Web and the iPhone. While the Industrial Revolution defaced the earth with its roads and highways, belching factories and endless pollution, high technology has a tendency to be much cleaner and more efficient. Due to the pressure of global warming, and possible melting of the Arctic zones, green technology is due to greatly accelerate. While modern civilization considered pollution a necessary evil, planetary civilization will regard it as abhorrent.

Planetary consciousness: The new consciousness is emerging as a profoundly spiritual world culture with a keen appreciation of the Universe, and the *Supreme Being* of which that Universe is a living expression. It increasingly identifies with Planet Earth as humanity's lowest common denominator and not its highest. The nature of *reality* as *Being, Consciousness and Bliss* is finally recognized on a quasi-scientific level, and the world has never been the same.

Planetary sourcebook/temple: While there are places of worship, spiritual training and *enlightenment* on every continent, distributed among the great faiths and religious traditions, there is no single temple or "Bible" uniting all faiths. This can be accomplished online in virtual space with relative ease. Recent developments, such as the virtual Internet environment called Second Life, point the way. What is envisioned is rich, interactive media with video and animation housing a vast, interlinked multimedia library, where people can elegantly explore the correlations among every tradition. This could develop like an online Disneyland, with sponsorship among the great *religions*, as well as universities and, possibly, even corporations. For this, we need a common spiritual language, literacy and intelligence *(see spiritual intelligence/literacy).* This book was written to point the way.

Play: The *being values* are awaken, create, play and celebrate. Children spontaneously play. Much of what could be play in life is work. Since few people totally choose their careers and jobs, work is rarely considered play. When one gets in touch with his or her divinity, it is possible to experience the job, however routine it may be, as play. There is a deeper sense of play, which is that we are living within a play—the *Megastory* and God is at play with and through us. All of history is really a vast play. The implication is that, due to endless attachments, we find it incredible that life doesn't have to be all that serious and that God has a superb sense of humor.

Play God or Be God: We ultimately have the choice to pretend that we are God or truly experience God. When we mistake our egos for our true Self, we *play* God and are preoccupied with proving ourselves. This is both our social mask and our *shadow*. When we surrender and allow that which is to BE, we needn't prove anything, least of all that we are God. At that precise moment, we experience God. The underlying insight is that there is only God and that we, as individuals, are delightful illusions and all part of the divine *play*.

Pluralism: This is an orientation that accepts all cultural expressions and faiths as equally valid, and often encourages and even embraces other points of view. It largely characterized the counterculture of the 1960s and 1970s, giving preference to ethnic minorities and demonstrating strong interest in Eastern cultures and *religions* within the United States. A common viewpoint might be that "all paths lead to God," and an affirmation that "with God as our Father, brothers all are we." Ken Wilber, in his work, critiques the view by encouraging people to go beyond it, maintaining that some faiths are more advanced than others. For example, does Voodoo have the same validity as *Zen Buddhism*? A key capability of the Dalai Lama and many highly realized beings is to be "omniperspectival," in the words of the late Lex Hixon, who thus characterized Sri Ramakrishna Paramahamsa. You are capable of appreciating all perspectives at once.

Protestantism: This historic reform in Western Europe of the Roman Catholic Church was focused on the individual and his or her own salvation, as opposed to reliance on the perceived authority of the church itself. With the advent of movable type and the printing press, the movement established the authority of the Bible and patterned itself after the early church in an attempt to renew itself. From this followed a wholesale rejection of icons and ritual. This movement became a separate tradition with a perpetual tendency to keep fragmenting into various denominations. It has resulted in great experimentation, with a subsequent loss of the pervasive feeling of unity as well as of the overwhelming mystery and majesty of God.

Ptolemaic thought: Claudius Ptolemaeus pioneered early astronomy in the 2nd century CE, as a Roman citizen operating out of Hellenistic Egypt. His theories were received by the Catholic Church with the same degree of sacrosanctity as was Aristotle, resulting in the famous standoff between Galileo Galilei, with his heliocentric theory, and the church. Ptolemaic theory regarded the Earth as the center of the Universe with the sun, planets and stars orbiting it in crystalline spheres, rather than the Earth rotating around the sun and the sun rotating within the Milky Way Galaxy. The mathematics were complex and contradictory and became difficult to maintain with the introduction of the telescope. In essence, it is the common-sense perspective of space by an untutored eye.

Quantum entanglement (*see* quantum leap, quantum mechanics *and* quantum revolution): This is the notion that two particles, which had originally been paired, can be linked and correlated even when they are on opposite sides of the Universe, and will maintain their spin. The implication is that each particle implies the other. Ultimately, it points to *nonlocality*; that time and space as such don't really exist but are only constructs of the mind; that things aren't really separate but just appear to be so.

Quantum leap: When a subatomic particle jumps from one layer to another within an atomic shell with no intervening steps, it is considered a quantum leap. This implication is of sudden, exponential growth as opposed to incremental, step-by-step growth.

Quantum mechanics: This is the physics of extremely minute, subatomic particles. Their movement and behavior completely contradict ordinary macroscopic movement. For example, particles suddenly appear and then disappear. They can move forward and backward in time. Sometimes they are seen as waves; other times, they appear as particles. This study is enabled by extremely high-energy experiments in tightly controlled laboratories. The stunning theories of quantum physicists have come out of their efforts to explain these strange phenomena.

Quantum physics Referred to as "particle physics," this is intimately tied in with high-energy experiments whose results cannot be explained, either by *the theory of relativity* or by classical Newtonian physics. It is the science of the extremely small, at the subatomic level, where a phenomenon can appear either as a particle or a wave—but not both at the same time—and the choice is entirely up to you. It can only be approached by factoring in consciousness itself.

Quantum revolution: With advanced-particle physics, a radically different view of the Universe emerged whose laws had little to do with the classic mechanics of Sir Isaac Newton. They were much more radical than the extraordinary insights of Albert Einstein, who unified space and time and considered space curved, with everything relative and nothing absolute. A couple of tenets were especially disruptive: the "uncertainty principle," which states that the process of experimentation alters that which is being observed, and the phenomenon being observed is an interaction of the observer and the observed expressed in terms of probability. Ultimately, this reduced the external world to what has been characterized as "mathematical ghosts," popularized by the phrase, "You create your own *reality.*"

Quantum theory: This is an alternative name for *quantum mechanics.*

Qur'an: This is the *sacred* book of *Islam,* dictated by the angel Gabriel to the Prophet Muhammad, who was considered illiterate. The word "Qur'an," also spelled "Koran," means "recite." The entire book is a collection of *divine* messages, from longest to shortest, that occurred to the prophet over a period of 20 years. They demonstrated familiarity with many passages of the Bible, both in the Old and New Testaments. The oral sayings were written down and codified within a generation of Muhammad's lifetime.

Ramayana: One of the two great Sanskrit epics of ancient India, this delightfully *divine* love story with a fairytale setting is about an exiled divine prince, Rama, and his wife, Sita, who are abducted from their forest hut by a demon king. Many contemporary Hindu names are drawn from this epic. It is both recited and reenacted to this very day throughout India. It would seem that hundreds of millions of Hindu's hold this epic as providing the very context of their lives.

Rational empiricism (see scientific materialism*):* This is *spiritual materialism* or scientism, the uncritical belief in, and adoption of, the scientific method to solve all problems. More particularly, it is the insistence upon the measurability and public verifiability of all phenomena. If anything is experienced that is not measurable, it is, for all practical purposes, considered unreal or illusory. Thus, most of the intangibles that make life truly worthwhile, such as love, truth and beauty, from an extreme position, are held to be illusions. The implications to humanity being able to feel at home in the Universe are profound. Some late modern thinkers, such as Alan Watts, attributed most of environmental destruction to this mindset.

Rationalism (*see* rational empiricism): This is the uncritical reliance on the processes of reason over empirical evidence on the one hand, or mystical intuition on the other. It is typically contrasted with both *mystical realization* and *revelation* and discounts intuitive processes. The notion might be that everything is reducible to mathematical symbols. It implies that the scientific method is the only vehicle to truth. It reigned supreme in the *European Age of Enlightenment*, and then met increasing criticism as time progressed. It has a strong appeal to self-styled *atheists*.

Reality: This is what people unreflectively assume to exist based upon their own sensory evidence—a world of objects, sensations and sounds—which all appear "out there." It is important to realize that our own bodies form a continuum with our perceived external world and other bodies. The scientific method insists on addressing only that which can be measured, that which is empirical. All other phenomena, including your inner experiences, are considered irrelevant or unreal for experimental purposes. Closer inspection deconstructs the modern myth. According to physiology, everything that appears external to us is processed inside our bodies through our brain and nervous system. We never actually see the object "out there." In order to operate in life, we make the assumption that objects exist external to our bodies. From the standpoint of *quantum mechanics*, the more microscopic we go, the more it becomes clear that all that is visible is simple fluctuations of energy, intervals of particles appearing and disappearing in a dance. This has been referred to as "quantum soup" and "mathematical ghosts." From the Eastern standpoint, such as *Advaita Vedanta*, there is no multiplicity; there is only The One. No in or out. The things that appear most real are most illusory; the things that are least apparent are most real. Thus, love, which is experienced within us, may be considered the most powerful force in the Universe, even though it is never directly seen, only felt.

Realization: This is the counterpart of revelation in the East. Realization is a favorite Hindu term for *"enlightenment,"* while Buddhists favor *"awakening"* and Christians favor being "*born again.*" In realization, revelation is experienced from within. From the perspective of *Advaita Vedanta,* the Hindu school of unity, God is seen as the Self. In that school, the Self is all there is; there is nothing apart from the Self.

Re-enchantment: This is the conscious effort to revive a mythical perspective on life. As people become aware that nothing is really "out there" in a classic objective sense, that we are looking at "mathematical ghosts" and "quantum soup," they accept the primacy of consciousness. God, the Universe, and humanity itself may now all be considered in terms of consciousness. Everyone and everything is alive.

Religion: In this book, religion refers to all the externalities of faith, including authority, scripture, institutionalized beliefs, rituals and observances, much like a sociological phenomenon. One might think primarily of the physical structure of a cathedral, mosque, synagogue or temple. It is all encompassing and refers to the persistent notion that there is an underlying order of *reality,* invisible and undetectable by any of our senses, which happens to fit well with the new physics. It can apply to any faith or tradition, even strict forms of *Buddhism,* which would not recognize a personal "God" in the Abrahamic sense, or *humanism.* Even communism, with its official atheism, might be considered religion when held dogmatically and adamantly. This is differentiated from *spirituality,* which refers to the inner practice and experience, as well as *mysticism,* which entails the direct experience of unity. Unity is the ultimate concern of religion, and the various traditions have tended to be founded by mystics. However, someone can practice a faith his or her entire life without a moment of true belief or inner experience, merely going through the motions, as it were.

Renaissance Man: This ideal emerged from the Italian Renaissance and described a great man who was well versed in all subjects and a virtuoso in his various accomplishments. It closely ties in with the values of a liberal education, where people are well read and highly literate, with a keen appreciation of the arts. Education is viewed as a cultivation of the highest possibilities and capabilities of an individual. Leonardo da Vinci serves as a supreme example, being an unparalleled artist, architect, philosopher and scientist. As the body of knowledge advanced through the centuries, especially in the 20th century CE, the ideal became impractical, and people felt compelled to specialize. This ideal is closely associated with *humanism* and tended to be secular. All that is worthwhile investigating are subjects directly related to people. In extreme cases, God is considered irrelevant.

Revelation: This is the counterpart of *realization* in the Western tradition. Since God is primarily thought of and experienced in the second person as the beloved "Other," inspiration and *enlightenment* are thought of in terms of revelation. With revelation, one perceives the profound, earth-shattering insights as being given directly by another being. A prophet is one who receives fresh revelation and who speaks for God, as though he or she were God.

Right-handed path: Right-handedness is the popular, mainstream way, as we see when Luke Skywalker fights Darth Vader in *Star Wars.* In the West, it is practicing white magic only, like the good fairy. In *Hinduism,* it corresponds with the god, Lord Vishnu, manifest as Lord Rama or Lord Krishna. The path of *mysticism* focuses on extreme devotion, or *Bhakti yoga,* or loving service to humanity, or *Karma yoga,* such as Mahatma Gandhi. All of us share these various traits, but we will tend to have a preference for *left-handed* or right-handed approaches to *spirituality.*

Sacred: This refers to that which has been specially set apart for a *divine* purpose. It connotes the immediate felt presence of God. While it can be explicitly religious in a social setting, it implies that which has the ability to utterly transform a person. The sacredness of life is a concept that speaks to the *Planetary Age;* that life itself, as opposed to machinery, is inherently sacred. It is the ever-deepening recognition that all is *Being, Consciousness and Bliss.*

Samsara: This endless cycle of suffering in *Hinduism* and *Buddhism* is due to false identification and attachments to ephemeral conditions. It correlates with the notion of reincarnation, where we all have endless lives, and the goal is to transcend the cycle by waking up into unity with our *Source.* In this book, it can be overcome by waking up to the nature of life as a play, movie or game. What is apparently real is only a dream to entertain us. It is possible to reenter the game as a conscious player, with the Creator playing within His or Her creation. *Samsara* is life played at effect; Self-realization is life played from cause.

Satori: This Japanese term of *enlightenment* connotes a sudden flash of insight into the true nature of things. It is roughly comparable to *cosmic consciousness.* In *Zen Buddhism,* it is often considered to be the first step towards Nirvana or ultimate awakening.

Scientism: This uncritical belief maintains that science has all the answers, thereby making all forms of philosophy and *religion* irrelevant. It is closely tied with *rational empiricism*, where only that which is observable by the senses and measurable may be considered real. In the late *Modern Age*, it connoted an uncritical acceptance of *evolution*—not merely as a brilliant theory but as an accomplished fact. Scientism is actually a form of religion that embraces extreme rationalism and abhors all sense of mystery.

Scientology: Created by the late L. Ron Hubbard, it is based on the concept of auditing, introduced with its founding book, *Dianetics*, using e-meters to measure a person's resistance to probing questions about a person's past traumas. The point is to complete the traumas and move on, achieving a state of "clear." Highly conscious beings are called "Thetans," with exceptional creative powers. It was developed in the 1930s and 1940s through world travel and extensive study. It is significant that Hubbard was a highly gifted science-fiction writer. He quipped that everyone should create his or her own *religion*. It ultimately achieved the nonprofit status of a church. It made important contributions to the development of Werner Erhard's *est*, especially "the anatomy of the Mind," which reveals how our thought structures have preemptive power over us, just like a machine. It has been highly controversial from the beginning and seems to have a closed culture. The possibility of a technology of *enlightenment*, which Werner Erhard developed and offered in much more open-spirited forum, is of broad interest. It is interesting that the word "tantra" means "technique" and the great schools within *Buddhism* are referred to as "vehicles."

Self-realization (*see* realization): This term describes the act of *awakening* to whom you truly are, your supreme Self, or "God." It is the Hindu version of Buddhist *Enlightenment* and the Christian experience of being *born again*. When you come to an appreciation that there is only "God," it dawns upon you that only "God" could be your true Self. The everyday "you" doesn't really exist. You are a dream character in a dream story, pretending that you aren't God so the show can go on. Within the dream, as a love story, your individuality is uniquely precious because of the underlying realization that you are truly *divine*.

Sermon on the Mount: Jesus of Nazareth gave his most important public address on a hill with people seated all around him, as recorded in the Gospel of Matthew, Chapters 5-7. It announces the principles of the *divine* kingdom with a new humanity, giving the highest standards ever annunciated to that date, most particularly, that one should love his or her enemies. If one has actually attempted to live in total accord with these precepts, one quickly finds out that it demands a transformed consciousness to fulfill them. It is noteworthy that Mohandas Karamchand "Mahatma" Gandhi was deeply moved by this passage and attempted to execute it on a mass scale. He declared that, if only 10 percent of the people who ever claimed to be Christian had truly lived by these precepts, the entire world would have gone to *Christianity.*

Shadow: This is the unconscious element of ourselves that we don't fully own but tend to project onto others. On the surface, we present our *persona* or social mask to the outer world. We literally make ourselves up in front of the mirror every morning. Below the surface, we are plagued by myriad petty, and often downright mean and nasty, thoughts and feelings. Because the shadow can go so deeply, it is easy for people to be completely out of touch with the *divine*; that deep within, far below the shadow, resides a *sacred* self of absolute love.

Shamanic consciousness: Indigenous people in hunting and gathering cultures are closely tied to creation and celebrate a continuum of people, animals and plants. All of life, even the very rocks, is seen to be conscious. If there is a God, He or She is not seen as apart or separate from life on Earth but imminent with that life. One prays to the animal he has sacrificed, thanking him for giving up his life that he might eat. The planet is often seen as a single gigantic being, with no single person standing apart. The shaman is the intermediary in the tribe between Heaven and Earth, the visible and invisible realms. Often derisively referred to as a "witch doctor," he is actually a combination of priest, healer and counselor. His role is as important at that of the tribal chief. In this book, this consciousness is seen as indispensible to the survival of humanity and the *transformation* of Planet Earth back into a Garden of Eden.

Shamanism: Sometimes disparagingly referred to as "witch doctors" or "medicine men," shamans play a healing role among indigenous people. They function as mediators between the seen and unseen worlds. It is not institutionalized in the same way as is priesthood in the Catholic Church, but is driven more by charismatic considerations that often involve having an out-of- body experience. While the *Modern Age* looked at shamans as being highly superstitious, the *Planetary Age* celebrates mystery and recognizes the validity of "primal religion." This is especially true in the face of *global warming* where we all must be citizens of the Earth and treat our planet like a green goddess and our cherished Mother if we hope to survive.

Singularity: This is the point where everything converges into infinity, such as dropping down into an ultimately dense black hole, as in an event horizon.

Sikhism: This very pure form of monotheism integrates the best of both *Islam* and *Hinduism*. It has over 25 million adherents, largely in the Punjab of India, with a gorgeous golden temple in Amritsar. The Adi Granth is the *sacred* scripture, which includes poems from Kabir, and is considered the ultimate guru. The founder, Guru Nanak Dev, had a mystical experience after bathing in a river where he declared, "There is no Hindu. There is no Muslim." God is formless and the only true *reality*. The name of God is of particular importance to invoke the presence of God. All men and women are equal. Because the faith originated under Islamic persecution of the various Hindu *religions*, it developed a posture of militancy, which was always defensive in nature. Sikhs have long held key military positions throughout India with an usually high regard for character.

Socrates: He is considered the pioneer of the dialectic, which was a method of questioning to help people arrive at the truth, which became the foundation of philosophy. In his later years, Socrates antagonized many people in his Athenian *democracy*, and was given the choice of either choosing banishment or drinking hemlock; he nobly chose hemlock. He was the direct teacher of Plato, who immortalized him. Plato, in turn, taught Aristotle, who became the personal tutor of the world conqueror, Alexander the Great. It is difficult to overestimate the importance of Socrates, and the Athenian philosophers, as they set forth a rational, deeply humanistic approach to life and the world that formed the foundation of much of Western civilization, with its linear thrust and uncritical optimism.

Source: This neutral word, which conveys the sense of God as Creator, was pioneered by *Scientology* and has been picked up for more general use. With regard to the Christian Trinity, it is an apt way of referring to God, the Father, as our ultimate Source. Other popular synonyms are *Higher Power*, the *Supreme Being* and Infinite Intelligence. God is both personal and impersonal, and ultimately *transpersonal*. God includes personality while transcending it.

Space/Time: Albert Einstein paired time and space, considering them an inter-related fabric, in that you can't have one without the other. Radical quantum theory suggests that these categories are ultimately subjective and conceptual. With no locality, phenomena reside outside space or time. With the growing recognition of the primacy of consciousness itself, in the scientific method, all the old rules have become obsolete.

Spanda: Hindus introduced this notion of the pulse of creation, where every-thing is vibrating. This resonates with quantum theory. It is as if we go in and out of existence millions of times per second. This all happens so fast that our brains cannot process it, so we see things as having a steady state. Sound and all of our senses entail vibration. Thus, *divine* speech *is* creation. "God said, let there be light, and there was light."

Special revelation: In Christian theology, the biblical scriptures, especially the Gospel proclaiming the incarnation of Christ, are considered to be a form of *revelation* set apart from creation itself. If we are created in the image of God, it would make sense that a God of infinite intelligence would want to directly communicate with His highest forms of creation, to actually talk with them, as it were. Thus, part of the vast drama of history is God directly intervening at various points to give the show away, to help humanity awaken to its inherent divinity and the perfection of creation itself.

Spiral Dynamics theory: Time in the West has been construed as a steadily ris-ing solid line, implying progression or *evolution.* Time in the East has been con-strued as circular. We keep coming back to the same day, the same week of the month and the same month of the year. We go from spring to summer to fall to winter every year, as well as with the seasons of our lives. The breakthrough is in putting these two together in an ascending spiral. For example, we go through economic contraction and expansion, yet the overall world economy keeps growing over the long term. While biological evolution may be debatable, the material progress of humanity, especially in recent decades and centuries, has been most impressive.

Spiritual intelligence/literacy: Recent studies have revealed multiple types of in-telligence and, by extension, literacy. Robert Kiyosaki, author of the best-selling series, *Rich Dad Poor Dad,* has championed financial education in schools that might develop children's street smarts and widespread ability to understand financial statements. By extension, there is a tremendous need for spiritual intelligence and literacy, something suggested by Ken Wilber. Spiritual intelligence and literacy need not be around any one religious tradition. It entails the ability to grasp ultimate issues and arrive at satisfactory answers with the assistance of all the great wisdom traditions, now accessible online.

Spirituality: This is the inner dimension of *religion* where one is actively seeking the mystical experience to come to a full *realization* of the doctrines of his or her faith. Being "*born again*" can refer to an enlightening experience where one's tradition becomes totally real and all consuming. One actually attempts to live it, and start on the path to becoming a saint or transformed being. In this book, spirituality is seen as the process towards mystical realization. Within the Christian tradition, one can "receive Christ" and try to be like Him. However, at certain points, one can experience an actual *transformation* of consciousness, which some might refer to as "Christ consciousness" or the "Holy Spirit," where one actually gets it and is empowered to live a radical new life. Increasingly, one hears of those who are "spiritual but not religious," characterizing tens of millions of people in the United States alone, who don't regularly attend any church, synagogue, mosque or temple, but who may be very enthusiastic about spiritual subjects. One need also think of television evangelism and the possibilities of online spirituality. As the old structures struggle to keep up with rapid change, this all makes sense. The contemporary world is more religious than ever, although not necessarily in the orthodox sense.

Spiritual materialism: The Tibetan guru, Chögyam Trungpa, widely celebrated in the United States, coined the term in his seminal book, *Cutting Through Spiritual Materialism,* to reflect how people inadvertently mistake a highly refined ego for *spiritual enlightenment.* He critiqued excessive reliance on positive states of mind, as any state of mind is transitory, feeling that positive thinking might actually cause greater suffering in the end than otherwise thought. Buddhists maintain that the individualized self is strictly an illusion. The term has been developed and extended to refer to grasping and cherishing outward forms of a spiritual path as opposed to appreciating their essence. It can also be a failure to grasp the nature of religious symbols and that to which they refer. For example, in the Christian doctrine of the Trinity, God is seen in three persons. Does that mean that there are three people up in the sky—Father, Son and a vague Spirit person? Joseph Campbell brilliantly clarified that all-powerful spiritual symbols are "transparent to the Transcendent," where you don't mistake them for God but they enable you to reach profound insight into the *divine*.

String theory: A branch of *quantum mechanics*, which attempts to reconcile it with classical physics and the *theory of relativity*, where different sets of laws apply at each level. It does this by postulating yet another level at the *Planck scale* of 10^{-37} meters, infinitesimally smaller than even subatomic particles. These are vibrating strings or membranes with varying shapes. They require extra dimensions, with M-theory specifying a total of 11. Speculations include the possibility of multiple, *parallel universes*. The theory struggles to establish scientific respectability among many of the more hard-headed physicists because no actual experiment has yet been conducted due to the tiny scale being addressed. It is thus considered unfalsifiable, impossible to prove true or false. There have been other times in the history of physics where theoretical physicists postulated phenomena that were later experimentally demonstrated, such as *nonlocality*. The theory seems to suggest that either we know nothing or the Universe is much weirder than we had ever imagined.

Sufism: This mystical edge of *Islam* was most recently celebrated in the poetry of Rumi and Hafiz. God is construed of as both friend and lover, most often appreciated and experienced through fellow human beings. It is a profoundly devotional path that seeks to transcend all conceptual models, experiencing and expressing spirituality directly on the being level. God is seen as much within as without. It is ultimately recognized that there is nothing but God, that there is only The One.

Summer of Love: In 1967, in the Haight-Ashbury district of San Francisco near Golden Gate Park, a festival ran for months on end, with youths wearing flowers in their hair and giving away candy laced with LSD, right on the streets. It was a brilliantly artistic movement with its own newspaper, *Oracle*, printed in living color. There was active interest in communes and all forms of "dropping out" in the face of an increasingly futile war in Vietnam. It was largely generational, young against adult, baby boomers against their forebears. This movement led to the growth of the counterculture in the late 1960s and 1970s, with an emphasis on creating alternatives. It was also extraordinary in pioneering a new interfaith spirituality. The impresario, Bill Graham, dubbed the youth, "The Love Generation."

Sunyata: This is the Buddhist doctrine of emptiness, or the *fertile void*. In the Far East, just as the color black is traditionally positive, the notion of emptiness is held to be a good thing, connoting infinite possibilities. The Mahayana tradition, with the Heart Sutra, equates form and void. Like the *yin/yang* symbol, these two are ultimately held to be one, a total reconciliation of opposites.

Supreme Being: A popular generic concept of God that can work in multiple religious traditions. It is monotheistic in recognizing that only one God is Supreme and open ended as to the nature of that God. It doesn't explicitly state that God is the only *reality* and is thus *exoteric*, yet it doesn't deny that possibility either. It is interesting that the term points to "being" as the essence of God. This notion has been applied to people by authors like Wayne Dyer as "being human for a time." This complements the term *"Higher Power,"* which is equally neutral. While "God" is by far the most widely held term, it is freighted with cultural baggage such that is difficult for all spiritual orientations to accept without further clarification.

Supreme Identity (*see* Supreme Being): This is Alan Watt's term for "God." God as perceived in the first person is our ultimate "I." It is an appreciation of the *sacred* coming from a profoundly personal orientation. It resonates deeply with the Western tradition. It contrasts with Joseph Campbell's term, "Transcendent Mystery," which goes beyond personality and is transpersonal in nature, or third person. The "Mystery" resonates deeply with the Eastern tradition.

Survival of the Fittest: In his groundbreaking study, *On the Origin of Species,* Charles Darwin attributes the ability to adapt to the environment as the key to whether any given species survives over the long term. Since his theory holds that life inherently evolves given enough generations, the species that adapts to changed conditions will have a better chance of continuing. This whole line of thinking soon adopted a predatory edge as it was extended into society in what became known as "social Darwinism." Colonialism and imperialism were justified out of hand with this theory. It became the law of the jungle: kill or be killed. With the emergence of *ecology*, the interdependent nature of species and systems has been increasingly recognized. Thus, this whole notion seems at best simplistic.

System: During the late 1960s, the counterculture increasingly saw the U.S. government, along with what it called the "military-industrial complex," as "the System" and "*the Establishment*," which was suppressing freedom and systematically destroying people's lives through a ruthless war machine. By then, it was increasingly apparent to the youth that the war in Vietnam was unwinnable and profoundly misconstrued, yet the war kept going. This whole sentiment was exacerbated by the suppression of psychedelics, along with a rigid adherence to the old consciousness, even though the government was ostensibly nonsectarian. President Lyndon B. Johnson's "Great Society," which took humanity to the moon, seemed more and more like a bad joke.

Tantra: Literally meaning "technology," this is an approach to accelerating *enlightenment* by using everything in life, both positive and negative, as a means of illumination. In many Hindu and Buddhist traditions, enlightenment is thought to take place over many lifetimes. However, in such traditions as *Zen*, *satori*, or sudden illumination, can come in seconds, even though the groundwork may take decades. In Tibet, Tantra is associated with Vajrayana, or the Diamond Vehicle, which encompasses mandalas, mudras or hand gestures, chants and visualization. Pressed to an extreme, Tantra could entail a type of sexual *yoga* where intercourse is deliberately sustained as a means of *realization*. Likewise, some Tantric masters might deliberately eat meat and drink alcohol, where normally they would never even touch such things. Tantra is sometimes referred to as the left-handed path, the infrequent way, as opposed to the right-handed, or common, path.

Theocracy: This refers to *divine*, as opposed to human, government. Usually, it is attempted in conjunction with a specific religious institution and has often, but not always, been associated with monarchy. The Dali Lama perfectly illustrates this, as he is considered both the legitimate secular and *sacred* ruler of Tibet. The Puritans experimented with this during the English Revolution. In the Middle Ages, the pope often held greater power than any particular monarch. In the ancient nation of Israel, God was considered the true ruler. The ultimate of theocracy would be law by the rule of love combining many elements of *democracy*. This was envisioned from a secular standpoint by the early communists with the idea of the withering away of the state, and by evangelical Christians in the Second Coming, with the idea of Christ, like King Arthur, as "the Once and Future King."

The One Life: Tied in with the "Circle of Life," it refers to the notion that all living things comprise a single life; that there is but one life that links us all. For example, if you take oxygen and carbon dioxide away from Planet Earth, we would all perish almost instantly. The term applies to life on a deeper level in that a single consciousness unites us all. The ultimate implication is that Who and What we call "God" is all there is. Eckhart Tolle brilliantly entitled a recent contemplative book, *Oneness with All Life: Inspirational Selections from a New Earth.*

Theory of everything: This is a highly sophisticated attempt to integrate Albert Einstein's *theory of relativity,* classical Newtonian physics and *quantum mechanics* through a more fundamental theory. This has actually been attempted by string theorists who seek to reconcile opposing physical laws in the different levels of the physical Universe. It is the holy grail of contemporary cosmology. The quest has been brilliantly narrated and illustrated by Brian Greene in the PBS documentary, *The Elegant Universe: Superstrings, Hidden Dimensions, and the Quest for the Ultimate Theory.* The contemporary American philosopher, Ken Wilber, has taken a different stance, maintaining that you can't have a "theory of everything" without maintaining the primacy of consciousness itself.

Theory of evolution: Charles Darwin brilliantly conceived a model to explain how life came to be that was purely mechanistic, based on random genetic mutations of species in their attempts to adapt to their environments and compete with other species. He was inspired by his voyage on the *HMS Beagle* to the South Sea Islands where he observed very strange forms of life. He then applied this same model to account for humanity, and the theory went on to become highly controversial. While the theory never sat very well with devout Christians, it appealed to intellectuals and scientists to such an extent that it was considered factual, even though numerous gaps in its overall understanding persist until today. The bitter contention point in Western *religion* is based on the idea of six days of creation, where God spoke life into being, which liberal Christians might extend to mean separate epics. If the first several chapters of the Book of Genesis are read literally, it will most definitely conflict. It is interesting that *evolution* maintains the exact order in the emergence of life as in Genesis, from sea to land, from simple to complex forms. The fatal flaw in classic evolution was that it was a very mechanistic approach that fit like a glove in a heavy industrial era rife with colonial exploitation, where *Survival of the Fittest* seemed to make sense. Facing *global warming*, it is apparent that we sink or swim together. Contemporary biology has had to forge new directions. A naïve, uncritical approach to evolution is most certainly obsolete. It is possible, as in *involution*, that God becomes the Universe. What is most certain is that there is an inherent mystery to creation and life that cannot be easily explained away, no matter how elegant the evolutionary theory. The *Modern Age* shunned such mystery; the *Planetary Age* is now deliberately seeking it out.

Theory of relativity: The famous theory, "$E=MC^2$," equates matter with energy. It maintains that light in a vacuum maintains a constant speed, and that moving objects can be determined and measured only in relation to one another. Further implications are that space and time are a unified phenomenon, referred to as a "fabric," and that space is ultimate curved. Before the explosion of the atomic bomb and space exploration, these notions might have been regarded as highly speculative and counterintuitive; afterwards, they became self-evident. The theory addresses huge distances and vast stretches of time, measured in light years. How far can you go at the speed of light? For example, Alpha Centauri, one of the nearest stars, is over four light years away, and the Universe is conceived to be over 14 billion years old.

The Secret: Australian television producer, Rhonda Byrne, recently introduced the key teaching of numerous American self-help teachers as the law of attraction, where you subconsciously attract everything into your life, whether positive or negative. This was first shown as a full-screen feature web video; then it went to DVD and then to a book. Its sales were unprecedented. For the sake of illustration, the emphasis was upon attracting material things. It brilliantly depicted the negative aspect of the law, where you inadvertently bring bad luck by dwelling on the negative. Gratitude was seen as a fundamental element in creating a virtuous spiral upward, where things get better and better.

Thousand-petal lotus: This term refers to the crown *chakra*, or energy center, just above the top of the head, which represents the highest state of consciousness—unity—in which there is no real separation between subject or object, or between God and oneself. In all the other chakras, one experiences a certain separation from The One. At this level, one experiences pure consciousness beyond any differentiation. In *Hindu* thought, distinctions and differentiation are tantamount to creation itself. At the crown chakra, you transcend these distinctions. A thousand highly integrated lotus blossoms symbolize it. It is significant that the location of this chakra suggests that, at that level, there is no distinction between body and its environment.

Three Faces of God: The contemporary American philosopher, Ken Wilber, popularized quadrant theory, where the basic distinctions to be made in our phenomenal world are inside and outside, and one and many. On a quadrant, three persons, or points of view, are identified. First person is "I," the one speaking. The second person is "you," singular or plural, those being spoken to; this can also be seen as "we." The third person, singular or plural, is that being spoken of. All human languages make this distinction. When we look at our experience of God, it can be broken down likewise, as if God had three faces. The first person is the experience of God as his or her own ultimate Self. The second person is the experience of God as the Absolute Other whom we worship and serve. The third person is the experience of God as a *Sacred Presence* that permeates everyone and everything. The breakthrough *realization* is that these are three faces of the same God. It is also intriguing to look at the Three Faces of God in relation to the Christian concept of the Trinity. The Father could be first person, the Son the second person and the Spirit the third person.

Torah: This is the Hebrew name for the five books of Moses. Sometimes the entire Old Testament is thought of as the *Torah*. It equates with the *Pentateuch*, the Greek name for Genesis, Exodus, Leviticus, Numbers and Deuteronomy.

Traditional Age: In this book, it represents every age before the *Modern Age*. Technically, there were various civilizations and many ages and eras, such as the Classic period of Greece. Because the Modern Age set the stage for a truly *planetary civilization*, it profoundly changed everything before it in scope and impact. The difference had to do with the emerging impact of publishing, literacy, democratic institutions, religious freedom, the scientific method and the Industrial Revolution. Industry actually sculpted the planet itself, stripping much of the natural resources and setting the stage for an unparalleled environmental crisis. In the Traditional Age, humanity was still struggling with nature and was no threat to it, moving out of the caves to be hunters and gatherers and eventually forging the great river valley civilizations. The world population was vastly smaller than in the Modern Age and life spans were much shorter. In biblical times, a man reached maturity by the age of 40. While people did live past 70, the norm was for people to die much younger. The practical ideal was that you would live long enough for your children to grow up and have their own children.

Transcendental Meditation (TM): The great modern guru, Maharishi Mahesh Yogi, devised a supremely simple path to *enlightenment* around a mantra and closed-eye meditation for 20 minutes in the morning and 20 minutes in the evening. Popularized by the Beatles, TM became a sensation in the late 1960s and early 1970s and continued to be a major force for decades. Much research was done demonstrating its calming effects on physiology and how the process impacted brainwaves. Maharishi stressed that thoughts become more and more subtle until they dissolve into nothing. When thoughts come, you just notice them, without accepting them or rejecting them. They pass through you, much like clouds in the sky.

Transcendent Mystery: Joseph Campbell coined this term to refer to God as inexpressible and beyond conception, incorporating everyone and everything. The term deemphasizes personality, as he thought of God in impersonalistic terms. His contemporary, Alan Watts, referred to God as the "Supreme Identity," which would fit monotheism as well as monism. These varying orientations are reconciled with the notion of the *transpersonal*, that God includes personality while transcending personality. The value of these terms has to do with its recognition of the primary role of symbols and intuition, that God can be directly experienced but not really defined.

Transformation: This is the process of the caterpillar becoming the butterfly, or metamorphosis. It is a neutral synonym for *enlightenment*. It can apply to the world as well as to humanity. It has an important connotation, which is that, in transformation, one shifts his or her identity from the stuff in his or her life to the space in which life appears. This is much like the Gestalt distinction of going from foreground to background. It is also similar to the Christian notion of the transmutation of bread and wine into the body and blood of Christ. Here, it is an alteration of substance, where you shift your identity from the material world to consciousness itself.

Transformational movement: An extension of the new age and human potential movements that is focused on the direct experience of enlightenment as a catalyst for a life that is, not only profoundly fulfilling, living up to its ultimate potential, but also capable of catalyzing the enlightenment of others, and eventually the transformation of the planet. Core is the notion of Self-responsibility, that there is no one and nothing outside you that causes your experience. This is enhanced by the insight of Carl Jung that whatever one resists, persists, that when you simply stop resisting, the problem has a tendency to disappear. The viewpoint is profoundly humanistic, taking a very experiential approach to the recognition of "God," who is viewed in the first and third-person far more than in the second person. The divine is recognized to be comprised of pure being. *Scientology* and *est*, along with its successor, Landmark Education, have played a key role in its diffusion. Werner Erhard was profoundly influential in the mid-to-late 1970's, and directly or indirectly inspired numerous spinoffs and groups. Like new thought, it is difficult to overestimate its impact and influence.

Transpersonal: This term describes that which goes beyond personhood while including it. In mystical discussions, one often hears that a view is either personal or impersonal. One either favors the experience of God as second person, the ultimate YOU, or third person, an impersonal, *sacred* energy. In *reality*, God is transpersonal, beyond any distinction of personal or impersonal. Hindus speak of Saguna Brahman, God with attributes, and Nirguna Brahman, God without attributes.

Ultimate reality: This is the notion that the apparent world or Universe is not all there is, but that there is a substratum, or ground of being, space or context, out of which the whole world springs forth. This comes down to the Hindu expression for God as *Being, Consciousness and Bliss*. This enables one to think of God in personal, impersonal or *transpersonal* terms. *Religion* in this context refers to matters of ultimate concern: life and death, who we are, where we came from and where we are going. This often entails a cosmology that necessarily transcends the scientific method but which can be informed by it.

United Religions Initiative: This international grassroots initiative, formed in 2000 and headquartered in California at San Francisco's Presidio, which is a former military garrison, aims to end religiously motivated and sanctioned violence and foster a planetary culture of peace, justice and healing. It functions through "Cooperation Circles," groups of seven or more individuals with at least three different faiths or spiritual paths. It is an early expression of a possible spiritual or conscious United Nations that transcends the modern paradigm of *humanism* to a more all-inclusive and profound approach to unity.

Unity in diversity: The One and the Many is a fundamental philosophic distinction. On the American dollar, we see the motto, *E pluribus unum* or "out of many, one." The notion is that there is an underlying unity in all people and all phenomena, no matter how differently each of them seems. One comes to relish the diversity as that which gives flavor to the whole, much like an international smorgasbord of many different cuisines.

Universe of being: Within life, we can either play from a universe of being or a *universe of doing*, or becoming. Action can either flow effortlessly through us as if we were surfing the waves, or we can act with great pretense and intense struggle, climbing a steep mountain in the face of an impending avalanche. True fulfillment comes out of the ongoing *realization* of the inherent perfection of being, that both everyone and everything are already perfect, always have been and always will be. This is, of course, shocking from the standpoint of the prevailing conception. This is referred to as "walking on the razor's edge." Jesus of Nazareth expressed it as being *in* the world but not *of* the world. It amounts to consciously creating your own experience above the line in your upper *chakras*. In unity with the Creator, whatever happens is your own creation, as your will is perfectly aligned with His. Practically speaking, life is a process of realizing completion or perfection, falling from that realization and then realizing it all over again, again and again, much like a dance.

Universe of doing: In this book, the universe of doing or becoming refers to experiencing life from the lens of survival; that everyone and everything is a potential threat to your own sense of self, your ego. There is so much struggle that you might as well be living in a completely separate universe from those who come from the Universe of *being*. In *reality*, it is a shift in perspective inherent in transformation. Before *transformation*, you identify with your individual self, and the stuff in your life has little or nothing to do with you. After transformation, you are the context or framework that holds all the stuff in your life, including your body and mind. You observe it without identifying with it. Clearly, this is the way out for contemporary humanity, beset by a series of increasingly pressing and urgent crises.

Velvet Revolution: This is the revolution within the Eastern European Bloc, where allegiance to the Soviet Union was dissolved and the direct oversight by the Communist Party was dismantled late in 1989. The term specifically refers to that process within Czechoslovakia. The term "velvet" refers to the nonviolent nature of the revolution, where the establishment actually cooperated in the transfer of power. Largely, the term refers to all the Eastern European nations gaining independence from the Soviet Union and the collapse of the Berlin Wall between East and West Germany.

What the Bleep Do We Know!?: Discovering the Endless Possibilities: This brilliant cult movie, starring Marlee Matlin, is replete with elaborate special effects and conversations with renowned physicists and biologists, such as Dr. Quantum, or Fred Alan Wolf, on the new paradigm of *reality*, largely focused on quantum physics and emphasizing uncertainty and infinite possibility. The multiple-worlds interpretation is brilliantly depicted. The whole point of the title is that we may not know what reality ultimately is, but it most certainly is not what we think it is. In the feature, common-sense notions of the world are brilliantly defeated. Its sequel, *What the Bleep: Down the Rabbit Hole,* features dozens of hours of interviews and even more elaborate animation. After seeing this production a couple of times, you will never look upon the world in quite the same way.

Wikinomics: How Mass Collaboration Changes Everything: This brilliant book by the Canadian Internet theorist, Don Tapscott, outlines the implications of the open-source method developed in software, especially the Linux movement, when applied to work, production and economics across the board. When people voluntarily contribute to a project in many parts of the world all at once over the Internet, the results are often better and more stable than a highly paid commercial team. It is amazing that companies like IBM and Boeing are standardizing on open-source methodology. Boeing, for example, is in alliance with companies in over 60 countries. They actually make their own blueprints available to their partners. This movement suggests an approach to life far more effective than socialism and an approach that might make capitalism, as we know it, obsolete.

Yahweh: Also known as "YHWH," meaning "I AM" or "I AM THAT I AM," God is the Self-existent One, this ultimate name of God in the Old Testament was revealed to Moses in the flaming bush. You don't measure God by other things but other things by God. This name was held so *sacred* that it was considered blasphemy to even utter it. In biblical passages, Hebrews would substitute the word "Adonai," meaning "the Lord." The implications of the name are profound as it points to the possibility that the *Supreme Being* is our own Supreme Identity. When Jesus of Nazareth declared, "Before Abraham was, I AM," the crowd picked up rocks to stone Him for blasphemy. It is highly revealing that He then quoted a passage in the Hebrew book of Psalms that "you are gods." This whole account is a critical link between Eastern and Western philosophy and *religion*.

Yin/yang: This is the ancient Chinese concept of the reconciliation of opposites, male and female, full and empty, drawn as a circle with a swirl of black and white with two eyes, one black and one white, suggesting that each contains the other. The implication is that we can't have up without down, cold without hot, good without evil. Each of the extremes actually contains the other. There is a hidden harmony to the Universe that they called the Way, or Dao.

Yoga: An integrated set of methods to directly realize the fundamental unity of all existence. God, humanity and all creation are ultimately found to be one *divine reality*. The root meaning is of being yoked or linked to the Ultimate. It is an ancient Hindu system uniting mind, body and spirit. Individuals are recognized as having different propensities and so can realize unity more easily through one mode than another. The most common form in the West is Hatha yoga, which leads its practitioners through a progressively harder sequence of postures designed to quiet the body and mind in preparation for advanced meditation. Classical meditation requires practitioners to sit for hours in an effort just to *be*, by closing their eyes and watching their breath, letting thoughts play out like a kaleidoscope without actively entertaining those thoughts. There are four basic types: Raja, which includes Hatha, *Jnana*, *Bhakti* and *Karma*. Raja focuses on managing psychic energy to drive consciousness from the base of the spine up through the crown of the head. Jnana focuses on contemplation and can be quite verbal, leading a person to realize that all of his self-identifications are false and that he is a uniquely precious reflection of the Ultimate. Bhakti focuses on devotion to various Hindu deities, best viewed as *manifestations* of the *Supreme Being*. Karma focuses on loving service to humanity as expressions of the Supreme Being. It is most apparent that these methods place greater or lesser importance on doing, thinking and feeling in an attempt to have people experience pure being.

Zen: This is the Japanese word for contemplation, called "Chán" in Chinese, as part of the Mahayana, or Great Vehicle tradition of *Buddhism.* It is best known for the clever riddles that Zen masters use to pop the minds of their students. Zazen, or sitting meditation, is heavily practiced. One might meditate, including conscious walking and breathing, literally 14 hours a day. Zen shuns concepts, preferring direct experience of ultimate being. They refer to Big Mind, who you really are, and Small Mind, who you pretend to be.

Ziggurats: These massive Babylonian temples, in what is now Iraq, were used for stargazing. They may have been the inspiration for the story of the Tower of Babel, where people attempted to build a ladder to heaven, ultimately realized in the modern space program.

TIMELINE
The Traditional Age

2000 BCE

Indus River Valley and Nile River Valley civilizations emerge.

1900 BCE

Abraham, father of monotheism, migrates to Canaan.

1500 BCE

Maya civilization of Central America begins.

Moses leads the Hebrews out of Egypt.

1000 BCE

1000 BCE: David, anointed king of the 12 tribes of Israel, consolidates a Hebrew nation.

961-922 BCE: Solomon, David's son, brings in the Golden Age of Israel.

700 BCE

700 BCE: The Prophet Isaiah envisions the millennium.

722 BCE: Israel, as separate kingdom, is conquered by Babylon.

600 BCE

587 BCE: Judah, as separate kingdom, is conquered by Babylon.

500 BCE

525 BCE: Siddhartha Gautama (c. 563-483 BCE) experiences enlightenment and promulgates it for 40 continuous years, founding Buddhism.

410 BCE: Western civilization emerges with the great humanistic philosophers, Socrates (469-399 BCE) and Plato (428-347 BCE).

400 BCE

400 BCE: The legendary oral epic, the *Mahabharata*, was first recorded, setting the stage for Hinduism as a religion independent of Buddhism.

343 BCE: Aristotle (384-322 BCE) personally tutors the World Conqueror, Alexander the Great (356-323 BCE), creating Hellenism, leading to humanism and early science.

300 BCE

300 BCE: The legendary oral epic, the Ramayana, first recorded, setting stage for Hinduism as an independent, syncretic religion.

264-238 BCE: Emperor Ashoka (272-238 BCE) reigns throughout much of India, standardizing Buddhism as the official religion, and sending out missionaries as far as the Mediterranean.

100 BCE

27 BCE-14 CE: Augustus (63 BCE-14 CE) begins the Roman Empire.

4 BCE-29 CE: Jesus of Nazareth, born in the Holy Land, begins the transformation of the Roman Empire, setting the stage for a world religion.

1 CE

29 CE: The Christian Gospel is first proclaimed.

64 CE: The Apostle Paul, the world's greatest
                    missionary, is executed.

300 CE

313 CE: With the Edict of Milan, Emperor Constantine
                    (285-337 CE; reigned 306-337 CE) legalizes
                    Christianity, preparing for its acceptance as the
                    official religion of the Roman Empire.

400 CE

400 CE: Huns, Vandals and Goths invade Western
                    Europe, initiating the Dark Ages.

427-1197 CE: Nalanda, an Indian Buddhist institution,
                    becomes the world's first university, an
                    institution later adapted by the Muslims, and
                    then the Christians.

600 CE

622CE: Muhammad (570-632 CE) founds Islam with the
                    Hijra, or Flight to Medina from Mecca.

700 CE

732 CE: Charles Martel halts the Muslim advance into
                    Europe with the Battle of Tours.

800 CE

800 CE: Charlemagne (742-814 CE; reigned 800-814 CE)
                    was crowned Holy Roman Emperor, officially
                    beginning the Middle Ages.

1000 CE

1095 CE: Pope Urban II calls the First Crusade to take back the Holy Land from the Muslims.

1100 CE

Troubadours in southern France begin to celebrate courtly love.

1200 CE

1258 CE: Rumi (1207-1273 CE), the greatest Sufi, begins writing his masterpiece, the *Masnawi*.

1274 CE: Marco Polo (1254-1324 CE) befriends Mongol Emperor Kublai Khan (1215-1294), grandson of the great conqueror, Genghis Khan.

1300 CE

1350 CE: The Black Plague kills as much as half of Europe.

1400 CE

1453 CE: Constantinople (Istanbul) falls to the Turks.

1455 CE: The Renaissance begins with Johannes Gutenberg's movable type and printing press.

1471 CE: The Incan Empire is at its height.

1485 CE: Leonardo da Vinci (1452-1519 CE) envisions human flight.

1492 CE: Christopher Columbus (1451-1506 CE) sets sail across the Atlantic Ocean in a mistaken attempt to reach India, accidentally discovering the New World, opening up the Modern Age as one of discovery and colonialism.

THE MODERN AGE

1500 CE

1510 CE: Nicolaus Copernicus (1487-1543 CE) initiates heliocentric theory.

1517 CE: Martin Luther (1483-1541 CE) nails *The Ninety-Five Theses* to Wittenberg Cathedral, sparking Protestant Reformation.

1519 CE: Sikhism is founded by Guru Nanak Dev.

1534 CE: Henry VIII starts the Church of England after a failed attempt to divorce his first wife.

1535 CE-1541 CE:

     Michelangelo (1475-1564 CE) paints the Sistine Chapel.

1598-1603 CE: Elizabeth I (1533-1603 CE; reigned 1588-1603 CE) patronizes William Shakespeare (1564-1616 CE).

1600 CE

1600 CE: William Shakespeare (1564-1616 CE) writes *Hamlet*.

1600 CE: Giordano Bruno is burned at the stake.

1610 CE: Galileo Galilei (1564-1643 CE) develops the theory of gravity, being forced by the Roman Catholic Church in 1632 CE to renounce the heliocentric theory.

1611 CE: King James authorizes the most famous English version of the Bible.

1618 CE-1648 CE:

The Thirty Years' War between Protestant and Catholic countries rages.

1637 CE: René Descartes (1596-1650 CE) writes *Discourse on the Method*, initiating modern philosophy with his famous dictum, "I think, therefore I am."

1649 CE: Charles I is beheaded in the English Civil War led by Sir Oliver Cromwell (1599-1658 CE).

1661-1715 CE: Louis XIV (1638-1715 CE) reigns in France as absolute monarch.

1687 CE: Sir Isaac Newton (1642-1727 CE) co-invents calculus, publishing his celebrated *Principia Mathematica*, introducing an intricate mechanical explanation of the solar system.

1700 CE

1776 CE: Thomas Jefferson drafts the United States Declaration of Independence, initiating the American Revolution. Democracy through representative government becomes the premier institution of the Modern Age.

1781 CE: Immanuel Kant (1724-1804 CE) writes *Critique of Pure Reason*.

1789 CE: The French Revolution begins with the Fall of Bastille on July 14. Unlike the American Revolution, it soon falters. Order is brought about only through the vigorous efforts of General Napoleon Bonaparte (1769-1821 CE).

1790 CE: James Watt invents the steam engine, leading to the Industrial Revolution.

| 1799 CE: | Napoleon ends The Reign of Terror on November 9. |

1800 CE

1801-1815 CE:	Napoleon Bonaparte is declared emperor, reigning over France and conquered territories.
1807 CE:	Georg William Friedrich Hegel (1770-1831 CE) writes *The Phenomenology of Mind*, introducing the dialectics.
1812 CE:	Napoleon invades Russia.
1815 CE:	The Battle of Waterloo brings about Napoleon's permanent exile in Saint Helena.
1819 CE:	The first steamship is created.
1820 CE:	The first railroad begins.
1837 CE:	Louis-Jacques-Mandé Daguerre pioneers photography.
1844 CE:	The first telegraph is created.
1846-1848 CE:	The Mexican-American War is launched by the United States as a land grab that eventually brings in the State of Texas.
1848 CE:	Karl Marx (1818-1883 CE), along with Friedrich Engels (1820-1895 CE), publishes *The Communist Manifesto* just before a failed European class revolution.
1849 CE:	The Gold Rush triggers the early adoption of California as a state, as well as a series of revolutions that last well over a century.
1859 CE:	Charles Darwin (1809-1882 CE) introduces the

"theory of evolution" with his *On the Origin of Species.*

1863 CE: Slavery as an institution is abolished by President Abraham Lincoln (1809-1865 CE; in office 1861-1865 CE) Lincoln's Union side ultimately wins over the Confederacy in the American Civil War (1861-1865 CE).

1871 CE: The telephone is invented.

1880 CE: Sri Ramakrishna Paramahamsa of Calcutta (1836-1886 CE) envisions framework for the harmony of all world religions.

1885 CE: The Indian National Congress is formed.

1887 CE: Paul Gauguin (1848-1903 CE) asks the ultimate questions in his painting in Tahiti, *"Who? Whence? Whither?"*

1890 CE: Motion pictures are invented by the Lumière brothers in Paris.

1899 CE: Sigmund Freud (1856-1936 CE) pioneers a scientific exploration of the unconscious, inventing psychotherapy with his masterpiece, *The Interpretation of Dreams.*

1900 CE

1900 CE: Guglielmo Marconi invents the radio.

1902 CE: Thomas Edison invents the phonograph.

1903 CE: The Wright Brothers fly for the first time.

1905-1906 CE: The early peaceful Russian Revolution is crushed by the Czar.

1905 CE:	Albert Einstein (1879-1955 CE) publishes his special theory of relativity and, in 1916 CE, his general theory of relativity.
1908 CE:	Henry Ford (1863-1947 CE) pioneers the mass production of automobiles by rolling out his Model T.

1910 CE

1914 CE:	Archduke Franz Ferdinand of Austria (1863-1914 CE) is assassinated on June 28, triggering World War I.
1914-1919 CE:	Sri Aurobindo (1872-1950 CE) pioneers evolutionary spirituality with *The Life Divine*.
1917 CE:	Vladimir Lenin (1870-1924 CE) leads the early Communist Party with a successful coup in the October Revolution of 1917, forming the Soviet Union.
1919 CE:	World War I ends in a negotiated armistice with the Treaty of Versailles.
1919 CE:	President Woodrow Wilson (1856-1924 CE; president 1913-1921 CE) unsuccessfully campaigns for America to join the League of Nations, a precursor to the United Nations.

1920 CE

1920 CE:	Women's suffrage enables American women to vote.
1925 CE:	Meher Baba (1894 -1969 CE) takes a vow of silence on July 12, which he maintains for the rest of his life.

1927 CE:	Copenhagen Interpretation of quantum mechanics formulated by Niels Bohr (1885-1962 CE) and Werner Heisenberg (1901-1976 CE).
1928 CE:	Mohandas Karamchand "Mahatma" Gandhi leads General Strike in India.
1929 CE:	U.S. stock market crash triggers the Great Depression (1929-1939 CE) on Black Tuesday, October 29.

1930 CE

| 1930 CE: | Mahatma Gandhi (1869-1948 CE) leads Salt March, establishing moral superiority of nonviolent approach to freedom. |
| 1939 CE: | Germany invades Poland on September 1, starting World War II. |

1940 CE

1941 CE:	Japanese bomb Pearl Harbor, leading to America's entrance into World War II on December 7.
1942-1946 CE:	America's Manhattan Project is initiated to develop the world's first atomic bomb.
1944 CE:	Allies invade Normandy, France on June 6.
1945 CE:	Germany surrenders to Allies on May 7.
1945 CE:	United Nations Charter is signed in San Francisco on June 26.
1945 CE:	United States drops an atomic bomb on Hiroshima on August 6. Japan surrenders unconditionally on August 14.

1946 CE:	Paramahansa Yogananda (1893-1952 CE), founder of Self-Realization Fellowship, publishes his classic, *Autobiography of a Yogi*, which shapes Westerner's conception of Hindu spirituality for decades.
1947 CE:	India and Pakistan are liberated from the British Empire on August 15, setting the stage for the British Commonwealth (inaugurated in 1948.)
1948 CE:	Mahatma Gandhi is assassinated on January 30.
1948 CE:	The Nation of Israel is formed on May 14.
1948 CE:	Bell Labs invents the transistor.
1948-1949 CE:	The Soviets blockade Berlin, Germany, leading to the construction of Berlin Wall.
1949 CE:	The People's Republic of China is created on October 1.

1950 CE

1952 CE:	United States detonates the world's first hydrogen bomb.
1954 CE:	The Soviet Union detonates its own hydrogen bomb.
1955 CE:	The Civil Rights movement (1955-1968 CE) begins on December 1 when Rosa Parks (1913-2005 CE) initiates a boycott of the Montgomery Alabama bus system.
1957 CE:	The Soviet's launch Sputnik, the world's first artificial satellite, on October 4, initiating the space race (1957-1969 CE) between the United States and the Soviet Union.

1959 CE:	Intercontinental ballistic missiles are deployed.
1959 CE:	Pierre Teilhard de Chardin's (1881-1955 CE) *The Phenomenon of Man* posthumously published, introducing the noosphere and Omega Point as the endpoint of human evolution.

1960 CE

1961 CE:	President John F. Kennedy announces "The New Frontier" of outer space in his inaugural speech, committing the United States to "landing a man on the moon" before that decade would run out.
1961 CE:	Soviet cosmonaut, Yuri Gagarin (1934-1968 CE), becomes the first human being to orbit the Earth on April 12.
1962 CE:	Rachel Carson (1907-1964 CE) publishes *Silent Spring*, which envisions springtime without any birds, creating the environmental movement.
1963 CE:	Women's Liberation movement emerges with Betty Friedan (1921-2006 CE) publishing *The Feminine Mystique*.
1963 CE:	Martin Luther King, Jr. (1929-1968 CE) marches on Washington D.C., giving his famous "I Have a Dream" speech.
1963 CE:	President John F. Kennedy (1917-1963 CE) is assassinated on November 22.
1964 CE:	The Civil Rights Act is ratified into the U.S. Constitution.
1964 CE:	The Beatles (1960-1970 CE) emerge as true "superstars" with their debut on the Ed Sullivan Show in February.

1964 CE:	Cal Berkeley activists pioneer the Free Speech movement in the fall.
1965-1980 CE:	Generation X emerges as a smaller generation than the post-World War II baby boomers.
1965 CE:	Affirmative action is introduced to reinforce the Civil Rights Act.
1965 CE:	Lyndon B. Johnson (1908-1973 CE; President 1963-1969 CE) initiates massive escalation of the war in Vietnam (1965-1975 CE), committing one-half million American troops.
1965 CE:	Intel co-founder, Gordon E. Moore (1929 CE -), correctly predicts in his paper on Moore's law that computing power will double every two years or so.
1965 CE:	A. C. Bhaktivedanta Swami Prabhupada, (1886-1977 CE) comes to New York City with less than $60 in his pocket. His International Society for Krishna Consciousness launches a global movement by the end of the decade.
1966 CE:	Alan Watts (1915-1973 CE) writes *The Book: On the Taboo Against Knowing Who You Are.*
1967 CE:	Hippies introduce the Summer of Love from April to October in San Francisco's Haight-Ashbury district, publishing the *Oracle* newspaper in living color. Their slogan is "Make Love, Not War." Timothy Leary (1920-1996 CE) wins notoriety at that festival for his motto, "Turn on, tune in, drop out."

1967 CE:	Janis Joplin (1943-1970 CE), Jimi Hendrix (1942-1970 CE) and Jim Morrison (1943-1971 CE) pioneer hard psychedelic rock, each prematurely dying through hard drugs and alcohol.
1968 CE:	Paul Ehrlich (1932 CE -) publishes the best-selling *The Population Bomb*, predicting that humanity's growth will outstrip environmental resources.
1968 CE:	Maharishi Mahesh Yogi (1918-2008 CE) becomes a global celebrity after the Beatles study with him in Rishikesh, India.
1968 CE:	Martin Luther King, Jr., is shot on April 4.
1968 CE:	Robert Kennedy (1925-1968 CE) is assassinated after winning the Democratic Party nomination for president.
1968 CE:	France undergoes a General Strike from May to June.
1968 CE:	The Cultural Revolution, interpreted differently, is concurrent in both the United States and China.
1968 CE:	"Black Power" and "Black is Beautiful" emerge as late 1960s slogans. "La Raza" emerges for people of Mexican American descent.
1968 CE:	The Beatles' animated film, *Yellow Submarine*, popularizes Einstein's "theory of relativity."
1968 CE:	Carlos Castaneda (1925-1998 CE) popularizes Native American shamanic culture with *The Teachings of Don Juan: A Yaqui Way of Knowledge*.

1968 CE:	Canadian media theorist, Marshall McLuhan (1911-1980 CE), introduces the concept of "global village."
1968 CE:	Fritz Perls (1893-1970 CE) popularizes Gestalt at Esalen with *Gestalt Therapy Verbatim*.
1969 CE:	U.S. astronaut, Russell Louis "Rusty" Schweickart (1935- CE), riding in an EMU (Extravehicular Mobility Unit) outside his space capsule, raptly gazes upon Planet Earth and declares, "No frames. No boundaries."
1969 CE:	New York's groundbreaking Woodstock Festival is celebrated in August.
1969 CE:	Richard Buckminster "Bucky" Fuller (1895-1983 CE) publishes *Operational Manual for Spaceship Earth*.

1970 CE

1970 CE:	Carl Rogers (1902-1987 CE), pioneer of humanistic psychology and nondirective therapy, publishes *On Encounter Groups*.
1970 CE:	Santa Clara, California, is dubbed Silicon Valley.
1971 CE:	The Trident submarine is introduced with multiple independently targetable reentry vehicle (MIRV) missiles. Each missile is programmed to break up into multiple warheads in its trajectory.
1971 CE:	Intel invents world's first microprocessor, setting the stage for a computer revolution.
1971 CE:	Baba Ram Dass (1931 CE -) publishes *Remember Be Here Now*.

1971 CE:	Werner Erhard (1935 CE -) founds the est training in San Francisco after an enlightenment experience driving across the Golden Gate Bridge.
1972 CE:	Richard Nixon (1913-1994 CE; president 1969-1974 CE) opens up Communist China to the United States, meeting with Chairman Mao Zedong and touring that country.
1973 CE:	Arab-Israeli War.
1974 CE:	President Nixon resigns from office in August after the Watergate incident.
1975 CE:	Henry Edward "Ed" Roberts (1941 CE -) of MITS in Albuquerque, New Mexico, introduces the world's first personal computer in January. William Henry "Bill" Gates sees a *Popular Science* article and leaves Harvard to join him, founding Microsoft to program it with BASIC.
1975 CE:	Fritjof Capra (1939 CE -) publishes the *Tao of Physics*, demonstrating the link between Eastern mysticism and cutting-edge physics.
1975 CE:	The United States evacuates Saigon, losing the Vietnam War.
1975 CE:	Steve Jobs (1955 CE -) starts Apple Computer, and introduces the Macintosh in 1994 CE, the iPod in 2001 CE, the iPhone in 2007 CE and the iPad in 2010 CE.
1977 CE:	Werner Erhard draws world attention in October to The Hunger Project, maintaining that "the end of death by starvation is an idea whose time has come."

1979 CE: The Soviet Union invades Afghanistan.

1979 CE: Proposition 13 passes in November, beginning
                steep escalation of housing costs in California.

1979-1981 CE: Ayatollah Ruhollah Khomeini overthrows the
                Shah of Iran. American hostages are detained.

1980 CE

1983 CE: American actress, Shirley MacLaine (1934 CE -),
                popularizes New Age spirituality with her book,
                Out on a Limb.

1984 CE: William Gibson envisions cyberspace with
                Neuromancer.

1985 CE: Mikhail Gorbachev (1931 CE -; Soviet General
                Secretary 1985-1991 CE) assumes power,
                initiating glasnost and *Perestroika* throughout
                the Soviet Union, successfully ending the Cold
                War with the peaceful fall of the Berlin Wall.

1985 CE: Margaret Thatcher (1925 CE -; British Prime
                Minister 1979-1990 CE) supports President
                Ronald Reagan (1911-2004 CE; president
                1981-1989) in November in Geneva's peace
                negotiations with Mikhail Gorbachev.

1988 CE: Joseph Campbell (1904-1987 CE) posthumously
                stars in Bill Moyer's sensational PBS Series, *Joseph
                Campbell and the Power of Myth*, firing popular
                imagination with the implications of mythology.

1989 CE: The Soviet Union withdraws from Afghanistan
                in February.

1989 CE: Massive youth protests occur in Beijing's
                Tiananmen Square from April to June, seeking

greater freedom and displaying a replica of the Statue of Liberty.

1989 CE: Raveendra "Ravi" N. Batra (1943 CE -), professor at the University of Texas at Austin, publishes *The Great Depression of 1990*, anticipating the collapse of both communism and capitalism.

1989 CE: The Berlin Wall falls in November in the Velvet Revolution where Eastern European nations successfully break away from the Soviet Bloc, forming independent countries.

1990 CE

1990 CE: Hubble Space Telescope is deployed in April.

1990 CE: Saddam Hussein (1937-2006 CE; Iraqi president 1973-2003 CE) invades Kuwait, setting the stage for the Gulf War.

1990 CE: Germany unites in October.

1990-1991 CE: Apartheid is repealed in South Africa.

1991 CE: Lithuania leads the Baltic countries in bringing down the Soviet Union with the nonviolent Singing Revolution.

1991 CE: George H. W. Bush (1924 CE - ; president 1989-1992 CE) bombs Baghdad in January as retaliation for Saddam Hussein's invasion of Kuwait.

1992 CE: The United Nation's Earth Summit is held in Rio de Janeiro in June.

1992 CE: William Jefferson "Bill" Clinton (1946 CE - ; president 1993-2001 CE) is elected, initiating the

Internet age with Albert Arnold "Al" Gore, Jr. (1948 CE -), in the "information superhighway." "The New Paradigm" is also introduced as cutting-edge environmental perspective on reality. The slogan "politically correct" characterizes the first Clinton administration (1993-1996 CE).

1993 CE:	The European Union is formed in November.
1994 CE:	Walt Disney's animated feature, *The Lion King*, introduces theme of the "Circle of Life," in tune with the growing environmental movement.
1994-2000 CE:	The dot-com boom emerges from Netscape in Silicon Valley, attracting massive investment into Internet start-ups. This all implodes in 2001 CE.
1994 CE:	Deepak Chopra (1946 CE -) breaks off from Maharishi Mahesh Yogi to launch a brilliant independent career as the leading American guru and popularizer of mind/body healing. *The Seven Spiritual Laws of Success—A Practical Guide to the Fulfillment of Your Dreams* becomes runaway bestseller.
1994 CE:	Nelson Mandela becomes president of South Africa in April.
1995 CE:	Ethnic cleansing occurs throughout Bosnia.
1997 CE:	Andrew Weil (1942 CE -) popularizes integrative medicine with *Eight Weeks to Optimum Health*.
1998 CE:	India and Pakistan run nuclear tests.

1999 CE: Brian Greene (1963 CE -) publishes *The Elegant
                Universe: Superstrings, Hidden Dimensions, and
                the Quest for the Ultimate Theory* on string theory,
                made into a brilliant television documentary in
                2003 CE.

1999 CE: The Y2K crisis anticipates a worldwide
                shutdown of mainframe computer systems with
                the advent of the new millennium. This was
                averted through a massive effort of primarily
                Indian engineers.

THE PLANETARY AGE

2000 CE

2000 CE: The United Religions Initiative is chartered in San Francisco, suggesting a United Nations of Religion.

2001 CE: *Monsters Inc.*, a masterpiece in 3D feature animation, is released, suggesting that our own shadows are more afraid of us than we are of them.

2001 CE: Al-Qaeda attacks the United States by destroying Manhattan's Twin Towers on September 11.

2001 CE: George W. Bush (1946 CE - ; president 2001-2009 CE), in retaliation for 9/11, first invades Afghanistan and then Iraq in 2003 CE, leading to a cycle of unwinnable wars.

2003 CE: Pakistan and India restore diplomatic ties.

2003 CE: Second Life successfully builds a 3D world on the Internet as an ever-expanding simulation.

2004 CE: Mel Gibson's groundbreaking feature, *The Passion of Christ*, is released, actually spoken in the ancient languages of Aramaic and Latin.

2006 CE: Vice President Al Gore (1948 CE -) stars in the documentary, *An Inconvenient Truth*, leading to his receipt of the Nobel Peace Prize.

2004 CE:	Implications of quantum theory are brilliantly explored in the cult feature classic, *What the Bleep Do We Know!?: Discovering the Endless Possibilities.*
2006 CE:	*The Secret* is released as a full-screen feature on the Internet by Rhonda Byrne (1951 CE -), creating a media sensation.
2006 CE:	Ken Wilber (1949 CE -) pioneers post-modern theology in Sound's True's audio, *The One Two Three of God.*
2006 CE:	Don Tapscott's (1947 CE -) *Wikinomics: How Mass Collaboration Changes Everything* is published, envisioning open-source economics.
2007 CE:	Apple's iPhone is introduced, selling well over 30 million units.
2008 CE:	Eckhart Tolle's (1948 CE -) *A New Earth: Awakening to Your Life's Purpose* is first published in 2005 CE, and celebrated by Oprah Winfrey (1954 CE -) with an unprecedented 10 full-screen webcasts.
2008 CE:	Barack Obama (1961 CE -) is elected the American president by leveraging both social media and networking booms. Green technology is a major theme of his first administration.
2008 CE:	Billy Graham (1918 CE -) accumulates a lifetime audience of 2.2 billion people to hear the Christian Gospel, entailing in-person evangelistic crusades worldwide as well as extensive radio and television.

2010 CE

2012 CE: Mayan calendar is due to end on the Winter Solstice, December 21, anticipated by intense worldwide speculation around planetary transformation.

LIST OF ILLUSTRATIONS

# Recommended Media
[B] = Book, [M] = Magazine, [A] = Audio,
[V] = Video, [W] = Website

Alir, Sunbul
The Muslim Next Door [B], White Cloud Press, 2008

Armstrong, Karen
Muhammad: A Prophet for Our Time [B], HarperOne, 2007

Arntz, William (with Betsy Chasse and Mark Vicente)
What the Bleep: Down the Rabbit Hole (Quantum Edition) [V], 20th Century Fox, 2006
What the Bleep Do We Know!?: Discovering the Endless Possibilities [B], HCI, 2007

Aslan, Reza
No god but God: The Origins, Evolution, and Future of Islam [B], Random House Trade Paperbacks, 2006

Attenborough, Richard
Shadow Lands [V], HBO Home Video, 1999
Gandhi, [V] (Widescreen Two-Disc Collector's Edition), Sony Pictures, 2007

Aurobindo, Sri
The Life Divine [B], Lotus Press, 1985

Barks, Coleman
The Illuminated Rumi [B], with Michael Green, Broadway Books, 1997
The Soul of Rumi [B], HarperOne, 2002
Rumi: Voice of Longing [A], Sounds True, 2005

Beatles, The
Yellow Submarine [V], MGM, 1999
Magical Mystery Tour (remastered) [A], EMI, 2009
Sgt. Pepper's Lonely Hearts Club Band (remastered) [A], EMI, 2009

Becker, Carl
*Heavenly City of the Eighteenth Century Philosophers [B], Yale University
    Press, 2003*

Beckwith, Michael
40 Day Mind Fast Soul Feast [B], Agape Publishing, Inc., 2000
*Spiritual Liberation: Fulfilling Your Soul's Potential [B], Atria Paperback,
    Simon & Schuster, 2008*
*Spiritual Liberation: Fulfilling Your Soul's Potential [V], Beyond Words
    Pub., 2009*
Life Visioning Kit [A], Sounds True, 2009

Berg, Yehuda
The Power of Kabbalah [B], Kabbalah Centre International, 2004

Bhaktivedanta, A.C. (His Divine Grace, Swami Prabhupada)
The Bhagavad Gita As It Is [B], Bhaktivedanta Book Trust, 1997

Campbell, Joseph
Power of Myth [V], Mystic Fire Video, 2001
The Hero's Journey: Joseph Campbell on His Life [B], New World Library, 2003
The Hero with a Thousand Faces, Third Edition [B], New World Library, 2008

Castaneda, Carlos
*The Teachings of Don Juan: A Yaqui Way of Knowledge, Deluxe 30th
    Anniversary Edition [B], University of California Press, 1998*

CBS
The Big Bang Theory, The Complete First Season [V], CBS, 2008

Chopra, Deepak

The Way of the Wizard [B], Harmony, 1995

Every Day Immortality [B], Gramercy Books, Random House Value
    Publishing, 1999

A Gift of Love [A], Rasa Music, 2000

How to Know God [B], Rider & Co., 2000

Deepak Chopra: The Essential DVD Collection [V], Wellspring Media,
    2000

The Spontaneous Fulfillment of Desire [V], Three Rivers Press, 2004

Buddha: A Story of Enlightenment [B], HarperCollins Publishers, 2007

Power, Freedom & Grace [B], Amber-Allen Publishing, 2008

Jesus: A Story of Enlightenment [B], HarperOne, 2009

Cohen, Andrew

www.enlightennext.com [W]

Living Enlightenment: A Call for Evolution Beyond Ego [B], Moksha Press,
    2002

Cooper, David A.

God Is a Verb: Kabbalah and the Practice of Mystical Judaism [B],
    Riverhead, 1998

DeMille, Cecile B.

The Ten Commandments [V], Paramount, 2006

Drury, Nevill

The New Age: The History of a Movement [B], Thames & Hudson, 2004

Easwaran, Eknath

Gandhi The Man: The Story of His Transformation [B], Nilgiri Press, 2007

The Dhammapada: A Classic of Indian Spirituality [B], Nilgiri Press, 2007

The Upanishads: A Classic of Indian Spirituality [B], Nilgiri Press, 2007

Eliot, T.S.

Four Quartets [B], Harcourt, 1943

Fox, Matthew
Meditations with Meister Eckhart [B], Bear & Company, 1983
The Coming of the Cosmic Christ [B], HarperOne, 1988
Original Blessing: A Primer in Creation Spirituality [B], Tarcher, 2000
One River, Many Wells: Wisdom Springing from Global Faiths [B],
        Tarcher, 2004

Frederick, Carl
est: Playing the Game the New Way: Collector's Edition [B], Synergy
        International of the Americas, 2007

Friedman, Thomas L.
The World Is Flat: A Brief History of the 21st Century [B], Farrar, Straus
        and Giroux, 2006

Fuller, R. Buckminster
Critical Path [B], St. Martin's Press, 1981
Operating Manual for Spaceship Earth [B], Lars Muller Publishers, 2008

Gach, Gary
The Complete Idiot's Guide to Buddhism, 3rd Edition [B], Alpha, 2009

Gladstone, William
The Twelve: A Novel [B], Vanguard Press, 2009

Greene, Brian
The Elegant Universe: Superstrings, Hidden Dimensions, and the Quest
        for the Ultimate Theory [V], Nova, WGBH Boston, 2004

Hanh, Thich Nat
Living Buddha, Living Christ, 10th Anniversary Edition [B], Riverhead
        Trade, 2007

Hart, Kevin
Postmodernism: A Beginner's Guide [B], Oneworld Publications, 2004

Hesse, Herman

Siddhartha: A New Translation [B], Shambhala Classics, 2000

Hixon, Lex

Coming Home: The Experience of Enlightenment in Sacred Traditions [B],
      Larson Publications, 1978
Living Buddha Zen [B], Larson Publications, 1995
Great Swan: Meetings with Ramakrishna, [B], Larson Publications, 1997
The Heart of the Qur'an, Revised Edition: An Introduction to Islamic
      Spirituality [B], The Theosophical Publishing House, 2003
Mother of the Buddhas: Meditation on the Prajnaparamita Sutra [B], A
      Quest Original, The Theosophical Publishing House, 2007

Houston, Jean

Jump Time: Shaping Your Future … [B], Sentient Publications, 2004

Hubbard, Barbara Marx

Conscious Evolution: Awakening Our Social Potential [B], New World
      Library, 1998
Emergence: The Shift from Ego to Essence: 10 Steps [B], Hampton Roads,
      2001
Humanity Ascending: Part 1: Our Story [V], Foundation for Conscious
      Evolution, 2007

Idilby, Ranya et al.

The Faith Club: A Muslim, A Christian, A Jew [B], Free Press, 2007

Judith, Anodea

Waking the Global Heart: Humanity's Rite of Passage From the Love of
      Power to the Power of Love [B], Elite Books, 2006

Kaku, Michio

Parallel Worlds: A Journey Through Creation, Higher Dimensions and the
      Future of the Cosmos [B], Anchor, 2006

Physics of the Impossible: A Scientific Exploration into the World of Phasers, Force Fields, Teleportation and Time Travel [B], Anchor, 2008

Kaufman, Philip
The Right Stuff (Two-Disc Special Edition) [V], Warner Home Video, 2003
The Unbearable Lightness of Being (Two-Disc Special Edition) [V], Warner Home Video, 2006

Kitaro
Best of Silk Road [A], Domo Records, 2003
The Essential Kitaro [A], Domo Records, 2007

Ladinsky, Daniel
The Gift: Poems by Hafiz, The Great Sufi Master [B], Penguin Compass, 1999
Love Poems from God: Twelve Sacred Voices from the East and West [B], Penguin Compass, 2002
Hafiz: The Scent of Light [A], Sounds True Direct, 2006

Lama, Dalai (His Holiness)
Seven Years in Tibet [V], Sony Pictures, 1998
Ethics for the New Millennium [B], Riverhead Books, 1999
The Universe in a Single Atom: The Convergence of Science and Spirituality [B], Broadway, 2006
Dalai Lama Renaissance [V], Waken Films, 2009
Not in God's Name—In Search of Tolerance with the Dalai Lama [V], Paradise Filmworks International, 2010

Laszlo, Ervin
The Chaos Point: The World at the Crossroads [B], Hampton Roads, 200
Science and the Akashic Field: An Integral Theory of Everything [B], Inner Traditions, 2007
Quantum Shift in the Global Brain: How the New Scientific... [B], Inner Tradtions, 2008
The Akashic Experience: Science and the Cosmic Memory Field [B], Inner Traditions, 2009

WorldShift 2012: Making Green Business … Work Together [B], *Inner Traditions,* 2009

Lewis, C.S.

Through the Shadowlands [V], *Vision Video,* 2004

The Chronicles of Narnia (Widescreen Edition), [V], *Buena Vista Home Entertainment/Disney,* 2006

The Complete C.S. Lewis Signature Classics [B], *HarperCollins,* 2007

Maharaj, Nisargadatta

I Am That: Talks with Sri Nisargadatta Maharaj [B], *Chetana Private Ltd.,* 1999

Awaken to the Eternal: Nisargadatta Maharaj [V], *Inner Directions,* 2006

Maharshi, Ramana

The Spiritual Teachings [B], *Shambala Classics,* 1998

The Essential Teachings of Ramana Maharshi: A Visual Journey [B], *Inner Directions,* 2002

Abide As The Self [V], *Inner Directions,* 2006

McLuhan, Marshall

War and Peace in the Global Village [B], *Gingko Press,* 2001

The Medium Is the Massage [B], *Gingko Press,* 2005

Merriman, Michael

Billy Graham: God's Ambassador [V], *20th Century Fox,* 2006

Neruda, Pablo

Selected Odes of Pablo Neruda [B], *University of California Press,* 2000

Pearson, Carlton

The Gospel of Inclusion: Reaching Beyond Religious Fundamentalism [B], *Atria,* 2009

God Is Not a Christian: God Dwells with Us, in Us, around Us, as Us [B], *Atria,* 2010

Peterson, Eugene H.
The Message Remix: The Bible in Contemporary Language [B], NavPress, 2003

Ram Dass, Baba
Remember Be Here Now [B], Hanuman Foundation, 1971
Miracle of Love: Stories About Neem Karoli Baba [B], Hanuman
        Foundation, 1995
Fierce Grace: A Film by Mickey Lemle [V], Zeitgiest Video, 2003

Ray, Nicholas
King of Kings [V], Warner Home Video, 2009

Redfield, James
The Secret of Shambhala: In Search of the Eleventh Insight [B], Warner
        Books, 1999
The Celestine Prophecy: What If Earth and Heaven …? [V], Sony Pictures,
        2005

Russell, Ken
Altered States [V], Warner Home Video, 2004

Russell, Peter
The Global Brain/The White Hole in Time [DVD], Penny Price Media,
        2006

Schaeffer, Francis
Trilogy: The Three Essential Books in One Volume [B], Crossway Books, 1990

Scorsese, Martin
The Last Temptation of Christ [V], Criterion, 1988

Simon, Robyn
Transformation: The Life and Legacy of Werner Erhard [V], Screen Media, 2008

Smith, Huston

The Illustrated World's Religions: A Guide to Our Wisdom Traditions [B], HarperOne, 1995

The Soul of Christianity: Restoring the Great Tradition [B], HarperOne, 2005

South, Stephanie

Biography of a Time Traveler: The Journey of Jose Arguelles [B], New Page Books, 2009

Tapscott, Don

Wikinomics: How Mass Collaboration Changes Everything [B], Portfolio Hardcover, 2008

Thurman, Robert A. F.

Inner Revolution: Life, Liberty, and the Pursuit of Real Happiness [B], Riverhead Trade, 1999

The Robert A.F. Thurman Collection [V], Wellspring, 2002

God and Buddha: A Dialogue (with Deepak Chopra) [V], Mystic Fire Video, 2003

Tolle, Eckhart

The Power of Now: A Guide to Spiritual Enlightenment [B], New World Library, 1999

Findhorn Retreat: Stillness Amidst the World [B/V], New World Library, 2006

Oneness with All Life: Inspirational Selections from a New Earth [B], Dutton, 2009

Tzu, Lao

Tao Te Ching (Translated by Gia-Fu Feng and Jane English) [B], Vintage, 1989

Vanamali

The Play of God: Visions of the Life of Krishna [B], Blue Dove Press, 1995

Wachowski, Larry and Andy

The Matrix [V], Warner Home Video, 2007

Watts, Alan

www.alanwatts.com [W]
This Is It: And Other Essays on Zen [B], Vintage, 1973
The Book: On the Taboo Against Knowing Who You Are [B], Vintage Books, 1989
Buddhism: The Religion of No-Religion [B], Tuttle Publishing, 1999
Zen: The Supreme Experience [B], Vega, 2003
Out of Your Mind: Essential Listening [A], Sounds True, 2005
Do You Do It or Does It Do You? How to Let the Universe Meditate [A], Sounds True, 2005
In My Own Way: An Autobiography [B], New World Library, 2007
You're It!: On Hiding, Seeking and Being Found [A], Sounds True, 2009

Wilber, Ken

Kosmic Consciousness [A], Sounds True, 2003
The One Two Three of God [A], Sounds True, 2006
Integral Spirituality: A Startling New Role [B], Shambhala, 2007
The Integral Vision: A Very Short Introduction [B], Shambhala, 2007
The Future of Christianity: A Startling New Vision, Integral Life, 2008

Wolf, Fred Alan

Taking the Quantum Leap: The New Physics for Nonscientists [B], Harper Perennial, 1989
The Yoga of Time Travel: How the Mind Can Defeat Time [B], Quest Books, 2004
Little Book of Big Ideas: Where Science Meets Spirit [B], Moment Point Press, 2005
Dr. Quantum Presents: A User's Guide to Your Universe [A], Sounds True, 2005

ABOUT THE AUTHORS

AUDRONE WIPPICH is a transformational catalyst in the emerging field of planetary consciousness. Born in Lithuania, she now considers herself a global citizen. The beauty, liberty and diversity of San Francisco helped Audrone's creativity blossom. She found herself in the midst of one revolution, which brought down the Soviet Empire, and then jumping to another. Relentlessly curious about the big picture, she found herself working in the multicultural milieu of Silicon Valley in digital media and marketing. From there, it was a short distance to exploring East/West relations as a means of developing a planetary perspective. Now she is planning to share this vision with the world through in-person and online events. Meet Audrone at www.audronewippich.com.

PHIL BRATTAIN, arriving in San Francisco from Phoenix, Arizona, plunged into social and cultural revolutions while still in school. The region's diverse international community inspired him to graduate from Cal Berkley in intellectual history, experimenting with the Human Potential movement.  Once in the corporate world, Phil found meaning as a peace and environmental activist. His foray into digital media led to international business development in software. Upon meeting Audrone Wippich, Phil was inspired to explore with her the cultural divide of East and West. This book emerges out of their ongoing conversation about matters of ultimate concern. Phil would like to open up this conversation to people everywhere, catalyzing planetary community. Meet Phil at www.philbrattain.com.

Joining The Authors

We invite you to join us in the rapidly growing revolution in consciousness around the world. We will be active online and in person with speaking engagements, seminars, podcasts and blogs. For any updates, visit www.awakenperfection.com.

For our individual calendars, please visit our websites:

- www.audronewippich.com
- www.philbrattain.com

Ultimately, we are creating a community around planetary consciousness. We invite you to join us and participate in its creation. Here are some of the things that we envision:

- We would like to build an "open-source" website, providing a forum for people around the globe to share their spiritual perspective on contemporary issues.
- We would like to sponsor dialogue among the full spectrum of traditions and outlooks.
- We would like to assemble a virtual media center of sacred text that will enable people of all faiths to compare perspectives and appreciate each other's views.

We welcome your thoughts and suggestions. Please email us:

- audrone@awakenperfection.com
- phil@theplanetaryage.com.

LaVergne, TN USA
23 August 2010
194402LV00005B/151/P